Belcher, Edward

Narrative of the voyage of H.M.S. Samarang during the years 1843-46

Vol. 1

Belcher, Edward

Narrative of the voyage of H.M.S. Samarang during the years 1843-46

Vol. 1

Inktank publishing, 2018

www.inktank-publishing.com

ISBN/EAN: 9783747781074

NARRATIVE

OF THE

VOYAGE OF H.M.S. SAMARANG,

DURING THE YEARS 1843–46;

EMPLOYED SURVEYING THE ISLANDS OF THE EASTERN ARCHIPELAGO;

ACCOMPANIED BY A BRIEF

VOCABULARY OF THE PRINCIPAL LANGUAGES.

Published under the Authority of the Lords Commissioners of the Admiralty.

BY

CAPTAIN SIR EDWARD BELCHER, R.N., C.B.,

F.R.A.S., F.G.S., &c.

COMMANDER OF THE EXPEDITION.

WITH

NOTES ON THE NATURAL HISTORY OF THE ISLANDS,

BY ARTHUR ADAMS, ASSISTANT-SURGEON, R.N.

IN TWO VOLUMES.

VOL. I.

LONDON:

REEVE, BENHAM, AND REEVE, KING WILLIAM STREET STRAND.

1848.

TO

THE RIGHT HONOURABLE

THE EARL OF AUCKLAND, G.C.B.,

FIRST LORD-COMMISSIONER FOR EXECUTING THE OFFICE

OF LORD HIGH ADMIRAL OF GREAT BRITAIN

AND IRELAND, &c., &c., &c.,

THESE VOLUMES,

CONTAINING

THE NARRATIVE OF

THE VOYAGE OF H.M.S. SAMARANG,

ARE, BY HIS LORDSHIP'S PERMISSION,

INSCRIBED,

WITH THE GREATEST RESPECT,

BY

HIS OBEDIENT SERVANT,

E. BELCHER.

PREFACE.

In appearing again before the Public as the Narrator of the leading incidents of a protracted Surveying Expedition, I wish the work to be regarded only as another effort in the performance of that duty which should be undertaken, to the best of their ability, by all Officers intrusted with the command of Scientific Voyages; and however monotonous the recital of the Service-portions of such duty may appear to those not immediately conversant with Naval affairs, I trust the observations here detailed on some of the Islands and Islanders of the Eastern Hemisphere, hitherto rarely visited, will not only prove interesting to the general reader, but will, in a political point of view, afford matter for consideration in our future intercourse with those Regions.

At the time of H.M.S. Samarang quitting England, on the termination of the war with China, the prominent feature of my instructions related specifically to "the Coasts, Ports and Rivers of that Empire, laid open by the new Treaty of 1842;" but the *veto* of Her Majesty's Plenipotentiary forbidding "all approach to any part of the Chinese Territories north of Canton," my attention was directed to the off-lying Islands of the Eastern Archipelago, including all that are comprehended within the limits of 50° N., and 10° S. Latitude, and as far as 175° of E. Longitude.

The territories of this wide domain were to be examined according to the tenor of my Instructions in H.M.S. Sulphur:—

"In all the operations connected with the several branches of the Service thus allotted to you, you will strictly guide yourself by the Instructions, *mutatis mutandis,* under which you acted in the Pacific," and which the following extract will illustrate.

"In carrying this great Survey into effect, their Lordships have placed the fullest reliance on the unabated zeal and talents which you have heretofore displayed, and they have cautiously and wisely abstained in your orders, from fettering you in the selection of your ground, or in that division and disposition of your time which the periodic changes of season, or the occasional necessities of the vessels may require."—*Voyage of H.M.S. Sulphur*, 1842.

The conclusion of the present ran :—

"On all these subjects we shall give implicit directions to the Commander-in-Chief; we shall prohibit his interfering with your proceedings, or permitting any casual Senior Officer, with whom you may fall in, to control, or meddle with you in any way, unless in cases of extreme exigency, and we shall direct him to keep up your supplies, so as to enable you to carry out this important Service with uninterrupted energy, and to continue on it till you receive further orders from US.

"(Signed) G. COCKBURN.

"W. H. GAGE."

Dated 13th of *January*, 1843.

The Instructions, therefore, confided to me the trust of selecting and examining those points most important to Navigation, and of using the intervals occasioned by the Monsoons, in enlarging the great net-work of Magnetic Stations over the limits assigned, with the aid of a most complete set of Instruments furnished from the Magnetic Observatory at Woolwich, to which twenty well-proved Chronometers (mostly prize) were added for the purpose of measuring accurate Meridian distances.

At the moment of my departure from Falmouth, a despatch arrived from the Admiralty, desiring me to visit Sarãwak, in Borneo, communicate with Mr. Brooke, and then proceed to Borneo Proper, where I was to examine and report on the Coal Measures of that district, and obtain a sufficient quantity for trial on board one of our Steamers.

The SAMARANG reached Singapore on the 19th of June, 1843, moved on to Sarãwak, and there, in the act of dropping down the river, grounded, heeled over, and filled. By the great exertion of the crew she was recovered, after eleven days' immersion, and having replenished provisions, and completed the object of her mission to Borneo, reached Hong-Kong on the 15th of September, 1843. Here the necessity for a diversion from the original Instructions became known, and avoiding the actual coasts of China, for the reason before mentioned, the off-lying Islands were examined, including in the following order, the Bashees, Meïa-co-shimahs, Luzon, Mindoro, Mindañao, Sooloo, Borneo, Celebes, and Ternate; whence, after a sharp encounter with the Illañon Pirates, off Gilolo, we returned to Singapore.

The Samarang then revisited Borneo, joining the Dido in her Sakarran Expedition. Subsequently, aided by the H.E.I.C. steamer, Phlegethon, placed at my disposal by the Governor of Singapore (for the search after an English Lady, supposed to be captive in Borneo), we transferred the Rajah Muda Hassim and family to Borneo Proper; leaving Mr. Brooke in undisputed possession of his territory. At this visit, the Phlegethon was moored in the main street of Brunai, and saluted the Sultan, at which period the original Document, wherein the Sultan offered to cede to Her Majesty the Island of Labuan, was received and transmitted by the Author to Government. Our search for the supposed female captive proving unsuccessful, the Samarang proceeded to Manila, where, hearing of the distress and captivity of the crew of the British barque, Premier, on the coast of Borneo, we returned to Sooloo, and, aided by the Sultan of that place, who sent his Ambassador, succeeded in liberating all who remained, and completed Treaties of Friendship with the Sultans of Gunung Taboor and Bulungan. The Samarang then revisited Sooloo, Manila, and Hong-Kong, with the Bashees, Meïa-co-shimahs, Loo-Choo, Quelpart, Korea, and Japan, where we were most kindly received; returned to Loo-Choo, and Hong-Kong; thence to Manila and the Mindoro Seas, to Mindañao, crossed to our old possession of Balambangan, and carried out the complete Survey from that Island to Labuan, revisiting Sarãwak and Singapore, where orders awaited us for England; and calling at Anjer (Java), the Keeling Islands, Cargados-Garajos, Mauritius, Cape of Good Hope, St. Helena, and Ascension, we arrived at Spithead after an absence of nearly four years.

In the collection of objects of Natural History, I was fortunate enough to possess an acute observer in the person of my Assistant-Surgeon Mr. Adams, whose remarks on the Plants and Animals of the countries visited, will be read with interest by all who can appreciate the delight experienced by the Naturalist, when transported to so prolific, and comparatively new, a field for observation as the remote islands of the Blue and Yellow Seas. In the department of *Mollusca,* to which I was myself chiefly attached, the zealous and successful exertions of Mr. Adams in obtaining drawings of the living animals, deserve my warmest commendation; and it is pleasing to me to know that the materials now preparing for publication are likely to furnish more important matter than has been contributed by any former British Expedition. It will be sufficient to notice, that the Molluscous division of the Zoology commences with an elaborate memoir on the anatomy of that remarkable Cephalopod, which has so long evaded the pursuit of the naturalist, the *Spirula,* or Ram's-Horn, by Professor Owen, the accomplished dissector of the Pearly Nautilus.

In conclusion, I thank my officers, Messrs. Browne, Richards, and Adams, for their skilful aid in preparing the drawings with which the Narrative is illustrated, and it only remains to ask a seaman's indulgence for any errors or ambiguity in the composition.

CONTENTS.

VOL. I.

CHAPTER I.

VOYAGE TO BORNEO AND THE SARAWAK RIVER.

CHAPTER II.

SARAWAK, BRUNAI, AND HONG-KONG.

CHAPTER VI.

SINGAPORE AND BORNEO.

CHAPTER VII.

BORNEO.

The unusually severe gales which then prevailed, compelling us successively to put into Weymouth and Torbay, we were prevented reaching Falmouth until the 5th of February; here I had been directed to swing the ship in order to determine the amount of local attraction; I had also to receive and fit Fox's Dipping Needle, and obtain final results on shore with Hansteen's Needles. These latter experiments were conducted at the house of Robert Were Fox, Esq., a gentleman to whom our Service and the whole scientific world are deeply indebted; and I must not omit to acknowledge the kind assistance derived on this occasion from the exertions of Capt. Ellice, commanding the Packet Establishment, who immediately directed the boats and masters of the packets in port to attend and aid our operations.

In the ordinary duties which will be required hereafter from every ship of war supplied with the compasses adapted by the Committee of the Royal Society, assistance from other vessels will scarcely be needed; but in instances where the Dipping Needle and other delicate instruments are to be observed on the quarter-deck, and the results of vessels equipped as the 'Samarang' to be regarded of authority, it is imperative that the ship be reduced to the same condition as she would be when such observations are to be made at sea; that all chance of error may be removed, or means pursued to arrive at data by which any may be corrected. These observations referring to the magnetic dip, intensity, and variation of the compass, must be taken throughout the voyage from a fixed point; prior to sailing, therefore, the ship is to be reduced to her sea footing; that is to say—to that state in which she would be found under ordinary breezes, away from the land and out of soundings. The cables, as well as her chain-messenger, should be unbent and below; all her boats up and stowed, and if provided with chain-topsail-sheets, particularly on the mizen-mast, they should be *home*. At Falmouth all this was easily provided for (the 'Samarang' had only two brass twenty-four-pounder howitzers on deck), and the ship being secured by hawsers to the mooring buoy was swung to thirty-two points of the compass for the Magnetic Variation, and to sixteen for Dip and Intensity. At other ports I should deem it sufficient to unshackle and pay down the after part of the chain-cable, and to hang the ship "before all" at the bitts—all other precautions observed.

On the evening of the 9th of February, 1843, we slipped our moorings and proceeded to sea. I had decided not to touch at any point before reaching the Cape of Good Hope, but strong breezes preventing our making westing, and pressing us almost to the entrance of the Straits of Gibraltar, I determined on nearing the Barbary coast, where I well knew that we should soon experience breezes calculated to facilitate a southerly passage. On the 25th of February we passed between the Island of Fuertaventura (Canaries) and the coast of Africa, where we took a fair wind. Here, in lat. 27° 7′ N., long. 14° 34′ W., we fell in with the wreck of a large vessel which we had observed on our homeward voyage in the 'Sulphur' off the coast of Portugal, the fore part of her bow timbers and stem still above water. As she was more than two-thirds immersed, and covered, probably, with barnacles (*Anatifa lævis*), she could not be much affected by the wind.

Her drift, therefore, between these two positions during this interval may safely be assumed as evidence of the prevailing southerly currents. I have little doubt that the next report of her will be from a more westerly position; influenced by the trade winds and intertropical currents of these regions, she will probably be driven past the Cape de Verds towards the West Indies. She is rather a dangerous object in the way of navigation, but having broken up from her centre and slipped all her weights, there is little chance of sinking much deeper. She might be mistaken for rocks at night, and may possibly have been reported as such.

On the 2nd of March we passed along the eastern side of the Island of Bonavista, and much closer to the breakers than we should have ventured had I been aware of the dangers reported in that neighbourhood; the next day we anchored in the Bay of Porto Praya in the Island of St. Jago, Cape de Verds. Here we remained four days, refitting, watering, and completing astronomical and magnetic observations; our observing position being upon Quail Island, rather nearer to the landing place than the centre of the island, and just below the highest ground.*

I deem it necessary to be particular in stating these facts, because discrepancies are frequently noticed by successive visitors to the same port, which may be traced to the differences of locality. Magnetic observations, for correct comparison, should always be conducted in one particular site, and especially amongst islands of volcanic origin; at Tahiti the differences of observation are often

* For notes on the Botany, &c. of St. Jago, *vide* Appendix.

considerable. The Consul, or principal merchant, should be apprized of the exact spot, and the place should be marked, if time permit, by some such effectual method as digging a hole and filling it with lime and stones, which will soon become a solid conglomerate. Three good angles to conspicuous objects would also assist in finding such a position.

The amount of Magnetic Variation, or Dip, is well known to vary on the eastern and western sides of islands, and therefore on basaltic or trap formations too much caution cannot be taken to select the same localities used by former observers; the data offered to prove the question of *annual change*, can be of little value otherwise, although we may notice in recent publications, the deduction of this element from the year 1600 to the present without any certain knowledge of the positions at which they were observed. The result of our observations at this position will be found in the Stations noticed in the Appendix.

On the 7th of March we quitted Porto Praya, but had scarcely cleared the bay when a ship-of-war was descried in the offing. On closing, we exchanged Numbers with H.M.S. '*Madagascar*', Captain Foote, senior officer on the coast of Africa. Having letters and parcels for her, it was fortunate we met; but for this circumstance they would have been delayed some months, being directed to be forwarded from the Cape of Good Hope!

Our onward course to the Cape was as monotonous as such voyages usually are; we did not, however, pursue "the beaten track", but endeavoured, by adopting an easterly route, to obtain a series of magnetic observations.

That my brother seamen may not be displeased with this remark, it may be stated that my reasons for selecting this almost abandoned track, were, in the first place, that many competent observers had already preceded me in the route towards the twenty-fourth degree of West Longitude; and, therefore, if I could pass ten or fifteen degrees more to the eastward, a parallel course would tend either to confirm or shake the theoretical lines of Dip and Intensity, particularly in the vicinity of the Magnetic Equator. Secondly, that as the Island of St. Matthew still remains on our charts, it might be desirable to add my testimony as to its existence or otherwise, in its "assigned position." These were points of research essential in a Naval Surveyor, and a further duty, which all Naval Commanders owe to their profession, is that of explaining why they have deviated from what is commonly received as the "main road", as well as the result of such deviation.

Having always considered the eastern route the preferable, I attempted, on my homeward voyage in H.M.S. 'Sulphur', to reach Porto Praya direct from Ascension; in this, however, I failed, owing to the occurrence of westerly breezes driving us towards the African coast until in the parallel of the Cape de Verd Islands, which proved that from the Cape de Verds southerly towards the Equator, in the month of June, favourable breezes without calms might be reckoned upon; and I was reminded that ships coming from Ascension and St. Helena generally make good passages, passing to the westward of the Cape de Verds. My experience whilst employed on the African Station, taught me that a fair passage from the

the Cape de Verds to Sierra Leone, or to the coast easterly, could always be anticipated, and that no retarding calms, are to be met with on the verge of African soundings. Vessels also from the African coast, seeking Ascension for change of climate, find this remark applicable, and it might be fairly assumed that if we could reach the Equator under light airs and moderate breezes in a less number of days than the average passage to the twenty-fourth degree of West Longitude (the increased distance being impeded by many days' calm), that by crossing to the eastward of the tenth degree of West Longitude, the westerly current would be avoided, and we should be able to fetch to windward of Ascension, or possibly sight St. Helena many hundred miles to windward of the "beaten track." The result proved as was anticipated. We experienced light and moderate breezes with a *south easterly* current. Between the 7th and 21st of March, or from Porto Praya to the Equator on the ninth meridian of West Longitude, we averaged eighty-one miles per day, and experienced no more than ten hours' calm! Here we passed over the position assigned to the Island of St. Matthews; the day was beautifully clear and the radius of vision at least twenty miles, but no traces of land were visible in any direction, whilst any moderate elevations could readily be seen at forty or more miles distance.

Before the south-westerly breezes quitted us, we had been carried as far as 8° west. On the 23rd of March experiments were made with the water-bottle and thermometers as low as 1,000 fathoms, as follows:—

		Depth.	Temp.	
Latitude of position	2° 32′ S.	300	46°	Fahr.
		400	38° ?	„
Longitude ———	8° 11′ W.	500	46°	„
		600	45° 5′	„
Sea at surface	79°	700	46°	„
		800	45°	„
		900	40° 25′	„
		1,000	42° 75′	„

The slight variations of the last two may be accounted for by the vibration of hauling the line in affecting the indices of the Six's thermometers. On the 25th, in lat. 4° 14′ S., long. 4° 41′ W., soundings were obtained at 1,615 fathoms, though a previous trial on the 20th, at the great depth of 3,065 fathoms, proved unsuccessful.

After light south-westerly airs we were enabled, on the 28th of March, by a succession of breezes from the S.E., to pass 150 miles to windward of Ascension in 9° 44′ E. On referring to a little publication by Henry Wise, Esq., termed "Analysis of a Hundred Voyages to and from China," it may be noticed, by way of comparison, that the 'Castle Huntly,' a fast-sailing ship in the China trade, which quitted the Lizard on the 15th of February, and had fair winds, crossed the Equator in 22° 5′ W., on March 23rd, and on April 4th reached the lat. of 22° 12′ S., and long. 28° 53′ W., taking twelve days to perform this distance. The 'Samarang' crossed the Equator on the 21st of March, in the meridian of 9° W., and on the 4th of April reached 22° 38′ S., and, long. 15° 43′ W., 790 miles to windward, without experiencing the "wear and tear" resulting from calms, and passing to the westward of 16° 18′ W., arrived in Simon's Bay, Cape of Good Hope, on the 25th of April.

We certainly ought to have reached the Cape on the 18th, and were only 200 miles distant from it on that day; I would therefore strongly advise keeping to the southward of 36° S, until near enough to the Cape to haul sharp in. Had we preserved southing instead of shaping our course to meet a suspected gale from the N.W., we should have reached the Cape easily. A good collection of well-recorded "Naval Passages", for each month in the year, would be highly valuable for the vicinity of the Cape. About six P.M., after experiencing two very heavy squalls, which caused the 'Samarang' to heel very much and to ship a great deal of water, we reached our anchorage in Simon's Bay in company with H.M.S. 'Thunderbolt', Capt. Broke. We found here H.M.S. 'Southampton,' Capt. C. Eden, bearing the Flag of Rear-Admiral the Hon. Josceline Percy, C.B; 'Acorn', Capt. Adams; 'Lilly', Capt. Baker,; 'Erebus' and 'Terror', Capt. Sir James Clarke Ross and Crozier.

The Admiral being absent at Cape Town, I was happy to join my good friends Ross and Crozier, and the night was far advanced before half our interchange of questions was expended; had the former not given me hopes of further detention, it is probable that we should not have parted until his anchor was at his bows, and that sullen monitor, the fore-top-sail, at his mast head.

After completing our observations to secure the time, I moved off to Cape Town, to pay my respects to the Governor, Sir George Napier, and Admiral Percy; I passed a very agreeable evening at the house of the former, where the Admiral and his family were staying, and afterwards visited the Observatory. On the day following I was joined by Lieut. Clerk, R.A., of the Magnetic Observatory, who was desirous of witnessing the operation of swinging the 'Samarang' for local attraction, and reached Simon's Bay in the evening. On the 30th H.M.S 'Thunderer,' &c., arrived with troops, and on the 5th of May, H.M.S. 'Cleopatra.' After a pleasant sojourn at Simon's Bay we quitted on the morning of the 5th, with a fair wind from the northward, and before noon were well to the southward of Cape Hanglip. Our observing position at Simon's Bay was the same as that used by Capt. Sir J. C. Ross, and by myself twelve months previously on my homeward voyage in the 'Sulphur'. It is marked by a post and well known to the people of the dock-yard, but somewhat liable to be overgrown by grass and shrubs; a spring at which cattle come to drink, serves, however, in some measure, to indicate the locality. Leaving Simon's Bay I now began to search for documents likely to assist me in selecting the best route for this season; Horsburgh's Directory proved to be of little or no service, and upon referring to the 'Analysis of a Hundred Voyages', before alluded to, that authority was equally unsatisfactory, although furnishing a better insight into general passages made at trading seasons. No warning of the discomforts, or even dangers, to which we should be liable occur in either; I had, however, already made the voyage to Ceylon in H.M.S. 'Southampton', in July, and was not unprepared for inauspicious weather. In that ship we split a close-reefed main-top-sail, and were reduced to our fore-sail for some days.

The 'Samarang', when deep, is an uneasy sea-boat;

she rolled viciously, and having nearly broken up one cutter, we were compelled to get the other in board before she sustained similar damage.

Our magnetic duties required us to carry the boats on our quarters, or they would have been stowed in-board before quitting the Cape. Ten days bad weather may always be contemplated in these regions until passing St. Paul's. Not obtaining any information from the books supplied by Government, I may add, that from present experience, as well as that of the Journals contained in the 'Hundred Voyages', I would recommend running a S.S.E. (compass) course from the Cape until reaching the parallel of 36° or 38° S.; then a course between S.E. by E. to S.E., as the local attraction may render necessary, in order to make the Island of St. Paul's.* About the 60th degree of east longitude we experienced light breezes, which continued, varying from north to south-west, until passing 70°. On the 19th we were again favoured with strong breezes varying from N.W. to S.W., but not sufficiently strong to prevent our carrying all plain canvas. During the night of the 22nd of May we passed the meridian of St. Paul's and expected to have sighted it at dawn, but had over-run our distance. On the 26th we reached the 95th meridian, and, with the expectation of meeting the S.E. trade near the tropic, altered our course, first to E. and E.N.E., and then to N.E.

* The daily observations for the Variation made on board each ship will accurately point out what is due to local attraction. After passing the Island of St. Paul's the course may be varied by degrees (as the variation decreases), so as to ensure cutting the Southern Tropic to the eastward of 100° or probably 105° E., where the S.E. trade may be expected from May until November.

My reason for keeping thus far to the eastward was to take advantage of the N.W. current, which usually prevails during this season; unless the wind be well free, the lee set considerably diminishes the rate of sailing, and if it haul, as it does occasionally, more easterly, time as well as velocity would be sacrificed. Soon afterwards we experienced a westerly current, and on the 30th, in lat. 24° 41′ S., and long. 99° 15′ E., the breeze suddenly chopped round to E.N.E., eventually to N.E , and notwithstanding the scud, or light clouds aloft, still preserved a a rapid motion to the eastward, fully proving that we were not far beyond the influence of a westerly wind. As the breeze did not admit of our lying better than N.W. by N., we tacked to the eastward, being at that moment in lat. 21° 15′ S., long. 98° 15′ E. It is important to notice these points, because I am satisfied the 30th parallel of latitude should not be crossed until reaching the 105th degree of longitude, in order to secure a comfortable passage, or to relieve the mind from the idea of being "backstrapped" *.

Every effort was made to preserve our easting, in order to sight Christmas Island, and we so far succeeded as to pass within ten miles to the westward of it. The result of our observations, on a running survey, give it an altitude of 1,115 feet. We passed the western extreme of the island on the 7th, at noon, and, calculating on our previous westerly current, steered a course to cut Klapp's Island; the following day, however, we found ourselves about thirty miles to the eastward of it, and about the

* Driven to leeward of a port and compelled to beat up.

same distance from Wine-Cooper's Island. On the 8th, at midnight, we passed Java Head, but the strength of the current prevented our getting much beyond the Second Point of the charts before daylight. Strangers may be warned to keep the Java shore on board and anchor when the breeze fails, otherwise they will find themselves drifted to the S.W. The 'Samarang', attending closely to this, arrived in Anjer Roads on the 11th, just five weeks from Simon's Bay.

Shortly after daylight numerous canoes laden with stock, fruit, &c., were noticed putting off to the numerous merchantmen endeavouring to work up. We received a visit from Capt. Hicks, of the Clipper Brig 'Anonyma', just arrived from China, who afforded us intelligence from the scene of our destination, and took charge of our despatches for Bombay. We also obtained from him much useful information relative to the navigation of this immediate neighbourhood, particularly as to the set and duration of the tides. Calm had compelled him to anchor the previous evening to the northward of the Strait, when he ascertained the flood tide to set N.E. three miles per hour. The tides are regular on both sides of the Strait, and the flood being strong, I gave up all idea of delay here and pushed on northerly. We were well supplied by the canoes with vegetables, stock, &c., at very low prices, but no edible, or sufficiently ripe, fruit was offered. Mr. Adams, my assistant-surgeon and constant companion on detached service, observed that " after a long and tedious voyage across the Indian Ocean, the Javanese who come off to barter, afford the European who sees them for the first time, much amusement. They are chiefly women, dressed with primitive simplicity in loose sarongs; their heads being protected from the sun by large hemispherical bamboo hats, and their long black shining hair streaming down their backs. In the canoes that venture alongside the ship, might be seen amusing monkeys, sitting among heaps of fruit and vegetables, chattering and making grimaces; huge turtles lying bound at the bottom of the boats; saucy Krocotoas, and gaudy-coloured Loris; pretty plantain squirrels in neat quadrangular cages, and domesticated Musangs.

The Straits of Sunda being considered the 'Gate of the East', the natives of the villages along this part of the coast of Java, find a ready sale for natural curiosities among the passengers of homeward-bound Indiamen. At Anjer, especially, a fair of the most remarkable character is held under the shade of a magnificent Banyan tree, where, for a few dollars, may be purchased long-armed Apes, hideous Baboons, pigmy Musks, Java Finches, graceful Doves, pert Paroquets, satin Grackles, gentle Love-birds, and splendid Peacocks. Among other quadrumanous rarities I noticed the *Hylobates syndactyla*, from the opposite Island of Sumatra, and among *Ophidians* a very large and handsome *Python poda*. The Kahau, or proboscis monkey of Borneo, was offered us for six dollars, and the pig-faced baboon might have been procured for half that sum. Baskets of Cowries (*Cypræa histrio, Argus, Arabica*, and *vitellus*, &c.), might be had for a mere trifle."

Before two o'clock of the same day we had weathered Java, but, owing to calms and variable airs, made little progress; and the prevailing easterly wind much impeded us. On the evening of the 13th we made the land of

Banca (drift-wood, Nipa Palms, and water-prahus abundant), passed Gaspar Island on the 15th, and entered the Straits of Singapore on the 19th. Keeping on the northern danger line in four to six fathoms, we groped our way at night towards Singapore, but several times found ourselves grazing the fishing stakes! To a lighter vessel than the 'Samarang' this might have proved dangerous, and, I think, considering the navigation of this Channel is considerably risked by these obstructions, the authorities of Singapore should prevent their being placed in any greater depth than three fathoms; they might then be made available as danger marks by day. On the 14th, we dropped anchor in Singapore Road, and having refitted and rated our chronometers, sailed for Borneo; on our passage through the straits we met and communicated with H.M.S. 'Wanderer', Capt. Seymour.

On the eve of our departure from Falmouth, I received instructions to call at the River Sarăwak, communicate with Mr. Brooke, and obtain the necessary information relative to that place; then move on to Borneo Proper and report upon the coal measures in that neighbourhood, and, if possible, obtain a sufficient quantity to test its value in one of Her Majesty's Steamers.

In order to appreciate the value of our connection with Singapore, it must be understood that the chief British traffic with Northern Borneo has been maintained through the medium of small Malay (or at times Bugis) Prahus, who collect the produce of that and the neighbouring islands in their voyages from Macassar, and (not unfrequently demanding it as tribute or Black-Mail) repair to this port to exchange their cargo for British goods, and return with them during the fair monsoon. This may, in many cases, prove to be the virtual object of these voyages; the immense profit (amounting, it is said, to nearly six hundred per cent) charged by the Dutch for similar commodities without any choice of quality, renders them doubly lucrative,—first on account of the higher price obtained for their goods at Singapore—and secondly, as just stated, in the more advantageous purchase of return cargo. By the laws which govern this trade, the Malay vessels are prohibited taking from Singapore any arms or ammunition beyond a limited allowance, or without a special pass; failing to produce this they are liable to be captured by the gun-boats belonging to the Indian Government, which cruize in the straits for the prevention of piracy. It was formerly the practice of the pirates, and from the fears expressed to me by those disposed to trade between Borneo and Singapore, I believe it still exists, to cruize amongst the numerous islands in the vicinity of the Anambas, and Natunas, for the purpose of intercepting the unprotected craft; and after robbing them of their cargoes, they would load a trading vessel of their fleet, and despatch her to Singapore, where the proceeds of the sale were expended in arms and ammunition. It is not improbable even that these returns were again disposed of in the neighbourhood of the Sarãwak, and furnished the means by which the disaffected intended to have attacked Mr. Brooke in his territory.

These ventures were not, however, restricted to the natural produce of Borneo, they extended even to the sale of human beings,—female children captured on the coast and sold as slaves to the Chinese at Singapore, who brought them up for their future wives. The laws of China strictly prohibit the emigration of females; and so strictly has this edict been enforced, I do not believe a case can be adduced of its infringement by any of the respectable classes; I learned, moreover, from one of the first Chinese merchants, that if the evasion of it did not entail death to the kindred left behind by the lady eloping, the expenses in the shape of hush-money would be too ruinous to allow of the risk. These piratical vessels do not belong, in many instances, to the neighbourhood of Singapore, and are nominally the friends and allies of the Dutch. It was by the prahus of the Sultan of Rhio that the boats of the 'Dido' were attacked, under an impression that they were the weaker party, and there is little doubt that had they been captured and the 'Dido' not at hand to resent it, all would have been murdered to prevent discovery. The pirates of these seas are of the same description, and we have only to refer to the exploits of the boats of H.M.S. 'Andromache' Capt. H. D. Chads, C.B., to prove their original haunts. It is much to be regretted that the case of the attack on the boats of H.M.S. 'Dido' was not referred to a competent Court of Admiralty, where the question of what constitutes an act of piracy might be defined. I am not prepared to admit that their act was not piratical, "because they were the forces of the Sultan of Rhio, not at war with us, and the friend and ally of the Dutch," or that because they failed in murdering the Dido's boat's crew, they had not committed piracy; indeed the very fact of this force being detached to collect tribute at the Anambas, has in itself a piratical complexion.

Before leaving Singapore I used every endeavour to obtain information which might assist me in finding the mouth of the River Sarãwak; but disappointed in this, I was compelled to trust to the pamphlet published by Mr. Brooke, a copy of which had been kindly furnished me by Mr. Wise. I did not imagine the published charts to be more in error than fifteen or twenty minutes of longitude, and confidently relied on obtaining a local pilot off its embouchure. On the 4th July we passed Tanjong Api, or "Fire Points"; a low wooded spit, forming the north-western angle of Borneo, and dangerous to approach within two miles. It has a slight elevation immediately within the line of trees, which are not Mangrove, nor is the ground swampy, as in other parts of the low coast; the trees are of hard wood, and the rocks and solid ground jut out at the point where a fresh-water stream oozes through the sand into the sea. The water inland is deeply tinged by leaves and decayed vegetable matter, but it percolates into a large sandy reservoir a little to the south, about ten feet above high-water mark, where it may be procured very pure. The knowledge of this fact is highly important to seamen; easy and safe landing may be found immediately to the southward of the large rock at the northern angle, and no similar facility for watering occurs in any part of the route by the Palawan Channel to Manila or China.

We looked in vain for Tanjong Datu of the charts; it is the first high land seen from Tanjong Api, and is situate in lat. 2° 6′ N. long. 109° 38′ E. There are several

c 2

rocky patches off its northern extremity, but they may be avoided by keeping in twenty fathoms until it is rounded, when Tanjong Sipang, capped by the high mountain of Santubon, points out the western or "Santubon entrance" of the Sarãwak, accessible to vessels of twelve feet draught by the chart, and of eighteen feet, aided by pilots, at high-water. Beyond Tanjong Sipang, off which a rock *a-wash* lies, a deep indentation called Ape's Bight occurs, and round the high peninsula, or where solid high land terminates (at Tanjong Po), will be found the Morotabas or eastern entrance to the Sarãwak. These facts being then unknown to us, and forced easterly by currents, we attempted the first great gap which seemed to correspond with Mr. Brooke's pamphlet, until we found the depth decrease to four fathoms; anchoring until the change of tide, and ascertaining by the charts that we were too far to the eastward, (being now at the mouth of the Batang Lupar), we worked an opposite course, and on the following morning found ourselves westerly of Santubon. I then determined to approach the river, now in sight, and anchoring in five fathoms off the mouth of a promising stream, which proved to be the Lundu, the boats were despatched for information, as well as to procure a pilot. Towards the evening they returned, having, after a smart chase, come up with a canoe, from which a very intelligent native, who happened to be an ally of Mr. Brooke's, volunteered to show us the way into the Sarãwak.

By 8 o'clock that evening we reached Tanjong Po, and by moonlight, assisted by our boats sounding, worked into the Morotabas, and anchored in safety. The ability of this native was remarkable; even by day I should hardly have given him credit, for conducting a square-rigged vessel of the size of the 'Samarang' into so narrow a channel as that formed at the entrance by the shoals. As he did not understand English, nor we Malay, our communication was chiefly by signs; a black board and a piece of chalk were procured, and we intimated to him our wish to know the direction and probable distance to Sarăwak. This he endeavoured to show, but suddenly recollecting a black silk handkerchief around his neck, which one of the officers had given to him, he immediately rolled it up like a snake, and kneeling on the deck, shaped it to represent the windings of the river; giving us to understand that Kapal Prahu (ship-of-war), was the nearest end, and Kuching, or Mr. Brooke's residence, the most remote. The intelligence expressed by his countenance, and the playful manner in which he executed his manœuvres, formed an admirable specimen of savage talent, affording us nearly as much information as might be obtained from a chart; of the distance, we were of course unable to judge.

Having advanced the ship as high up the river as I thought our present knowledge of it warranted, she was anchored in a safe berth, and I proceeded with my gig in search of the town of Kuching, which we reached about four P.M. I was received most warmly by Mr. Brooke, and he immediately despatched Mr. Douglas, his naval aide, to assist in piloting the ship up; after touching on one or two banks, she eventually found a safe berth off the city of Kuching, nearly in the same spot occupied by H.M.S. 'Dido,' Capt. the Hon. Harry Keppel, who had visited the river shortly before. Previous to the arrival of the 'Samarang,' Capt. Keppel had been appointed to the command in the straits of Malacca, and in the execution of the duties entrusted to him, had visited Sarãwak, in order to repress some piracies committed in the vicinity of the territory ceded to Mr. Brooke. The pirates, as I before mentioned, threatened to attack Mr. Brooke, and but for the timely aid of the 'Dido,' for an account of which I must refer the reader to Capt. Keppel's very interesting work, he might have been defeated before the 'Samarang' could have rendered any assistance; the arrival of our frigate at this particular period, was estimated therefore, beyond doubt, by the people of Sarãwak as a jealous interest on the part of the British Government in the affairs of Mr. Brooke.

On the second day of our sojourn at Kuching, we paid a formal visit to the Rajah Muda Hassim; it appeared to gratify him much, and the arrival of a second British ship-of-war added in no small degree to the importance of the 'Tuan besar' (great man), the term by which Mr. Brooke was known to the natives, who concluded he must be a very important chief for his Government to send two large war ships to support him.

Preparations were now made for ascending the river, and for visiting the mines, as well as Mr. Brooke's friends, the Dyak tribes, in their native holds. On the morning of the 11th we started, accompanied by all the Officers who could be spared from duty, and well stored with provisions, in three covered canoes and my gig, and shortly before sunset reached Siniavan; here we slept, and on the following morning proceeded to Toondung, a distance of about twelve miles.

The scenery throughout the river is somewhat uninteresting, being much confined by the lofty trees which intercept the view; but the small cleared patches which frequently present themselves, give promise of a rich luxuriant soil elevated about fifteen feet above the ordinary level of the stream. We first met with elevated land at Siniavan, about nine miles direct from Kuching. The Chinese appear to have made some progress here, in their gardens, the plateau, on which their houses are built, being above thirty feet above the level of the river, to which it gradually descends. We observed the customary products of tropical gardens, but upon a critical examination of the soil, found it to consist of a great preponderance of clay, which in this climate, where torrents of rain are succeeded by intense heat, causes the ground to cake and become rent. The inhabitants endeavour to overcome this by the introduction of wood ashes into the pits which they make for their plants, and although they have both loam and sand in the vicinity, do not appear to understand the value of these materials for improving the soil, nor are they disposed to be advised.

At Toondung, which, by the sinuosities of the river, I assume to be about twelve miles distant, we found the stream perfectly clear, with a pebbly bottom, and enjoyed the luxury of a cool bath without the apprehension of being selected as a delicate meal by any epicurean alligator. The narrowness of the river in this part, caused the lofty trees on the banks to approach so nearly as almost to complete an arch, and thus, shaded from the sun's rays, kept the stream at the same temperature as that in which it descended from the mountain; it was not, however, free from disagreeables which annoyed us in the form of leeches.

Having duly equipped ourselves, we proceeded, about nine A.M., on our journey to the Antimony Mines, distant about five miles inland; the intermediate country does not merit any particular notice, being merely an uninteresting gently undulating tract, which rises gradually until it reaches the mountains where the ore is obtained, about 700 feet above the level of the river. Here we breakfasted, or rather lunched, and examined the ore *in situ*, as well as the process by which the Chinese work it; not by blasting, but simply by making large fires upon the heavy masses, and throwing water on them to cause them to split; by this rude process, the purest portions become fused and dissipated. As the entire mountain is a mass of ore, any improvement in their *modus operandi* would not be of much importance to the present generation. It is paid for by contract, at a certain price per picul of 140lbs. delivered at Kuching, where the ore is strictly examined and that of doubtful quality rejected. Having refreshed ourselves, and amused the Chinese by practising with rifles at our empty bottles, we continued our march to the Gold Mines at Selingok, which I should estimate at about three miles further inland; on our arrival we were saluted by several gingals, very much to the risk of all parties, if one might judge from their rude construction, as well as the heavy charges put into them. Here we remained to sleep.

The Gold Mines are worked by a Chinese party, at a rental, and as it is not their interest to allow any one to ascertain the amount of their returns, the property may be retained on these conditions, until Mr. Brooke can put it into better hands. The gold is obtained by washing, from a very loose disintegrated granitic debris, containing detached crystals of quartz (dodecahedrons, or six-sided pyramids, base to base), pyrites, antimony, and traces of tin. I have been informed that late experiments prove their current of water to be too powerful, and that they lose a very large portion of light gold.

On the morning of the 13th, we returned to Toondung, and thence by boat to Siniavan, where we passed the night; on the 16th, after an early breakfast, we started for the Dyak village of Sarambo. We were apprised that this excursion would put both our walking and climbing to the test, but as I suspected that our land brethren must have under-rated our powers, I had treated the matter rather in jest; indeed, we were all simple enough to carry our guns, in the hope of shooting objects worthy of preservation. As we approached the base of the mountain, which I should describe as a cone compressed literally with an oval base, it presented the appearance of prepared ground, that could readily be maintained by a small power against a formidable opponent. The advances appeared to proceed by terraces, and the access to each guarded by steps, up which we could only ascend by notched logs; the first were easily overcome, but as we proceeded they became more frequent and more slippery, the angular edges being worn away, and, as fewer intervals for breathing occurred, our strength rapidly diminished. I notice these objects in a war-like view, as the attacking or scaling party would be but a poor match even for the female garrison left in the village, by the time they reached the outer lines. Those who accompanied me maintained their ground until we made good our lodging in the Great "*Head House*", but we amounted only to three; forty-five minutes afterwards (by watch), when we had recovered ourselves, we noticed the rest of our party advancing, some *towed* along holding a stick by which a Dyak helped them forward, whilst several were reduced in dress to nearly the same limited garb as their Dyak assistants; yet, upon subsequent examination we found that the height to which we had ascended was only 950 feet above our point of departure at Siniavan.

After refreshing ourselves with cool cocoa-nut milk, aided by the contents of our baskets, we examined the village and our apartment, which was the "Head House," *par excellence*, of this tribe. It is a building elevated on posts, about thirty feet above the ground, of an octagonal form, with the roof, commencing at the height of six feet within the room, carried up to a very sharp peak; the flooring, which in all buildings in the country, is sufficiently open for the passage of a kris, is formed of the outer rind of the Nibon Palm (*Areca tigillaria*), an exogenous wood of flinty hardness towards its exterior, and pith within; from some cause, however, not yet determined, it does not endure long, the decay, arising probably from the fermentation of its juices. Suspended from the ceilings of this building are the heads of the enemies captured by the tribe, those of the higher caste being ornamented according to their taste by red and white paint, with Cowries for eyes, but the generality simply smoke-dried. We examined a few of them, but it is highly probable their numbers had been very much diminished out

of respect to Mr. Brooke, whom they were prepared to receive. When we consider that every man in the village had to obtain a trophy of this revolting description before he could be permitted to pay his addresses to his lady love, it is highly probable that the living members had abstracted theirs in order to afford us the shelter which this building offered, independent of its being the chamber of the honoured guest! The village itself contributed little to interest; the houses were all in the same style, built upon posts, not raised more than three feet from the ground, and as filthy as can well be imagined.

The dress of the male is simply a cloth about the loins, descending about half way to the knee, with a jacket of tough material woven by the women, and frequently padded with bark cloth to withstand the point of the arrow; the legs and arms are generally ornamented with rows of brass wire rings covering them to the extent of about a foot. The female dress is mostly a short sarong of very substantial workmanship, displaying no want of taste in the pattern, and not extending below the knee. The sarong generally in use throughout other parts of the eastern islands, consists of about the same quantity of material as may be required to make a gown of the present style, or three times the circumference round the shoulders; it is open at top and bottom, and, extending in length from the shoulders to the heels, is generally overlapped, twisted round the waist by the upper edge, and, with the twist turned in, is retained like a petticoat; sometimes it is thrown loosely over one shoulder and under the opposite arm, at other times over the head and held crossing over the breast, cowl fashion, and is worn by both men and women. The ornaments displayed by the women are of brass, similar to those of the men, but they are distinguished by wearing stays formed by a continuous spiral band of rattan, which, extending about a foot above the hips, presents a beaded black band not unbecoming; they also use a light jacket composed of the same material as the sarong.

During the period of our visit, the women were occupied in drying rice upon a slight platform in front of their houses; they are well formed, and, with pleasing features, are free from the shyness exhibited by the Malay; of their strength we had a convincing proof by witnessing two girls not exceeding ten years of age, ascending the steep hill we had laboured to surmount, with enormous faggots on their backs. In one or two of the houses visited, a considerable degree of neatness prevailed, for this untutored tribe, and there was a manifestation of domestic happiness among the younger couples, which would not suffer if placed in competition with European manners. They were much amused in examining our dresses, and comparing them with textures of their own manufacture; it was plain, however, that the gilt buttons of our uniform excited their greatest admiration, and we returned home with the loss of not a few in consequence; as an example of their affection, however, I noticed the ladies begged them only to adorn their husbands.

During the afternoon we visited one of the minor peaks of this mountain, whence we had a magnificent view of the whole country, and complete outline of the land from Tanjong Datu to the most eastern point,

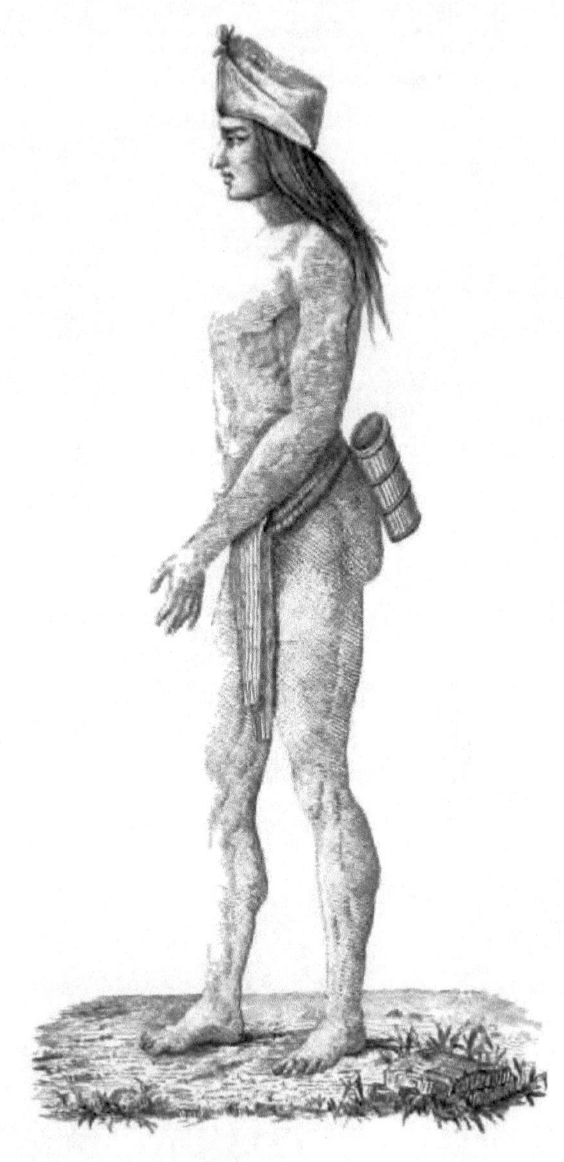

Native Hill Dyak.

furnishing us with important observations for its future delineation. Here we found another 'Head-House,' smaller and neater, but of inferior calibre to that at Sarambo. On our return to the village in the evening, we joined an assembly of the principal inhabitants in which their chief, Meta, a compact and handsomely formed young man about twenty-five years of age, addressed a very energetic speech to Mr. Brooke, which was interpreted to us. He commenced by expressing his satisfaction, as well as that of his allies, at the interest which Great Britain had been pleased to take in their affairs, and bore witness of the increasing benefit they derived from the residence of a man of such activity and kindness of disposition as Mr. Brooke among them. Formerly, the Dyaks effected the cultivation of their territory at the risk of life, and half their strength was expended in the village in the protection of their property; now, they were not only free from the piratical incursions of their neighbour, but were able to visit their "Great Friend" at Kuching in safety, and to supply their wants from his stores. The oration was long and much applauded, and those who knew the Dyak language described it to be not only interesting but brilliantly expressed; the evening terminated with dancing and singing on the part of the natives varied by that of my gig's crew, and on the ensuing morning, after taking leave of our Dyak friends, we returned to Siniavan and reached Kuching the same evening, with the prospect of softer repose than that afforded during the course of our eventful excursion.

The 'Samarang' was now ordered to prepare for sea,

and also to be in readiness for the reception of a visit of ceremony from the Rajah Musa Hassim and his suite. As it was contrary to the custom of vessels employed upon surveying duty to fire salutes during the period of rating the chronometers, or until after the necessary observations are made for the determination of the meridian distance between the ports of departure and arrival, we could not risk the disturbance of them; but having three boats on the water fitted with brass guns, it was arranged that the compliment should be paid by them; and, it seemed to afford more amusement and interest than might have been experienced had the guns of the ship performed the office. The Rajah and his suite arrived in due state, and after inspecting the ship, expressed themselves better pleased with her than with the beautiful 'Dido,' nearly double our tonnage; two decks and better shelter weighing more in their estimation than capacity or beauty, and our main-deck cabin, with free passage of air by the ports and windows, seemed more consonant with their ideas of comfort; the difference in the description of gun mattered little, and they could hardly be brought to comprehend that our twenty-four 32-pounders were not preferable to the eighteen heavy guns of the same calibre mounted by the 'Dido.'

The progress made by Mr. Brooke during his short sojourn amongst these people, not only in acquiring a moral command over the affections of the Malay race, (hostile, often, to the Christian in feeling as well as religion,) but also in allaying the fears and exciting the affections of the Dyaks or natives of the interior, is truly wonderful; this great philanthropist has in a comparatively short period entirely overcome the antipathy felt by the Malay to the residence of an European and a Christian amongst them; by representing the sovereign ruler and proprietor of the Sarãwak district, he has, moreover, advanced to an elevation, unparalled in the history of any remote aboriginal tribe. The Malay has yielded up his tyrannical sway over the Dyak; and his systematic pursuit of piracy, the terror of their tribes, has been successfully arrested. With the example and influence of Mr. Brooke, the Malay, Dyak, and English have combined their forces, and, under the command of one of our spirited captains, have entered the strongholds of their lawless neighbours, and dealt a blow from which piracy will never recover; the particulars of which have already been forcibly narrated by my friend Capt. Keppel.

The next question which naturally suggests itself is, what is to be the end of the splendid advantage resulting from the energy of our countryman? Are the unfortunate Dyaks, and no less unfortunate Malay rulers to be left to the savage vengeance of the neighbouring pirates, by the withdrawal of British protection, upon the bare plea that the occupation of Borneo is against the spirit of our Treaties with Foreign Powers? Let us refer to our Treaty with Holland, and I think it will be clear to any unprejudiced mind that it contains no article inimical to our taking possession of any part of Borneo, even by force:—

"TREATY 1824, 17th of MARCH.

"Art. 6. It is agreed that orders shall be given by the two Governments to *their Officers* and *Agents* in the *East* not to form any new Settlements on any of the Islands in the Eastern Seas, without *previous authority from their respective Governments* in Europe.

"Art. 12. His Britannic Majesty, however, engages, that no British Establishment shall be made on the Carimon Islands, or on the Islands of Battam, Bintang, Lingin, or on any of the other Islands *south* of the Straits of Singapore, nor any Treaty concluded by British authority with the chiefs of those Islands."

But the case assumes a very different aspect when viewed under a gift, sale, or transfer, by the Power acknowledged by the laws of nations to be authorized in conferring part of his Dominions upon a subject of his most ancient ally. Such a proceeding was not attempted to be cavilled at when the Sultan of Sooloo, a sovereign, not even of Borneo, conferred upon the subjects of Great Britain not only the Island of Balambangan, but also a greater portion of the northern coast of Borneo (extending from Maludu Bay to Pulu Tiga) than that now under discussion. Great Britain had then a factory within the river of Borneo Proper, within sight of the city of Brunai, and also the fortified Island of Balambangan, from which her subjects eventually withdrew, not by the interference of any European Power, but by the continued depredations of the pirates, and unhealthiness of the climate.

Mr. Brooke, by formal Treaty with the reigning Powers of Borneo, having obtained, or, for a consideration, purchased, his estate of Sarãwak, seeks for that protection which should be, and usually is, extended to British subjects from the mother country; anxious also not to lose sight of the interests of those with whom he has consented to settle, and willing, at the same time, to advance their security, by obtaining the countenance of Great Britain, he has further induced the Borneon Powers to seek by Treaty a closer alliance with our country, and to offer, as a pledge of their sincerity, the cession of part of their territory for the foundation of a military position. Kuching does not offer such a position; it is inland, approachable only with a favourable tide, and by a circuitous route, nearly twenty-five miles from the sea; nor are any spots to be met with either at the Santubon or Morotabas entrances desirable for forming a settlement. The ground is too precipitous, and the difficulties of clearing away and levelling too heavy an operation for an infant colony to undertake. If compelled to select a spot in this neighbourhood, the most eligible is probably on the Santubon or western entrance; but it is much to be feared that the percolation from the mountain in the rear would create fever, and take off the young colony before any efficient mode of draining could be carried out. It is more than probable that to this cause alone may be attributed the original lamentable sickness at Hong-Kong.

Under these considerations it was thought that the Island of Labuan would offer a better naval position, a more central point from which the pirates could be overlooked; and under the supposition that its coal might be rendered available for the use of steamers employed upon the

D

station, it was considered advisable to make a further examination of its capabilities.*

The river Sarãwak is safely navigable up to the ridge of rocks which occasioned the unfortunate accident to the 'Samarang,' to be described in the succeeding chapter. All dangers may be avoided by the aid of beacons or pilots, and care should be taken not to pass them until the proper times of tide, certainly not at dead water or change of tide to ebb, as the rapidity of the ebb produces many eddies and causes a vessel to veer so much that she becomes unmanageable. The banks of this river do not afford any firm landing, or spots eligible for cultivation, until within the neighbourhood of Kuching; above this town, the banks are level, in many places cleared, and apparently of a rich diluvial granitic soil. The Chinese possess excellent gardens, where the sugar cane and common vegetables appear to thrive. The climate is particularly healthy, and no greater proof of this can be

* At the moment of going to press with the observations above recorded, intelligence has reached England that the Island of Labuan is ceded to the British authorities for a naval and military station.

The following is from a letter dated "Labuan, East coast of Borneo, December 25th, 1846:—

"We are now at the Island of Labuan, which was taken possession of yesterday by Captain Mundy, of the 'Iris,' in Her Majesty's name. There is to be a grand expedition against the pirates next April, and we may be detained on the station till May. The treaty ceding the Island of Labuan was signed and sealed by the Sultan. I have no doubt that there will be a flourishing trade here in a few years; there is a brig laden with long cloths in the harbour, so that the merchants of Singapore have their eyes here already. If the piracy could be suppressed, a large market would be opened."

adduced than the circumstance of the 'Samarang' losing only two men out of a crew of two hundred, during the arduous surveying duties of this river, and neither of which cases was fairly attributable to climate. The great drawback which occurs to me is the want of a labouring population; the Malay is too indolent and independent, and will hardly work for the maintenance of his own family; the Dyak may be induced to quit his mountain holds when he finds security and a better market for his labour, but at present he prefers the air and retirement of the mountains, with the cultivation of his Paddy fields, without which necessary article of provision the town population would probably suffer.

The Chinese are the only people to be depended upon, but the present race is little better than Ladrone; they belong to their captain or headman, and it is difficult to obtain their labour excepting through him, with whom they are under bond. Under the countenance, or protection of Great Britain it is not improbable that a more civilised race will flow in. A feeling of greater security will naturally be engendered by the formally taking possession of any portion of the northern coast of Borneo, or even by the frequent visits of our cruizers for the suppression of piracy. If the highly important advantages which Mr. Brooke has obtained, are not followed up by some decided act on the part of Government before any misfortune befal him liable to annul them, this territory will gradually recede into its former insignificancy, or be transferred to the hands of some other power.

The forests of Borneo do not appear at present to offer any very desirable or valuable wood; poon is abundant,

D 2

and apparently of finer quality than that procured at Singapore, approaching in some parts to the hardness of good mahogany or cedar. With the advantages which the river offers for the construction of saw mills, poon and cedar plank might afford a lucrative article of export to Hong-Kong.

With respect to the position which Mr. Brooke now occupies in Borneo, I am firmly of opinion, that it would be unsafe to trust the power which he has so firmly but mildly wielded in the hands of others. His acceptance of any appointment under Government, which would interfere with the absolute power which he exercises would destroy the charm by which he has maintained himself amongst the unruly Malays. Nothing but the vigorous exertion of power, untrammelled by law, will avail with them. As the British population increase and become better able to protect themselves, the necessity for this power may decrease, but so long as Mr. Brooke exists, he should not descend from his princely position.

CHAPTER II.

SARAWAK, BRUNAI AND HONG-KONG.

Preparations for leaving Kuching—The Ship grounds—Inclines forty-five degrees to Starboard—Instruments saved—Construct Houses on shore—Royalist dispatched to Singapore for provisions and assistance—Measures adopted for raising the Ship—Zeal of the Crew—Speedy and succesfull issue—Cockpit Hall—Newspaper report of the Disaster—Departure from Sarāwak—Navigation dangerous—Arrival at Borneo Proper—Visit to the Sultan—Reception—Brunai, a City of the Waters—Floating Bazaar—Futile search for Coal—Lema Islands—Arrival at Hong-Kong—Improvements at that Island—Its Physical and Natural History.

On the 16th of July, preparations were made on board the 'Samarang' for quitting Kuching, but in unmooring it was found that sufficient attention had not been paid to securing her in the stream, and she had been forced by the tide on a slaty ledge immediately below Mr. Brooke's residence. I was then absent, and on my return found the ship inclined to port, twenty-two degrees, a most unpleasant predicament, and one which in the event of the tide falling lower, might be attended with danger. She was battened down and every precaution observed in case of slipping from her hard bed; shortly after midnight she righted, and by dawn, preparations commenced for moving down the river. It was my intention to warp the ship against the last quarter flood, through the narrow pass where the rocks bar the mid-channel, but the delays occasioned by grounding the previous evening, prevented our reaching the spot until slack water; indeed, the tide of ebb had made, and our kedges for dropping through were already laid with strain on them. An eddy tide, or under tow, having laid the ship athwart the river, with her stern towards the rocks, orders were given to drop one of the heavy quarter kedges in shore, but, unfortunately, the proper officer was not in the boat, and the youngster, finding the 'Royalist' in his way, waited to let her pass instead of dashing athwart her bows. No time was to be lost, and the kedge was ordered to be instantly let go where he was; alas! it was now too late, the bow hawsers had stretched, and the tide pressing the ship towards the reef, caused her to ground by the heel on a projecting rock, the leads giving not less than four fathoms all around. The strength of the ebb now came full upon us, and the ship turning upon the pivot formed by the rock under her heel, stretched the hawsers and, finally, brought home the anchors; she then lay with head down the stream until she bedded herself in the line of current upon the inclined side of the reef, having six fathoms on her starboard side, and nine feet under her port, fore, and main channels.

In the expectation, that being grounded by the heel and the boats sent to sound having reported deep water a-head, she might be hove into deeper water, the starboard anchor, of 15 cwt. was laid out, but the bottom being of rock and smooth slate, it was unavailing. The small bower of 30 cwt. was then laid out a-head, or down stream, and held in mud, the tide, however, had now fallen so as to render any attempt to move futile; moreover, we had discovered that a patch of rock with only nine feet of water over it lay directly under our bow. All efforts were now directed to prevent the ship falling over to starboard, as we had no less than six fathoms on that side, our draught of water being sixteen feet, and fall of tide at this period about nine feet. To obviate this, the coasting sixteen inch hempen cable was secured to the trunks of trees on the left bank, with double runner purchases leading from it to the fore and mainmast heads, and a steady strain kept up as it continued to stretch; this service was much retarded by the opposition of a swarm of hornets, which stung our men so severely that they were glad to precipitate themselves into the river; they soon, however rallied, and effected their object. By this time the ship had taken her inclination to starboard, and in defiance of all our efforts to the contrary, fell over to twenty-two degrees, or the same inclination as that experienced the previous night. All attempts to get spars over, as shores, were rendered futile by the rapidity of the current, and, to add to the dilemma, those peculiarly required for such service, being stowed in the channels (in order to afford room for the two barges on deck), could not be got at on the declining side; we had, however, embarked several large spars cut up the river as specimens of the wood to be obtained here; and as the tide slackened, we succeeded in getting three of these well placed on the starboard side, and a good vertical strain brought upon them by purchases lashed through the starboard main-deck ports. These measures, aided by our horizontal purchases on the coasting cable, tended to prevent her keel from slipping.

The usual preparations having been made by battening down the hatchways, and the ship having only inclined twenty-two degrees, or to what had been ascertained the previous night to be not attended with danger, no doubts were entertained of her righting herself with the ensuing flood tide, particularly as more decided measures had been adopted to aid her by the horizontal purchase from the mast heads on the coasting cable to the shore. Upon the rise at flood, the chain pumps were put in motion to free her from nine inches water, reported in the well, this being merely two inches beyond her ordinary depth in the well. A serious difficulty, however, not hitherto contemplated, now presented itself; the 'Samarang' being fitted with the old chain-pump, it was found that the inclination caused the slack part of the chain to fall into a curve, and the descending discs to overlap the trunks so much as to render them useless. Before time allowed of any effectual remedy being applied, a report was made of the water "gushing in full streams into the hold," and that the ship had five feet, the rise of tide rapidly overpowering her. The carpenter then discovered that the water found its way through the air-holes bored through the casing between the beams above the shelf-piece, and passed down by the vacant timbers left out to afford ventilation. These holes being ornamental, could only be stopped by nailing plank over them, and by this time they were some feet below water; the tools of the carpenter and crew were submerged, and subsequently, it was ascertained, that the water not only flowed through these air-holes, but that it found its way *out* on the receding tide by the butts of the outer planking, as well as spirketting at each port. It was therefore apparent that she could not be righted without more decided measures; namely, that the weight of the ship and stores could only be overcome by displacing the water within her holds and lower-deck, and lightening her of every possible weight. As soon as the water was observed to gain upon us, means were taken to withdraw all the chronometers and instruments through the cabin windows; they were despatched to Mr. Brooke's house at Kuching, within sight, at the distance of about a mile, but unfortunately overtaken by a deluge of rain on their way thither. Immediately Mr. Brooke ascertained that no hopes remained of the ship righting this tide, he despatched all the native craft which could be mustered, and such clothing and hammocks, belonging to the crew, as could be got at, were sent away to the town for safety.

At eight o'clock that evening, the crew, having been, more or less, incessantly on the alert for the last twenty-four hours, and since four, P.M., under a continuous torrent of rain, were withdrawn, leaving a guard-boat at anchor, to prevent pillage; by this time the ship had inclined to forty-five degrees. Natives were now hired to construct houses on shore for the accommodation of the crew, and parties were appointed to receive, and stow away, the various stores landed to lighten the ship, which was soon cleared of her top hamper. Orders had also been given to the native chiefs to employ their people in cutting and bringing down the river the largest and lightest timber which they could procure, and we continued daily to receive rafts varying from twenty to thirty spars each. I hoped to have been able to right the ship on the evening of the 23rd, without their aid, but the flow of water was found to be overpowering, and our chain-pumps, in their present condition, inadequate to reduce the level of the water in the hold. In this dilemma I resolved to husband the powers of the crew until the next spring tide, when, with the means at command, I calculated upon every chance of success. Upon receiving intelligence of our situation, as well as the loss of provision, Mr. Brooke, in the most handsome manner, placed the 'Royalist' at my disposal, also his store of nails, iron, and other important articles, without which, as our carpenter's stores were under water, we should have been greatly distressed.

Mr. Hooper, our zealous and indefatigable purser, having immediately volunteered his services, was directed to proceed in the 'Royalist' to Singapore, communicate our disaster to any vessels of war that he might meet there, and return with all possible despatch with bread, and as much salt provisions as he could find room for. The 'Royalist' took her departure on the night of the 22nd, the day prior to our first attempt to recover the

Method adopted for raising H.M.S. Samarang.

ship; and when my letters, antecedent to that failure, spoke confidently of ultimate success.

To overcome the difficulties of the occasion, it now became necessary to adhere to a more decided system. Our crew continued to fail from fever and diarrhæa, and at one time more than half were either in their hammocks or disabled; the three warrant officers fell ill, and not an individual seemed to entertain the remotest idea of the 'Samarang' being ever brought to float again on the bosom of the ocean. Severely afflicted myself, with partial loss of my right arm and hand, as well as suffering mentally, I continued, however, to superintend my plans.

The three upright spars before mentioned were replaced by larger ones, arranged as follows:—the first was stepped just abaft the fore-channels, in three fathoms mud, the second between it and the starboard gangway, and the third on the fore side of the main-channels. The two last were used as sheers; and to these and the foremost, the main strain was to be applied; their length enabled their heads to reach above the tops, and a spar was lashed horizontally, to keep them steadily in their places. To the heads of these the vertical purchases were attached in the following manner:—

On the head of the main, an iron-strapped top-block, *a*; on the lashing, which was formed by the bights of the breeching hawser passed through each of the main-deck ports and over the skid beams, a lashing block, *b*; the top pendant was rove through *a*, down through *b*, and secured round the head of the spar. The top tackle purchase was brought upon this, and, by a leading block on the starboard gangway, direct to the capstan. A similar purchase was also applied to the foremost spar, and all hove to an even strain.

The mast head purchases attached to the coasting cable were arranged as follows:—

From each mast head, a lashing block *c*; lashing block on the cable, *d*. The runner, of five inch hawser, rove through *c* and *d*, and its end secured to the mast-head over the shoulders of the rigging; on this double runner the barges long purchase, falls four inches prepared rope with double blocks, was used for the runner tackle, the hauling part rove through a block at *e*, below the cap, and led amidships; when taut, luffs were clapped on these falls. The power of these purchases was sufficient to bring about ninety fathoms of the fifteen inch cable *taut*, and during the day it stretched sufficiently to let its bight fall into the river. Until required for further use, a strain was maintained sufficient to keep it just out of the water. Of the heavy spars which were floated down the river, a powerful raft was constructed, consisting of eighty pieces of timber, and disposed as follows:—the twenty largest were first formed into a single raft, occupying an area of about sixty feet by twenty; four strong cross riders were secured on these, and the raft increased in this manner to four tiers, the outer, upper spar, being calculated to admit of the bilges of the water casks taking between it and its neighbour within, so as to render them independent of their lashings, their floating powers enabling them to press heavily into their proper positions. As such a mass of timber attached to the side of the ship might, during the spring tide, cause her to shift her position to greater disadvantage, this raft was secured by independent moorings. The next object was, to derive the greatest power from this raft; if lashed alongside, the yielding of the hempen, or chain fastenings, would very shortly render it useless, if not a hindrance. Two very powerful trees, exceeding seventy feet each, of available timber, were selected from our raft supplies; they were got across the ship by the aid of our uprights, attached solely to them, for fear of oppressing the ship still further, by bringing any lifts from the masts. As they were intended to act in a double capacity, some description of their application will be necessary.

Their heels being lodged on the foremost and after skid beams, on the Port side they were there securely cleated, lashed, and the lashings wedged; the outer ends were supported by topping lifts from the sheer heads, and they were thus prevented from affecting the ship by the action of the stream. From the ends of these outriggers to the heads of the sheers, heavy double runners, with the cat and fish blocks as purchases, were attached, similar to those already described as *a* and *b*. The leading blocks of these purchases were at the outer ends, and long luffs were led from their heels the whole length of this lever, in readiness to clap on when required. The object of this lever purchase, was to act in conjunction with the power of the raft, which could not be attached before the moment for concentrating our forces. . The upperworks had been well caulked, and all the air-holes between the beams closed and plastered with pipe clay, obtained from a pit found in the vicinity of our huts, the hatchways were closed in by double platforms, ten inches asunder, the space between made water-tight with old hammocks and a bed of pipe clay; the chain-pumps had been fitted with leading or conducting boards, which obviated the overlapping, and we had now only to await the lowest tide. As the tide ebbed, scuttles were cut in the decks to allow the water to flow out, and boards covered with greased felt were kept in readiness to close them at a moment's warning. The crew were previously schooled at the pumps, and an estimate having been made of the least number required to work fifteen-minute spells, they were formed into divisions; and by the appointment of special officers to each division, we secured eight spells, or two hours full power before again calling upon the first division to resume their spell; I fully calculated, however, that before half this period could elapse, the fate of the ship would be decided. Arrangements had been made that each spell coming off duty should retire into a large Tope, or native vessel, alongside; there receive a pint of sherbet, and take repose if they desired.

It now only remains to describe what we anticipated from these operations. Our first purchase was a double runner and luff *vertically* exerted on the immersed gunwale; No. 2, the levers. These were allowed to bear the full weight of their outer ends on the raft, and at the period of low water, lashings were securely passed over them, through strops, already passed through the main-deck ports, and over the skid beams. By this arrangement, the buoyancy, or floating power of the raft, was fully communicated, *without loss*, on the lever ends, and acted, *directly*, in raising the lee gunwale; this was leverage resulting from the rise on the flood tide, at this period equal to twelve feet. Two mechanical powers were now applied in aid; the first was the direct purchase to the gunwale from our sheer heads, which inclined at an angle of fifteen degrees inwards; the second was the topping lift runner purchases to the heads of these sheers, which afforded its whole power directly in connection with the raft at the lever ends. It will be apparent, by consulting the diagram, that the tendency of these topping lifts to draw the sheers into a vertical position, (as the difference between the hypothenuse and perpendicular) would furnish a very considerable lifting power on the immersed gunwale. The final working, but variable power, was that exerted in the horizontal line, by the purchases from the mast heads to the coasting cable attached to the trees on shore.

It may be as well to notice, that the strength of our crew was at this time considerably diminished; the substitution of rice, resulting from the loss of bread and other changes of customary diet, upon men enduring heavy fatigue, had, in addition to fever and diarrhæa, at one period, withdrawn more than half our force, and particularly our leading petty officers. As the time, however, approached for bringing our whole energies to the anxious experiment about to be made for raising the ship, it afforded me extreme gratification to notice a marked disposition among the crew to rally, and when the important day arrived, not more than thirty were absent.

The 17th having been fixed upon for our great effort, the crew were exposed as little as possible, and arrangements were made for their accommodation in the Tope or native vessel alongside. About four, P.M., they were directed to take five hours sleep, and at nine o'clock orders were issued to embark. The inclination of the ship remained at forty-five degrees, and a long plumb line was attached to the foremost cabin bulk head to indicate the slightest alteration. The water on the ebb fell as low as the starboard main-deck waterways, and until near dead low water continued to flow out of the scuttles made in the decks for its escape; these were afterwards closed, as well as the scuppers and main-deck ports, as high, at least, as the lashings would admit. The chain pumps were put in motion, and cleared the holds to five feet. The lever lashings were then brought taut and wedged, and the greatest strain brought upon the sheer, as well as the topping lift purchases, which were then belayed; by which arrangement our whole remaining force could be employed for the pumps and mast head purchases.

Our first division at the pump had just been relieved and sent into the Tope for their sherbet and rest, when we found that the water in the holds was rapidly diminishing. The speedy rising of the flood tide gave very ominous notice of the great strain on the levers; they cracked with one or two reports which made me very uneasy, but as it was confined to their inner ends I still retained confidence in them. About the same moment, the plumb began to vibrate, and the officer watching it reported her "*moving*". This excited those stationed at the mast head purchases, and the leading man, striking up an improvisation adapted to the moment, or a burlesque on the croakers who declared the ship never could be recovered, they ran the falls rapidly in, and she righted to thirty degrees. The pumps soon freed her, and she continued gradually to assume her upright position. The moment she became free from the rocks, we found it necessary to cut our important aids adrift, particularly the mast head purchases which tended to press her on the reef. At two, A.M., the ship was hove off to her anchor, and warps having been already laid out, it was weighed and the ship dropped up to a secure berth above the rocks.

At dawn, the crew were sent to rest, and at about ten, A.M, to the inexpressible satisfaction of all concerned in the welfare of H.M.S. 'Samarang', we resumed our former moorings off Kuching. As the hand pumps kept the drainings under, it was obvious that she had not received any material damage under water; divers were employed, who reported some ruffling of the copper but nothing materially wrong. The state of the ship was inconceivable; the coal tar, as well as that forced out of the rope stowed in the holds, had smeared the paint-work within, the river mud had accumulated to a depth of several inches between decks, and in the hold had filled every open space below the level of the tanks. The bread, which was stowed in bulk in the sail room, tinned for that purpose, relieved from the pressure of the water, had commenced fermenting, and the combination of effluvia was dangerous even to those who had hitherto preserved their health. For the removal of the bread we were fortunately able to hire natives, and this service having been completed, the ship was freed from everything, thoroughly scoured, large fires made in the holds, and white-washed.

About ten, P.M., on the evening of the 3rd of August, as we were all seated at Mr. Brooke's hospitable table, after the harrassing duties of the day, we were surprised by an addition to our party of Mr. Hooper, our purser, as well as Lieut. Chads, first of the 'Harlequin', Capt. the Hon. G. F. Hastings, which vessel, in company with the 'Royalist', had reached the Morotabas entrance of the Sarãwak, bringing provisions, as well as rope and purchase blocks to our relief; a noble example of zeal, and executed with extraordinary despatch, only twelve days having elapsed since Mr. Hooper left the river in search of assistance. Both vessels joined us, and although our grand effort to raise the ship, unaided, was completely successful, I feel bound to record my warmest acknowledgement of the important service subsequently derived, not only from the force of the 'Harlequin's' officers and crew, but from her excellent captain, in particular, who zealously superintended the land duties, and by his kindness in anticipating my wishes, relieved me of a load of anxiety. The duties of cleansing, rigging, &c., not requiring my presence, I planned an excursion to the exterior coast, with a view to improve the health of those employed with me; the barge and gig were fitted with *Kedjangs*, or palm matting, to protect us from rain, and I proceeded to make a survey of the coast as far as Tanjong Datu. The result of this examination, directed principally to the entrances of the Sarãwak river as adapted for positions for building, should Her Majesty's Government determine upon taking possession of this territory, was unfavourable, and on the night of the 18th, we returned to the 'Samarang', now ready for sea.

Thirty-three days had elapsed since entering the Sarãwak river, and what exciting events had occurred during that limited period! On the 16th of July, the 'Samarang' grounded and filled, and not a member of her company seemed to entertain the slightest hope of her recovery. The garbled reports which found their way into the English papers, and which must have emanated from some illiterate person at Singapore, were really ludicrous; the following is from *The Times*:—

"Loss of Her Majesty's Ship Samarang, 26 Guns.—During the last few days the Lords of the Admiralty have received accounts from Singapore, containing intelligence of the loss of one of Her Majesty's frigates, the Samarang, 26 Guns, Commander Captain Sir J. Belcher, C.B., off the Island of Borneo. The circumstances attending her loss are reported to be as follows:—The Samarang, which was launched at Portsmouth in the year 1822, was in the latter part of last year fitted up as a surveying ship in order to make a survey of the Chinese Seas, and in the course of the spring of the present year she sailed from Portsmouth on the expedition, and arrived at Singapore on the 22d of June. On the 28th of the same month she proceeded to inspect the River Burrawak, off the Island of Borneo. They had favourable weather and the voyage was equally successful. On the 17th of July she had gained about forty miles up the river above named, when in the early part of the day the master, Mr. Lozey, left her in one of the galleys, accompanied by another officer and a party of seamen, for the purpose of taking soundings along the coast. The ship was under weigh at the time, and was making but very slow pace, when suddenly the ebb tide, which runs remarkably strong, carried her right on to a sunken coral rock, which she struck with considerable violence, producing the greatest alarm amongst those on board. For a few minutes she kept an upright position, and then partly slipped off the rock and fell over on her beam ends, when she instantly filled, and it was only by the greatest exertion that the crew could save themselves; in fact, many of them as the ship rolled over were precipitated into the water, and no doubt would have perished, but for others who caught hold of them as they made their appearance on the surface of the water. Having reached the shore, which was not far distant, they commenced saving from the unfortunate ship, as the tide permitted, as much provision as they possibly could get at, as also the arms which they needed in order to protect themselves from an attack by the natives. An order was instantly sent by the commander, Captain Sir G. Belcher, C.B., to Singapore for assistance, and in the subsequent day until fresh arrivals every means were resorted to to save the vessel. Her guns were thrown overboard and her masts cut away, but it had not the slightest effect. When the mails left Singapore she remained in the same position, and it was very possible that she would become a total wreck. The following is from an extract of a letter dated Singapore, Aug. 3, which furnishes some additional facts:—'The wreck at high water is covered by four feet of water, and we fear she is bilged, as she is lying completely on her side. Her Majesty's ships Harlequin and Wanderer have since arrived from Singapore for the purpose of attempting the raising her, which it is feared will prove ineffectual, although Captain Sir G. Belcher entertains very sanguine hopes. There were 32 valuable chronometers, and an immense number of mathematical and scientific instruments, as also several rare surveys and charts on board of her, and which were estimated at about 32,000*l.*, all of which are lost. We have dragged several of them out of the sunken ship, but find them perfectly useless, and not worth repairing. Sir G. Belcher and several of the officers have taken up their quarters at the British Consul's residence at Borneo, and the crew are living at a small settlement about three miles off, and on half allowance.' "

Such is the history of the disaster of the 'Samarang', copied *verbatim et literatim*, from the "Leading Journal"; thank God, however, she was restored to the navy, after eleven days immersion only, and, in a few more, floated proudly on the water complete with stores and provision, and ready for service. Not an instrument was injured; the losses incurred to Her Majesty's Service were trifling, and the recovery of the ship was effected entirely by our own exertions. The only store needed, viz., ammunition, was obtained from the 'Harlequin', and this being only wanted for salutes, was not of very material importance. Of our stores of powder, rockets, and live shells, not any had escaped the water, although prepared and fortified in the usual manner; indeed, the water of the Sarãwak appeared to have affected everything which suffered immersion in a most extraordinary manner. As the river consisted of pure fresh water, the stores saved were subsequently washed, and dried under a powerful sun, with the expectation that they had not sustained much damage; subsequent experience, however, proved that experiment to be unavailing.* Before quitting the Sarãwak, Mr. Brooke, who kindly consented to accompany me with his interpreter, received from the Rajah Muda Hassim a letter addressed to Her Majesty, to which he would receive the Sultan's seal at Borneo Proper, intimating his wish to aid Great Britain in the suppression of piracy, and extension of trade.

Thus ended our eventful sojourn with this zealous mediator of peace and civilization in the Sarãwak; the alternations of distress, hope, and gratitude that affected me during this exciting period my pen cannot portray; nor can I find language to convey the satisfaction I enjoyed, of being able to resume my duties, and avert the disappointment that would have been otherwise experienced by those who had entrusted me with this important command.

The house allotted to the Junior Officers of the 'Samarang', by their kind friend Mr. Brooke, is thus described by Mr. Adams:—

"Our house, which some of us facetiously christened 'Cockpit Hall', was situated on the banks of a small branch of the Sarãwak river, embosomed in a grove of Coco-nuts, Areca Palms, Papiaas and Plantains. A slight

* Excepting, however, those sails and other stores which had been previously immersed in Sir. W. Burnett's valuable solution.

Nibon fence enclosed its *atap* * walls. The habitable portion of our domicile was elevated on piles, four feet from the ground, and consisted of three separate apartments, with open windows, some made by ourselves, and a floor made of split Nibon, covered with neat mats. A ladder mounted to the door, some rude planks formed our table, and our wardrobes hung around the walls.

"Bamboo and sugar canes formed little plantations around our garden, but all beyond was wild uncultivated jungle. At a short distance, a dark forest upreared its stately trees, where the plaintive cry of the Wou-wou might be heard, and where the lively squirrel and a hundred other interesting animals gamboled among the branches.

"A pleasant spring was near our house, Capsicums and Pine-apples grew abundantly in our garden, and close under our dining-room windows was a magnificent specimen of the *Cassia grandis*. The glories of 'Cockpit Hall' are now, however, departed; the progress of improvement has been fatal to its picturesque character, and the total aspect of the grounds in its vicinity has been changed. During the whole period of our detention at Sarãwak, the conduct of Mr. Brooke was kind in the extreme. We were ever welcome at his hospitable board, his visits were frequent to the house occupied by the Lieutenants, and on numerous occasions he enlivened 'Cockpit Hall' by his presence, ingratiating himself with all by the winning kindness of his manner, and I am sure every individual will unite with me in acknowledg-

* Leaves of Nipa Palm.

ing the great pleasure they derived from the society of this truly great and good man."

On the 19th of August, the 'Diana' steamer, belonging to the Honourable East India Company, which had been despatched by Mr. Church, the Resident Councillor at Singapore, joined us, and on the morning of the 20th, having embarked Mr. Brooke, and his interpreter, Mr. Williams, our number being increased by the 'Royalist', Mr. Brooke's yacht, and 'Ariel' brig, belonging to Mr. Stewart, lately arrived from England with stores for the settlement, she towed us down the river; we very soon found, however, that the power of the 'Diana' was inadequate to the work, and about 9 o'clock she entangled us in the trees on the right bank. Just at this moment we were joined by Capt. Seymour, of H.M. Brig 'Wanderer', and, in the confusion occasioned by this accident, the hawser catching his gig threw the coxswain overboard; fortunately he was saved. After disengaging the ship, the 'Diana' again took us in tow, but a second time put us upon a bank near the junction where we had to await tide. Shortly we espied flags, exhibiting above the mangrove trees, the number of H.M. Steamer 'Vixen', and we soon had the pleasure of adding Capt. Giffard to the list of our supporters. Upon the rising tide, this powerful vessel took both 'Samarang' and 'Harlequin' in tow, and rapidly carried us to the river's mouth, where we found the 'Wanderer' awaiting our arrival. Misfortunes still inclined to attend the 'Samarang'; although the 'Vixen', drawing fifteen feet, *preceded us* towing, and the 'Harlequin', drawing the same water, followed in our wake, still they escaped, whilst the 'Samarang' struck on a rock on which we eventually found but twelve feet; she jumped over it but not without experiencing a sensible concussion.

Arrived at length in the open sea, the 'Wanderer' and 'Diana' were despatched to Singapore, and accompanied by the 'Harlequin', 'Vixen', 'Royalist', and 'Ariel', we proceeded on our passage for Borneo Proper. As the charts of the coasts of Borneo could not be relied on, it became necessary to advance with caution. Light airs would not permit the sailing vessels to make much way, I therefore placed myself on board the 'Vixen' by day, and visited the prominent features of the land, in order to fix their positions. During these operations, nothing worthy of note occurred until the 28th, when having sighted Labuan, situated about fifteen miles to the northward of the entrance of the river of Borneo Proper, the 'Vixen' was sent a-head in order to secure our anchoring after dark, by showing a light at the anchorage, or warning us by signal of any danger lying in our course. Owing to the currents driving us to the northward, and Great Roossocan Island intervening, she became eclipsed, and her signals were not perceived by us. After passing over some uneven ground, having as little water as four fathoms, and perceiving breakers between us and the island, I deemed it prudent to drop our anchor in thirteen fathoms, which we afterwards found 'Harlequin' had done after the first cast of shoal water. At daylight, a large rock was exposed, about ten feet above water, and close under the cabin windows! The breeze favouring our escape out of this dilemma, we weighed, and towed by 'Vixen', anchored off the Island of Moarra, just within the entrance of the river, where we found Mr. Brooke's yacht, the 'Royalist', as well as the 'Ariel', belonging to Mr. Stewart, had preceded us. Leaving the vessels at anchor, we proceeded in our boats, accompanied by Mr. Brooke, Captains Hastings and Giffard, to the city of Borneo, to pay our respects to the Sultan, as well as to obtain information respecting the coal, and the different sites at which it might be found. Mr. Williams, Mr. Brooke's interpreter, started in advance, and on our arrival we found arrangements already made at the palace for our reception.

The Palace of Borneo, as well as the entire city, is constructed on piles driven into the mud on the sides of the river; on these is placed the main platform, which is of substantial beams, crossing these piles about sixteen feet above low-water mark, leaving not more than two feet water at the outer posts. On this stage the palace is erected, consisting of a wooden pitched frame-work, thatched with the leaves of the Nipa palm (*Nypa fruticans*), which do not inflame; the flooring formed of the split outer rind of the prickly or Nibon palm (*Areca tigillaria*), leaving interstices of a quarter of an inch, through which the river effluvia ascends pretty strongly at low water, when the ebb leaves the mud bare.

The large audience hall is matted, decorated by hangings of coloured cottons, and at the furthest extremity is a throne or kind of highly gilded and painted bedstead, devoted to His Highness the Sultan. Our party being European, chairs were provided, and having been duly ushered in by the prime minister, Pangeran Usop, we were seated on either side of His Highness, who was not only surrounded by his guards, which lined both sides, but out of extreme compliment, I suppose, two very suspicious looking characters were posted behind my chair, with rusty blunderbusses pointed towards my head. I perceived, however, that they were not in fighting order; being without flints or priming, I was not much alarmed by them. The business of explaining the object of our visit having been duly executed by Mr. Brooke and his interpreter, and the ceremonial compliments passed, we were invited to a repast, in a neat little detached chamber where it had been prepared for us, with chairs and table in the European style. The repast consisted of curries and other dishes of fowls, rice, vegetables, &c., served up in very fair style; but however good the mulligatawny or currie soup in the centre vessel might have proved, there was a certain want of taste in the selection of the utensil, which, although like a tureen, it had a cover, excited a hearty laugh, and certainly destroyed any inclination to partake of its contents.

The Sultan, who is a nephew of the Rajah Muda Hassim, appears to be about forty years of age, very heavy and timid, whilst a degree of stupidity or idiotcy is strongly exhibited in his features; he has also a deformity in the right hand, in having two thumbs. He did not join us either in the room, or at table, but deputed his Pangeran Usop to do the honours.

In relation to the capital of Borneo, Mr. Adams, our Assistant-Surgeon, makes the following observations:—

"Brunai is truly a city built upon the waters, and

Sultan of Borneo Proper

although it does not offer a very apt similitude to Venice, yet reminds one somewhat of that 'glorious city in the sea', for at Brunai—

> "'No trace of men, no footsteps to and fro
> Lead to her gates.'

"The gondola is represented by the rude canoe, and the marble palaces by a mass of houses built on piles. Persons entering its watery streets, may see the platforms on either side thronged with swarms of swarthy beings half naked, dirty, and exceedingly lazy. The city appeared to be very populous, but at the period of our visit the small-pox was raging with fearful fatality. Mr. Tradescant Lay, who visited Brunai in the 'Himalch', estimates the number of souls at twenty-two thousand five hundred; and further states, that the chiefs affirmed to him that they were originally a colony formed by a migration from Johore in Malacca. One of the most amusing features of the place is the floating bazaar, composed of many hundred boats, which commence in small numbers at one end of the city, increasing gradually as they proceed; and, finally, exhibit a dense mass of enormous conical hats entirely concealing the female traders, who thus protected from the sun, dispose of their small wares. The circulating medium consists of flat square pieces of iron, as heavy and cumbrous as the money with which Lycurgus supplied the Spartans.

"The appearance of Brunai as seen from the summit of the Kianggi mountains is very novel and curious, particularly at high-water, when there is no communication with the dense mass of houses in the middle of the river except by boats. At low water numerous mud banks appear, on which are also great numbers of rush-roofed houses; many dwellings, moreover, are situated on the firm banks of the river."

Having completed our business with the authorities, we moved on to Pulo Chermin and Areng,* to examine the coal, and ascertain how far it could be worked at the surface without going to the expense of unwatering the beds. Either by the misinterpretation of former visitors, or too great a desire to set forth the riches of this part of Borneo, these strips of coal have been much over-rated. I was informed, that by great exertion, the Honourable East India Company's steamer 'Diana' obtained two tons from Pulo Chermin for trial. On my arrival I was promised *thirty tons* for H.M.S. 'Vixen', in which vessel I proposed to test its quality, having in some measure detained her to accompany me for this express purpose; with all our exertion, however, not more than thirty pounds of good coal could be collected, without clearing away to a depth of six feet, rubble, below high-water mark, and all the native labourers that could be collected would not have procured one day's consumption for that vessel in less than a week. This coal, although of good quality in the small strips in which it occurs, is merely an indication of what may be found underlying, and that cannot be worked (if prudent to do so) without the assistance of pumps or steam machinery. The cost of procuring it from the natives, which I imagine would be from sources of which we are at present ignorant, (probably up the river near the city) would be near thirty-four dollars per ton,

* The Malay name for coal.

even for surface rubble long exposed to the sun, and the authorities have imbibed such a notion of its value and importance, that the first price paid (even for trial) would be assumed as its future standard. Under these circumstances we merely employed our crew to collect specimens of the coal with its attendant strata of sandstone, &c., from the Islands of Chermin and Areng, and returned to our vessel.

As the small-pox was now raging at Borneo, any further delay in the neighbourhood would have been not only dangerous, but impolitic, on account of the quarantine to which we should have been subjected on our arrival at Manila; we were detained, however, a short time to cut fire-wood sufficient to enable us to pursue our voyage with the 'Vixen', having been greatly disappointed in our expectations of procuring a supply of coal.

The services of the 'Harlequin' being no longer required, that vessel was directed to land Mr. Brooke at Sarãwak, and proceed with the despatches to Singapore, and on the 4th of Sept. after experiencing the great value of Mr. Brooke's services in our present expedition, as well as in the co-operation of my good friend Capt. Hastings, we parted for our different destinations.

Before taking leave of Borneo, I must be permitted to repeat my acknowledgement of the public as well as private obligations we were under to our worthy and hospitable friend Mr. Brooke. From the moment our disaster became known to him, his Yacht, stores, house, and table, were pressed upon us, and during the tedious and harrassing interval which occurred, between the time of our immersion and the departure of the 'Samarang' from Sarãwak, his kindness and attention to every individual under my command was most unremitting.

On the 4th of Sept. the 'Samarang', towed by the 'Vixen', left Borneo Proper, but at noon on the 5th, having cast off our tow-line, being then barely in sight of Labuan, 'Vixen' signalled five fathoms, and for *one hour* both vessels were picking their way, steering to avoid the rocks, clearly visible beneath us, and in one or two instances finding as little as three fathoms. Having cleared these dangers, we shaped our course through the Palawan Channel, and arrived without further incident in the neighbourhood of Manila on the 9th, when, in pursuance of the instructions from the Admiral, the 'Vixen' was despatched into that port in order to obtain stores for the squadron, as well as coal sufficient to enable her to reach Hong-Kong. Passing the Lema Islands, the 'Samarang' entered that port on the 14th; here we found the Cornwallis, Capt. P. Richards, bearing the flag of Sir S. W. Parker, G.C.B; 'Agincourt', Capt. Bruce, flag of Sir T. Cockrane; 'Castor', Capt. Graham. Steps were immediately taken by the Admiral to make good our defects and complete us for sea, and as the report of the 'Samarang's' recovery from her disaster in the Sarãwak River was deemed by him to be satisfactory, the customary inquiry by Court Martial was dispensed with, and a memorandum was communicated to the captain and crew, thanking them for their conduct on the occasion. On the 28th of October, the Admiral visited Macao, in H.M. S. 'Spiteful', followed by the 'Samarang' on the 30th, in order to obtain the meridian distance from that spot.

The improvements made at Hong-Kong since our first

visit to that station are almost incredible. We landed from the 'Sulphur' to take possession of this island, and commenced the operations of the survey in March 1841. At that period, its northern face was blank, the site of the town was not even fixed upon; now, after a period of little more than two years, an imposing city, still in the course of extension, occupies a frontage, of above a mile in extent, and the buildings, erected and habitable, are of the first order, both as regards comfort and magnificence. The sickness so much dreaded, and which seemed at one period almost to paralyse advancement, has ceased, and the busy hum of the artificer, as well as of active commerce, has succeeded to the barren and gloomy solitude which had reigned previously. All this sudden advancement, and in the vicinity of a country which is accounted to be among the earliest civilized regions of the earth, was the work of a handful of British adventurers, and unaided by any great comparative outlay on the part of their Government; well may they be styled the 'Merchant Princes of the land.'

The following remarks on this New Settlement of ours are by Mr. Adams:—

"Hong-Kong has been said to be void of interest in living forms, and some have declared that its vallies have the silence of the grave; but in looking towards the Bay a dense mass of Tanka boats is seen, which, with other Chinese crafts, added to the crowded shipping of every nation, afford proofs of the most active state of commerce and civilization. Turning to the land, the patient and labourious Chinese may be seen toiling at their daily avocations, children gamboling in the roads, Sepoys,

Bengalese and European soldiers, in their varied and gaudy dresses, and here and there some tiny-footed damsel, toddling awkardly along, followed by her swarthy page, or elderly Duenna, bearing a huge umbrella. In our rambles over the mountains the steep ascent is cheered at every step by some scarce plant or sparkling insect. Showy Orchideous and Composite flowering-plants, huge *Carices*, and singular *Graminea*, uprear their fragile forms, and, on every side, the Ferns, Grasses, and Lichens, are particularly beautiful, though of small dimensions. Huge *Grylli* spring up from among the brushwood, and Caterpillars spin odd-shaped cocoons among the stunted trees; Ants are busy in their granaries and citadels, Lizards glide among the prickly Aloe leaves and painted Butterflies spread their gorgeous wings on every barren spot. The fish-market of Victoria, when the boats that swarm among the islands have just discharged their cargoes, offers a rich ichthyological treat to the naturalist. Brilliant Mullet, fresh, and leaping on the boards, strange looking Balistes, in their coats-of-mail, curiously formed Pleuronectes of various shapes, and marked with red, brown, and grey; enormous Perch, with glittering silvery scales, hugh mis-shapen Skates, and the fins of monstrous Sharks; gigantic Eels, and Chætodons, with bright-banded sides; Gudgeons, and Sturgeons, Rays and Diodons, and the snake-like *Gymnothorax*, with its pointed mouth and elongated jaws; while numerous tubs are placed around filled with living fish, including *Palinuri* red and green, and Crabs of the most fantastic forms; Frogs tied up in animated bundles may also be seen in prodigious numbers."

CHAPTER III.

BASHEE AND MEIA-CO-SHIMAH ISLANDS.

Macao—General features—Camöens' Cave—Sail for the Bashee Group of Islands—Batan—Natural History and Resources of that island—Visit the Meïa-co-shimah Group—Arrive at Pa-tchung-san—Reception by the Mandarins—Exploring Excursion—Interesting co-operation of the Natives—Integrity, kindness of disposition, and general habits—Laborious mode of dressing the hair—Cleanliness and domestic comfort—Temples and Groves for worship—Oblations—Mode of sepulture—Want of mechanical skill—Success in agriculture—Chiefs entertained on board the 'Samarang'—Port Haddington—Ty-pin-san Group—Mr. Adams' account of the Meïa-co-shimahs—Return to Hong-Kong—Sail for Manila—Courtesy of the General Alcade—Scenery and general features—Pass the islands of Cabras, Luban, and Panagatan—Arrive at Mindanao—Anchor off the town of Samboanga—Cordial reception from the Governor, Colonel Figueroa—False alarm—Shooting excursion into the interior—Departure for the Island of Sooloo.

WE now steered our course for Macao, where I had the pleasure of meeting, at the table of Mr. Alex. Matheson, Rear Admiral Cecil, commanding the French Squadron in these seas, as well as Captain Roy, formerly of the Madagascar Frigate, wrecked on the Bombay shoal, off the coast of Palawan, in 1840, and with whom I became acquainted on my first visit to Singapore in the 'Sulphur'; the latter had now arrived in the 'Cleopatra', and after exchanging frigates with Admiral Cecil, would return to France.

"Both Hong-Kong", says Mr. Adams, "and Singapore offer great variety of costume to the notice of the traveller, but no place in the course of our wanderings, amused me so much as the strange and populous city of Macao; particularly on account of the endless succession of oriental figures that are there continually passing before the eye. For example, the intelligent Parsee with high-crowned cap and snowy robes, contrasts with the sable garments and odd-shaped hat of the demure and sanctified Catholic Priest; the swarthy son of Portugal, with haughty step, and dark flashing eye, with the Brahmin, mild, observant, and serene; the wealthy British Merchant, with the influential Mandarin; the respectable monied Armenian, in his picturesque and splendid dress, with the French officer and English sailor; while Portuguese damsels, gliding along to mass, with lustrous expressive eyes, and drapery thrown gracefully over the head and shoulders, complete the attractive picture. In every quarter of the city, swarms of narrowed-eyed Chinese, acute, cunning, and industrious, eager to barter, greedy for gain, are importunate, impudent, but always good-natured. Some of these worthies, may be seen sitting in groups, in the middle of the squares, quietly pursuing their various occupations. Here may be seen the grave empiric, busily engaged in gently beating or tapping the head or breast of a patient, afflicted perhaps with some grievous malady; and there, you will notice the operations of the barber, who removes the wiskers, and shaves the head, the ears, the nostrils, and even the eyelids.

"Passing through Macao, I visited Camöens' Cave, the burial place of the immortal Portuguese poet, author of the 'Lusiad'. It is situated in a beautiful garden, belonging to Madame Pereira, not very far from the city of Macao, and close to the European burial-ground. The so-called cave is a rude, picturesque archway, formed of two enormous blocks of stone, with another large rock placed upon them, and elegantly shaded with splendid showy trees, which wave their feathery branches over the entire mass—fit resting place for a poet's "mortal coil". On the summit of the roof-block, they have placed a small hexagonal summer-house, chiefly remarkable for the ridiculous number of silly signatures of unknown visitors, who ignorantly deface and mar whatever is curious, hallowed, or beautiful. Most of these debasing autographs are English; the only one, worth noticing, was by some inspired Portuguese, who had written, in the devotion of his heart, "Luis Camöens te adoro!" a sentence, however trite, singular for its affecting simplicity. In the solitude and retirement of this garden, and in the midst of the rocks that now form his grave, the immortal minstrel is said to have delighted to wander, and "chew the cud of sweet and bitter fancy". The verses, with the composition of which his tender soul beguiled the tedium of his lengthened banishment, now serve to decorate the marble of his tomb. The poet's bust surmounts the pedestal, and shows a head, at once benevolent and animated. Many a pilgrimage is made to this hallowed spot, and the effective scenery of the

F 2

ornamental gardens that surround his tomb, tends materially to increase the soothing influence of the feelings that arise when visions of the past, and the dreamy fancies of a poet's life, crowd around. A good effect is wrought upon the man who breathes a genuine sigh in memory of the great, whether the object of his regret has poured forth the melody of his nature in streams of living verse, or has given to his country laws, or liberty, art or science."

Our observations at Macao being complete, and having finally taken leave of our Commander-in-Chief, Sir W. Parker, now about to quit this station, we took our departure on the 2nd of November, with the intention of making the shortest passage to the Meïa-co-shimah group of the charts, against the S.W. monsoon; fully aware that this would prove a most unpleasant service, and that great caution would be necessary in carrying canvas, in order to preserve the efficiency of our Chronometers, so that the operations depending upon them should not be entirely frustrated.

After a tedious beat along the coast of China, in order to clear the Lema islands, we stretched off easterly, and on the 11th of November sighted Sabtan, one of the Bashee or Batanes group; all these islands are termed 'Bashees' on the existing charts. On the morning following, we beat up between Ibugos and Sabtan, and anchored in fifteen fathoms. During the time employed in beating up, several canoes came towards us, and often sufficiently near to communicate, but as often a sudden panic seemed to inspire them, and they betook themselves to the island of Sabtan. On anchoring I landed immediately at Ibugos, on what is termed "Bashee Island" of the charts, and succeeded in obtaining sufficient data for securing its position. As strong gales prevailed outside, we then commenced the survey of the immediate neighbourhood, and had completed the western sides of these islands, when a letter from the Alcade and Commandant at San Domingo, induced me to shift my position to that bay, in the Island of Batan. On reaching the bay of San Domingo, I found the Spanish colours flying; the remains of two forts; and was shortly waited on by the Alferez or Ensign, and Corporal of the guard, in their proper costume, with many apologies for the non-appearance of the Captain or Alcade Mayor. On my visit to the Casa Real I was received with much warmth by the Alcade, and offered every facility in supplies of bullocks, vegetables, &c.; every demonstration of assistance was also personally afforded by the Alcade, Padres, and natives, with a view to forward our operations. Having remained a few days at San Domingo, I moved the ship to the bay of San Vicente on the western side of Batan, completing the survey of these four islands, as well as securing several points on Ibayat and Round Island, to the northward, in anticipation of their completion at a future period.

The bay, or barely anchorage, of San Vicente, erroneously termed Ivana in the chart, is merely the landing-place for the Pueblo of Ivana, which is situated on the S.W. angle of the island, and about one mile from San Vicente, where only a few huts remain.

The group of Batanes subject to this Alcade consists

of the following, commencing at the northernmost, or north Bashee of the charts—

Siayan, Mabudis, Ibayat (orange Id.); Diogo (high Id.); Dequey (Goat Id.); Ibugos (Bashee Id.); Subtan, or Seminanga, Batanes, Calayan, and Babuyan, and the rock Crista Gallo, of the Babuyanes group, frequently visible in moderate weather. The Alcade resides at San Domingo, Batanes, supported by a military force, consisting of an Alferez or Ensign, Serjeant, Corporal, and twenty-seven Privates.

The Casa Real, or residence of the Alcade in San Domingo, is situated in

Latitude	20° 27′ 26″ N.
Longitude	121° 57′ 0″ E.
Variation	0° 23′ 0″ W.

The Island of Batan has three convents, with Padres; one at each of the three principal Pueblos, viz: San Miguel, on the N.W. extreme bay, San Carlos in the centre, and Ivana, on the south-west; the present principal resides at Ivana.

The natives, who are a cheerful and remarkably well-built race, much resembling the Dyaks, do not generally understand Spanish, but speak a language resembling Ilocos, or that of the province of Cayagan, on the northern part of Luzon, but peculiar to this group; even the Alcade is compelled to refer to the assistance of the Padre in his communication with them. Both men, as well as women, are well featured, with remarkably agreeable countenances; but mistaking us for freebooters on our first arrival, were not easily induced to approach.

The Islands of Batan and Sabtan are mountainous,

with many broad cultivated spots; the highest peak, apparently an old volcano, is about 5,000 feet above the level of the sea, thickly covered with trees; the former is, however, the richer in soil, and produces abundantly yams, sweet potatoes and its varieties, maize, onions, garlic, rice, grain, &c.; indeed the only want appears to be variety of seed. Cattle, pigs, goats, sheep and poultry are abundant; deer are found on Sabtan and Ibugos, as well as quail on all of the islands. Wood is reasonable and plentiful, as well as water; but this latter necessary is difficult to procure, as the rivers are barred by reefs, which prevent boats from approaching or rafting off in sufficient quantities for ships of war; this, however, would soon be remedied if the visits of vessels rendered it advantageous, and I have already impressed on the authorities the necessity of some arrangement to meet this most important desideratum.

Speaking of this group of islands Mr. Adams observes:

"The Bashee or Bachi Islands, were so called by Dampier, from the name of an intoxicating liquor, which is much drank there.* This Bashee is a thick yellow fluid, of a subacid taste, between that of cyder and toddy, and is not very potent in its effects.

"The Indians inhabiting these islands are most probably an old branch of some Malay colony, from Luconia. They retain the practise of masticating the areca nut, and betel leaf, though the lower orders do not smear the latter with lime, like the Malay, or add gambier, like the Chinese. They are moreover passionately fond of tobacco.

* Millet-Mureau in 'Perouse's Voyage' p. 483.

Their ordinary dress is a cloth about the waist, and a perineal band like that of the Dyaks of Borneo. They have pleasing features, and are by no means similar in disposition to the indolent and vindictive races of Malasia. Their houses are rudely built of grass and canes, and display but little taste or comfort in the internal decoration. In their villages, the sheds for the goat and pig, are hardly to be distinguished from the dwellings they use themselves. They clear the ground by firing the grass; eradicating the stubble afterwards with wooden pegs.

"In Batan, there is some very beautiful scenery, more especially in the interior of the island. The mountain peaks are verdant to their summits, and in the gullies that groove the hills, run numerous water-courses. The fertile glens are rich with varied stores of useful vegetables, mingled with wild flowers. Patches of highly cultivated ground planted with yams, batatas, and sugar-cane, interspersed with groves of plantains, bread-fruit, and cocoa-nuts, extend in every direction; and on the naked acclivities of some hill-sides clusters of Orchideous plants, and wild raspberries are met with in abundance.

"Add to this, dense grassy brakes, where the Landrail hides; sunny glades where

'The butterfly is basking in the paths,
His radiant wings unfolded':

green shady thickets, where beautiful Snails* are feeding

* *Helix speciosa*, Jay, and three varieties of a species believed to be new.

on the lily leaves; quiet pools, where the white Heron sits disconsolate on a stone; and marshy swamps, where the long-billed Snipe is busily engaged probing the yielding soil for worms.

"At Ibugos, an excursion was planned to hunt deer; we started at daylight, with fourteen marines, intending to beat the ground regularly from one end of the island to the other. Deer, of small size, were numerous, but somewhat shy, and difficult to follow on account of the long rank grass. Troops of wild cattle were also seen grazing in various parts of the island; our leader, Lieutenant Heard, succeeded in procuring a buck, which was not secured until after considerable resistance."

Having received much civility from the Alcade and Padres, we quitted Batan on the 27th of November, under a promise to return, and with a fair breeze from S.W. started afresh for the Meïa-co-shimahs. On this northerly course we gradually fell off to N.N.E., but found we had made the Island of Samasana instead of Botel Tobago; we then worked along the eastern side of Formosa, and stretched off for the Meïa-co-shimah group. On the 30th of November we sighted Hummock and Sand Islands, and passing close under the southern reefs of the latter, stood on in the hope of reaching Ty-pin-san, or at least of sighting Ykima of the charts; but not finding it in the position assigned, and bad weather preventing our getting to windward, I made up my mind to seek the nearest shelter, and commence operations. We then succeeded in reaching the S.W. angle of Pa-tchung-san of the natives, where nothing but reefs presented themselves. The customary good fortune of Exploring Vessels, however, attended us, and we soon discovered a gap in the reef into which the 'Samarang' was warped, and before sunset, securely moored; although with not more than room to swing. Vessels should not venture near these islands after dark, until their dangers have been more closely examined, and charts published. From the western limit of Hummock Island to the eastern range of the Ty-pin-san breakers, the space is dangerous. Independent of the many reefs which connect the islands, the constant strong winds, with haze and rain during the N.E. monsoon, render the approach at that season very hazardous except on a clear day.

On the morning after our arrival I landed, accompanied by our Chinese Interpreter, Aseng, formerly a boy of Mr. Morrison's, who both spoke and wrote the court language, and was met by one of the Mandarins and his attendants, at a hut hastily constructed on the beach. All were evidently alarmed, but after a short conference with our Interpreter (by written communication in the Chinese court dialect), the object of our visit was soon understood, and confidence established. In a short time I succeeded in effecting an arrangement permitting four Officers and myself to survey the Islands, by land; undertaking upon my part to prohibit any of our crew from entering their villages, or penetrating into the interior, and that their operations should be strictly confined to the sea limits.

On the 6th of December, attended by Lieut. Baugh, Messrs. Richards, M'c Dougal, Adams, Assistant Surgeon, and the Chinese Interpreter, we commenced our examination of the territory of Pa-tchung-san. The official

QUAND-TUND TSZE

(Chesterfield)

Native of Pa tchung san

interpreter of the island and several minor officers, attended by numerous coolies, swelled our party to at least fifty persons. A little spice of independence, or rather desire to inconvenience the inhabitants as little as possible, induced us to commence our adventure as pedestrians, but the second and following days found us mounted on small sturdy ponies. At sunset the first evening we advanced about five miles, and took up our quarters for the night in a Joss House, or religious temple, which had been prepared for us; our companions, or rather conductor, on this excursion, having begun by this time to enter into the spirit of our operations, and understand our wishes. The Chief or Interpreter, Kien Anchee, a red-capped Mandarin from Loo-Choo, proved to be a very intelligent, polished, as well as energetic character, and certainly exerted himself in every way not only to facilitate our movements, but also to secure our comfort. He was seconded by another, Shanghai, who from the knowledge he exhibited of the hydrographic features of the islands, and his constant exertions in forwarding my surveying duties, received the appellation of Beaufort; others obtained names adapted according to their manifestations of ability, not omitting, however, "Chesterfield", the secretary to the Embassy. The moment we were housed, the conducting authority, Kien Anchee, despatched letters, as well as written orders, to the surrounding outposts, to report, as we conceived, that all was safe. During our examination of Pa-tchung-san, which occupied us twenty-one days, the routine observed daily was similar; we generally mounted our horses after breakfast, or about 8 A.M., and by sunset had reached some station to dine and sleep, prepared in readiness for us; and upon our expressing a wish to send to the ship, a swift messenger was instantly despatched, and returned with wonderful celerity, considering that he was not unfrequently commissioned to bring bottles or other articles requiring to be conveyed with care.

The natives, or persons inhabiting the Meïa-co-shimahs, may be divided into three or more classes:—first, the Mandarins, who understand the Chinese written characters, and have either been educated at Loo-Choo, or sent from thence charged with authority; secondly, those who are, probably, the first-class natives of these islands, enjoying the second rank, and who appear to have received some education, inasmuch as they write the Loo-Choo characters, and in some instances understand Chinese; thirdly, those who possess sufficient property to entitle them to separate themselves from the working classes or slaves; of which class I assume the coolies to be.

In the Pa-tchung-san group we were given to understand that they had five yellow- and one red-capped Mandarins, deputed from Tah-Lieu-Quiew, or great Lew-Kew, who remain about five or more years; but at Ty-pin-san they appeared to be in greater proportion.

The two western islands of Pa-tchung-san and Koo-kien-san, including the adjoining low islets, appear to be under the government of a superior Mandarin, with five of similar rank, as a council; these are aided by numerous chiefs, or men of property having the control over the lower castes of labourers, &c., of which the bulk of the population consists, confined to quadrangular hamlets as if they either feared aggression or considered

Boy of Pa tchung san.

it necessary to keep them within command, a disposition sufficiently obvious in a penal settlement. The upper classes are readily distinguished by their deportment, the superior texture of their dress, their attention to the hair, as well as by a more intellectual expression of countenance, with a very urbane and polished manner. Occasionally one can detect amongst the lower castes the elongated and peculiar eye of the Chinese, leading to the probability of some admixture of that race rather than one of Korean or Tartar origin. The same observations apply equally to the people of Ty-pin-san, although on that island we found a much larger population for its extent of cultivation, and a greater number of Mandarins; there were also traces of warlike habits, such as the possession of a battery, and less restriction upon the interchange of goods.

The people of these Islands are not only independent of each other, but either pretend to be, in great measure, ignorant of the other's affairs; and it was not without some pressing that I persuaded the chief of Pa-tchung-san to communicate to the authorities of Ty-pin-san the nature of my visit, and our peaceable observance of their habits and customs. As far as we had opportunities of noticing (and we lived in contact, although not amongst them, for six weeks), their moral excellence was conspicuous, and formed an agreeable contrast with the piratical disposition of the Malays; crime seemed indeed to be a thing of rare occurrence among them. They might have been frequently tempted to rob us of articles valuable to them, though of insignificant value to us; but whenever such happened to be thrown away, or left behind by us, they were brought in with unusual ceremony and much apparent concern on the part of the chief; on one or two occasions when by some negligence, parts of our instruments were mislaid, even upon the summits of mountains, we did not fail to remark the distress of mind exhibited in their countenance, through their anxiety to restore them. Such manifestations of integrity prove that they have a sound perception of the principles of right and wrong; even the coolies employed in transporting our effects were characterized by these remarkable traits, and in an insulated tract so far removed from the seat of civilization, it could not but excite the most agreeable reciprocity of feeling.

In general manners I incline to think these islanders differ from their friends of the Loo-Choo district, being much more resolute and active, and not unsparing even in their methods of coercion, substituting often the bamboo for the fan. This rendered them in my opinion far more interesting than their monotonous neighbours, the Loo-Chooans; they exhibited a greater disposition to be friendly, and many excited a degree of attachment that was not broken at parting, nor, as far as the eye witnesseth, without emotion.

I cannot leave this remote people without testifying still further to their amiability of disposition one towards the other; they seldom quarrel, or even betray feelings of resentment, the use of fire-arms or of any offensive weapon is unknown among them. All crimes of any enormity are submitted to trial at Loo-Choo, and we were given to understand, as well as our interpreter could explain it, that the culprits were sent in the monsoon junks to be tried, and if guilty executed at Loo-Choo, but that death was not inflicted by their own authority at the islands; all bad characters were sent to labour at the off-lying low islands, where produce is probably scarce, labour heavier, and water difficult to obtain.

Their laws must however be stringent, as the most abject permission and endurance of punishment, though we saw nothing beyond that inflicted by a stroke of bamboo, appeared to be submitted to cheerfully, and to have a powerful effect on the bystanders. That their decisions in special cases extend to the penalty of death, we had evidence, in the case of two parties found guilty of adultery, whose skeletons in the same coffin were shown to us; the law awarding in such case the horrible impalement of both the offending parties together, by a stake passed between the two lower ribs.

From the information obtained by our Chinese interpreter, who was admitted into some of the private dwelling houses, as well as from our own observations, in the houses vacated for our habitation, it appeared that the women of the better classes occupy an apartment distinct from the ordinary sitting room of the family; that they wear the 'eschaw', or robe, and the oosisashee, already described, the hair being loosely secured in a larger knot, without the head being shaved, as in the male portion of the community; and that their feet are permitted to enjoy their natural freedom of growth, subject only to the slipper and stocking, made after the fashion of the Chinese. I had an opportunity of noticing one dressed female arranging her house, and a little girl, very neatly attired, brought by her papa to see the Barbarians; both were pleasing, even pretty, but the females mostly seen during our tour of the island were of the lowest order, ill-looking, dirty, and bare-legged.

Amongst the males the mode of dressing the hair, which is generally performed by a youthful valet, appears not only to engross much time, but also to require some dexterity to arrive at the pink of fashion; after manipulating with an oleaginous matter, their long black hair is worked up evenly on all sides towards the crown of the head, where the operator, confining it with one hand, continues to pass turns of silk band between the hand and head, straining every hair to its root, and apparently causing some little moisture to flow from the eyes; it is then tied, and he proceeds to comb out the remainder, and, doubling it back over two fingers, expands the remainder of the tail over the ligature on the crown, and passing the kamesashee and oosesashee through the under part of the tied hair, confines the top-knot securely. It is an elaborate process, and exhibits a considerable degree of neatness and cleanliness. The moustache, as well as the hair on the chin, is suffered to grow to its natural length; but all the hair and whisker to the tip of the chin is closely shaved.

Throughout the Islands, the construction of their villages appeared to be nearly similar, the houses being arranged within the squares or parallelograms, intersected by narrow lanes or streets, bounded by stone walls. Each house appears to stand separate, with a neat and picturesque garden of shrubs and shady trees; they are constructed of massive wooden frame-work, and slightly raised above the earth, having a very sharp-pitched

J. Richards, del. — Brothers imp.

HOUSE OF THE MEIA CO SHIMAHS.

sketched at Pa-tchung sang.

thatched roof. The sides, as well as internal divisions, are of moveable sliding pannels, which can be opened at pleasure; and the floors are covered with neat mats, of prescribed dimensions, formed of rice straw, generally of three inches in depth, each mat being intended to serve as a bed. Cleanliness was predominant throughout, and they invariably put off their shoes on entering their dwelling, to prevent anything being soiled. It was evident that amongst the better classes, or in the houses devoted to our occupation, very great attention was bestowed upon their domestic comforts; in each of these we noticed, in the principal room, a species of family altar surmounted by the customary board, containing a representation of some favourite, but, to us, incomprehensible deity, as well as choice moral maxims; nothing, however, was to be seen that could lay claim to the designation of furniture.

Their Temples, or Groves for Worship, are generally situated in some thickly planted wood near the sea-shore; no images were observed; a few tablets, with some moral maxims and the names of their favourite deities inscribed, and some jars, containing flowers or green leaves, formed the extent of their religious service. The place was held sacred, neatly swept, and had invariably a symbolic figure, approximating to one of the Chinese characters, as a gateway; on one occasion, it appeared at the head of one of the tablets.

Regarding their mode of sepulture, they sometimes bury their dead in caverns hewn out of the sides of the rocks, in natural caves or holes near the sea, the apertures being carefully closed, in wooden coffins; and, not un-

G

frequently, in simple cerements only. The better classes erect stone tombs, surmounted by piles of loose stones, and, in one instance, at Pa-tchung-san, we noticed a very extensive plastered mausoleum. In most cases they appear to select the more picturesque and secluded spots, overshadowed by trees. Oblations, much in the style of the Chinese, particularly of flowers and water in the Clam shell, are offered at the tombs, for the solace and refreshment of the departed on their weary pilgrimage. In examining these tombs, or disturbing their contents, I was at first particularly cautious, but I soon found that they were not so sensitive on this point as the Chinese; and as the elevations of their tombs offered, in many instances, good stations for surveying, I found that they did not hesitate an instant in making apertures to receive the marks, which, indeed, they generally erected for us.

Of their mechanical abilities but very little can be adduced, indeed they appear to be far behind the most ignorant of the eastern islanders in this respect; notwithstanding they are known to be in possession of the customary Chinese tools, they do not exhibit, excepting in fitting their houses, any skill beyond that of providing shelter. They weave a very coarse kind of cloth for home purposes, with frame and shuttle, and manufacture very indifferent nets and fishing gear. They do not make the most of the advantages afforded by their proximity to the sea; their canoes are of wretched construction, and, excepting a few stragglers occasionally noticed at low tides in quest of *Mollusca*, they never appeared to follow fishing as an occupation; sustaining themselves almost entirely by agricultural industry.

Their chief object of cultivation is the cotton-plant, although a considerable portion of arable or productive land is devoted to the Batata and large Radish; the low marshy grounds are principally arranged in Paddy fields, on which they expend much pains and labour; the Yam, Sugar-cane, and a kind of Wheat, are found amongst them, but not common. The soil is turned up by a plough of very simple construction, worked by a single bullock; and this, with hoes and trowels, sum up the amount of their agricultural implements, whilst the pestal and mortar are in ordinary use, for pounding rice. The sides of the mountains and uncultivated grounds are covered with a high rank weedy grass, serving as food for their black cattle, of which they have a tolerable abundance, and, like the people of Loo-Choo, were not disposed to part with them. They have a numerous race of rough but sure-footed ponies, which we found of great service, particularly in ascending the mountains.

The people of these islands affected an ignorance of having at any period been visited by another nation, notwithstanding we have decided proof of the wreck of the 'Providence', Capt. Broughton, in the year 1796, upon the Island of Y-ki-ma, on the northern coast of Ty-pin-san, and of the assistance rendered by them in constructing a vessel in which they reached China. I closely questioned men of seventy years of age, but no recollection could be adduced, either of the wreck, or of the residence of the crew amongst them. One circumstance, however, is remarkable; notwithstanding their apparent ignorance of navigation, we found a stone on the most elevated mount on Y-ki-ma, and near the spot where the disaster of the 'Providence' must have occurred, having the points of the compass cut upon it. It was a column or pedestal of stone, on a mount used as a look-out, or lounging place for smoking; a similar stone was also noticed upon one of the highest islands of the northern coast of Koo-kien-san, elevated about 1,500 feet above the level of the sea; in both cases the direction of the Magnetic Meridian, tested by theodolite, was found to be correct.

We entertained the chiefs of both groups of islands on board the 'Samarang', and amused them on shore by the exhibition of the magic lanthorn; it did not, however, create much surprise amongst them: at Pa-tchung-san the chiefs expressed a wish to see the guns fired, but even this did not elicit particular astonishment. They had probably occasion, at some distant period, to think of defence; as at Ty-pin-san, near their largest town, I observed walls which only required the presence of guns to constitute a battery, and was furnished with a loop-holed screen in front to serve the use of archers or matchlocks. These works might have been constructed either as a defence against ths Chinese or Ladrone pirates, which formerly infested these seas, or they may have furnished a stronghold to the pirates themselves. The houses in the immediate vicinity were also of stone, roofed with tiles, and the road for a considerable distance well paved; but this was the only spot, on any of these islands, which exhibited any marks of strength. The inhabitants were not disposed to prevent our entry, but, on the contrary, offered the walled position, on which a staff and

MUND

Native of Pa tchung san.

colours were exhibited, as our resting place for the night.

The Islands of Pa-tchung-san and Koo-kien-san afford several commodious harbours, and are, with good charts, perfectly safe of approach. One, on the Kee-chee side of Pa-tchung-san, which we named Port Haddington, in compliment to the first Lord of the Admiralty, would shelter a large fleet, but it abounds with coral patches, rising suddenly from ten or fifteen fathoms almost to the surface. In clear weather, all those having as little as five fathoms over them, are clearly discernible, and of course easily avoided. Except on the northern side of Koo-kien-san and that just spoken of, watering would be found very difficult, as the reefs extend a great distance from the mouths of the streams, which are of frequent occurrence. I must except, however, Seymour Bay, on the S.W. angle of Koo-kien-san, where we spent the first of the year 1844. There a fine stream enters the sea in deep water, and a vessel might be moored sufficiently close to lead the hoses from Hearle's pumps into her, without the intervention of boats and casks.

The Pa-tchung-san group consists of ten distinct islands, of which five only are at all mountainous; the remainder are flat, like the Coral islands of the Pacific, and similarly belted with reefs, such as in this instance connect the ten islands into a distinct group. Besides these, Hummock Island, a high uninhabited mass of rocks, is near the coast, and to the W.N.W., the Island of Y-na-koo, with its lofty peak and table base, offering further interest for an examination at some future day. Y-na-koo-is probably the Koumi of the old charts.

On the 18th of January, 1844, we quitted our anchorage in Port Haddington, and steered to pass to the northward of the two low coral islets situated off the N.E. extremity of Pa-tchung-san, but suddenly finding ourselves in seven fathoms water, with a heavy swell setting from the northward, tacked and ran between them, upon recollecting that our friend, "the Hydrographer", had so advised. During the latter period of our examination of the northern extremity of Pa-tchung-san, we obtained sight of these islands, and upon getting angles to them from one of my positions, I had informed our intelligent friend alluded to, that I should call there on my passage towards Ty-pin-san. At that moment he was surrounded by many spies, and probably afraid of making any communication without the sanction of Kien-Anchee, he therefore watched for an opportunity the ensuing day, and motioning me to follow him behind the house whilst the others were deeply engaged, drew out these two islands upon the sandy walk with his staff, and with a motion full of meaning, formed a line between them to signify that such should be our course; this done, he immediately defaced his outlines and pretended to be in search of something in the sand. We thought at a late period that the fact of his affording this, and other similar information, had been discovered, as his spirits were less buoyant. These islands I suspect to be Tă-lă-mah and Yer-rah-boo, names given by the natives of Ty-pin-san to islands reported to be visible from the summit of Koo-ree-mäh, on that bearing.

The Islands of the Ty-pin-san group are Ty-pin-san, Koo-ree-mäh, Y-drah-boo, Y-ki-mah, and Oo-gă-mee.

SHUNG HOO

Native of Ty pin san.

(Winter Dress)

The S.W. angle of Typinsan is situated in Lat. 24° 44′ N. Long. 125° 14′ E. var. 1° 23′ W.* The anchorage of Ty-pin-san is in a hollow, formed by the junction of Ty-pin-san and Koo-ree-mah reefs; two other dangerous outlying reefs lie half a mile off the southern end of the latter island. The anchorage is rocky with sandy patches between, and is not secure in any season. Ty-pin-san should not be approached at all on its northern side, the reefs extending beyond the clear radius of vision from the summit of Y-ki-mäh; on the southern side, the reef extends about one mile from the land, and vessels, during northerly breezes, might lie to, under its lee until morning, the drain of current is southerly. As yet, safe anchorage has not been found in the vicinity of Ty-pin-san or its islets.

"In describing the principal features which seem to mark the character of the people of this hitherto unknown, or rather unvisited group, termed Meïa-co-shimahs by the authorities, it will be immediately apparent how very near they approximate, in general, to the inhabitants of Loo-Choo, so well detailed by M'c Leod and Basil Hall in the Voyages of H.M.S. 'Alceste' and 'Lyra'. Like those mild and inoffensive islanders, their physical appearance much resembles that of the Koreans and Japanese; their dress also consists of a similar loose robe, of varied pattern, having large wide sleeves, and which is secured about the waist by a long sash. Like them, also, they strain back their long black hair, which is secured in an elegant top-knot, through which they pass their ornamental hair pins, or kamesashee and oosisashee; the former bearing an ornamental head evidently copied from

* For corrected Latitudes and Longitudes *vide* Appendix.

a small hexapetaloid flower, a species of *Xyris* noticed on their island; the latter is a slender instrument with a spatulate extremity, serving various purposes, from ear-pick and nail-cleaner, to even that of chop-stick. These ornaments are of gold or silver, according to the rank of the wearer. With the females, only the latter is worn, and instead of the narrow spatulate form, it resembles a long mustard spoon, with a slightly curved point. On state occasions the grandees wear red, yellow, or blue caps, of office, and in pursuance of the customs of the Chinese, their women are strictly secluded.

The chiefs are sent from Loo-Choo, or as pronounced by them Tah-Lieu-Kieu or great Loo-Choo; and we believe this to be a penal settlement from those islands. The yearly tribute payable to the Emperor of Loo-Choo, is forwarded by two junks quitting Pa-tchung-san and Ty-pin-san with the favourable monsoon, and returning with a cargo of material for clothing, cooking utensils, crockery, tea, pipes, and other necessaries conducive to the happiness and comfort of these poor islanders. This tribute is but of trifling value, and consists of Rice, Batatas or sweet Potatoe, and Tobacco; and is probably received more as a mark of submission than for its intrinsic worth, as by their own estimate, the return cargo (the gift of Government) far exceeds in value any thing which they could send. Although they pretend to be ignorant of the use of money, as a medium of interchange amongst the islands, the chiefs are well aware of the value of the silver dollar. Their general disposition, however, is averse to receiving any thing as remuneration from strangers, and it was not without considerable difficulty that we even-

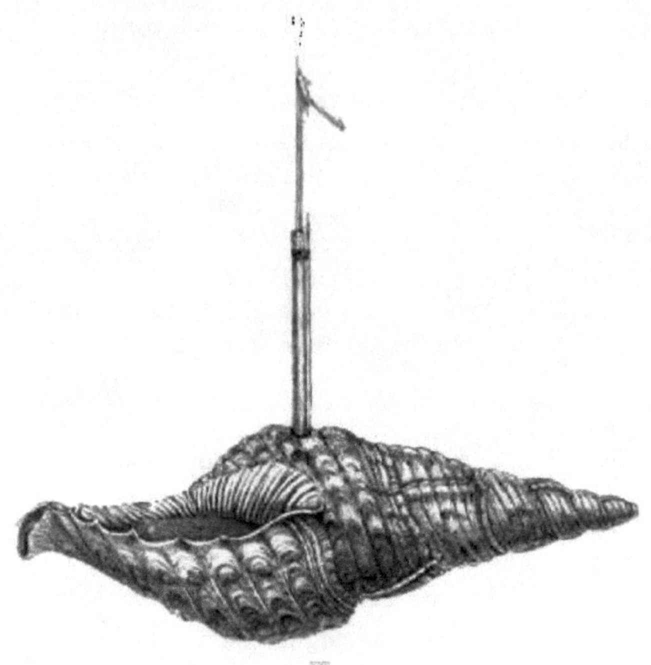

Triton Tea-Kettle.

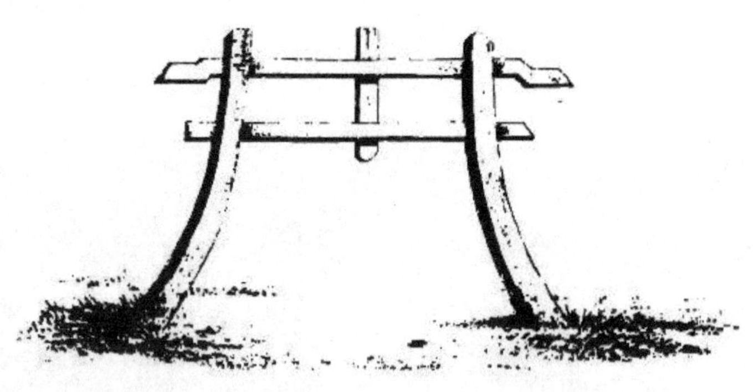

Symbolic Entrance to Religious Grove.

tually succeeded in pressing them to accept of cloth and flannel in return for the supplies with which they had liberally furnished us during our journey round the island.

"It would be an easy task to designate this people as a set of tea-drinking old women, imbecile and apathetic; void of energy and enterprise, living in contentment on a group of islands the value and facilities of which they are almost entirely ignorant, and of whose position and resources they are unable to take advantage. But on contrasting them with the insidious, fawning, and deceitful Chinese; or the savage and vindictive, bloodthirsty Malays, I cannot but fancy their character amiable, and their condition one to be envied.

"Their food is extremely simple, consisting chiefly of the Batata, Rice, and other vegetables, varied with the produce of the deep, including molluscous animals, such as the Cuttle Fish (*Sepia*), the large Clam (*Tridacna gigas*) and others. In their adaptation of the shells, which abound in this region, for various household and other uses, they display considerable ingenuity; two instances in particular excited my attention, and are worthy of notice. The first was in the use of a valve of the large Clam shell just spoken of, for the purpose of swinging the gates to their inclosures; they place it under the heel of the the main post, in the middle of which it revolves upon its point with ease, and its upper end being confined to the standard by a neat ring or grommet of rattan, serves for the hinge; it works very smoothly. The second instance was the construction of a tea-kettle out of the well-known Trumpet shell, *Triton variegatus*, the operculum forming the lid, the canal the spout, and a wooden hook, let in upon the principal of the *lewis* for lifting stones, forms the handle. This rude vessel was adopted several times for our convenience, and answered its purpose admirably. They appear to indulge constantly in smoking tobacco, and seem as passionately fond of tea as their continental friends the Chinese; that which they had in use was, however, of a wretched quality, and afforded us the opportunity of gratifying them with some of a superior kind. Sweet wine was also found to be acceptable; I believe it was given to their wives, for we never observed that they drank it, though I urged it upon them as a medicine. Of the mysteries of the healing art they appear to be profoundly ignorant, trusting almost, if not altogether, to nature, in the progress of their maladies.

"They appear to be acquainted with the potter's art, as tiles of various shapes and sizes were observed about their villages; and in the moulding of their large water-jars and cooking utensils, they evidently evince considerable ingenuity. Some of their vessels, used for containing their 'saki' or Sam-shoo, assume even a classic elegance of form, as represented in the accompanying figure.

"Exclusive of the Mandarins, there would appear to be two distinct castes in the island, the one being rich, intelligent, and altogether superior to the people they govern and control, which is expressed by the more intellectual expression of their features, their more erect bearing, and urbane and polished manners. Their mode of salutation is graceful in the extreme, consisting of a low bending of the body and inclination of the head.

Bridle

Pa - tchung - san

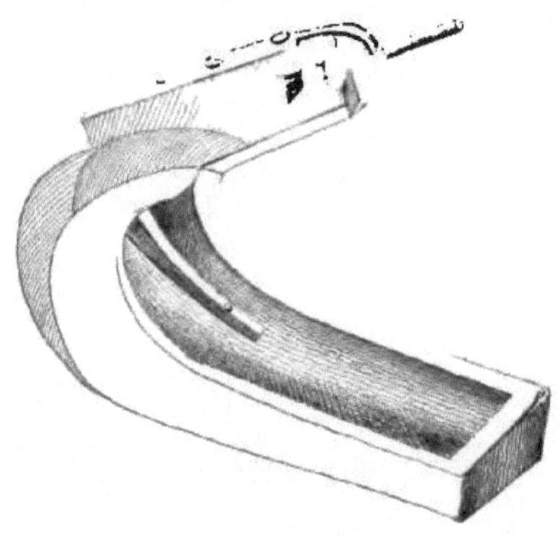

Wooden Stirrup

Meia co shimas

This better class seem to be held in great respect by the inferior, who are ill-clad, and of a flatter cast of features, their physiognomy more resembling the lower orders of the Chinese, while the former assimilate rather to the Mantchouan Tartars.

"I remember, on one occasion, being much amused at our reception by a large assemblage of the natives of Ty-pin-san; as we approached their village, three Mandarins received us standing, and, bowing low, prevailed on us to be seated on their mats, offering us at the same time their pipes, with hospitable *empressement.* Many hundreds of the natives then crowded on the hills overlooking their large and populous village, all stationary and solemn, with eager curiosity depicted in their features. As soon as our magic tripod was erected, and the mysterious theodolite removed from its case, the impatience of the crowd was with difficulty restrained; such, however, is the in-born sense of good-breeding of these poor people, that they did not press and jostle each other, much less incommode the surveyors, but, on the contrary, formed a large semi-circle around us, those nearer sitting or kneeling down, and others in the background standing in regular rows. Our horses were carefully attended to, and small pages held umbrellas over our heads to screen us from the sun. The observations having been completed, we remounted and proceeded to the village, followed by the multitude all scampering in the same direction, and, wearing long robes or gowns, and being all bare-headed, the whole scene made a novel and somewhat ludicrous impression.

"Perhaps the following short sketches of character

may serve, not only to amuse the reader, but also to give some idea of the amount of intellectual and moral energy to be found among these interesting islanders:—

"There was an old man, a native of Pa-tchung-san, hale and active, of the name of 'Mung', with a quick and piercing restless grey eye, a venerable beard depending to his breast, and moustachios to match, a man evidently of high authority amongst them, who was especially jealous of our movements; if we strayed from the party it was he who spurred on his little wiry horse in pursuit. He very soon earned for himself the appropriate soubriquet of "The Spy"; and yet the old fellow was fond of a joke, and would sing as he journeyed on his way, and excite you to a race across the sands. I have seen the old man, however, frequently assume a stern look and fierce demeanour, when the lower orders showed themselves refractory or insolent; then his ire would get the better of his dignity, and, seizing a stick, he would belabour them unmercifully. 'Kien-Anchee', a magnate of the highest rank, who accompanied us as guide and interpreter round Pa-tchung-san, ever showed himself a perfect gentleman and a most intelligent host, explaining everything in a clear and impressive manner, and evincing considerable knowledge and acumen. Open in his manner, he yet had an eye of speculative discernment, and a brow expressive of judgment and discrimination. Joyous in his temperament, he seemed to inspire all with cheerfulness and confidence, leading us on, in the most gratifying manner, from village to village in the circuit of the island. Possessed of a varied and extensive knowledge of the geography and topography of these islands,

Grandee of Ty-pin-san.

his maps and sketches were of great use. 'Shang Hai', surnamed the 'Beaufort', on account of the interest he invariably took in our surveying operations, was a man about forty, with a fine, good-humoured, expressive countenance, and an exceedingly bright and anxious eye. Of an eager and somewhat sanguine temperament, he wanted the self-control and placid demeanour of his brother magnates. Impetuous in his motions, he performed his multifarious functions with energy, giving his orders and seeing them obeyed in person; punishing, with his own arm, any infringement of civility, or any neglect of the comforts of the pale-skinned foreigners, and acting as a willing guide in every excursion. Inquisitive and fond of our society, he passed much time in our company, acquired many words of our language, and proved himself a very usefnl and important sort of personage. In process of time he adopted also some of our vices, loved sweet wine, begged for sugar, and did not altogether eschew rum. Through his means, batatas, onions, fowls, radishes, and turnips were always forthcoming edibles in our encampment; our horses were good, and our coolies obliging and civil.

"The better classes are great writers, composing many long letters, and filling large scrolls of their Chinese paper with singular hieroglyphic, Japanese characters, a dialect of Japanese being the vernacular tongue of the islands. It is a highly interesting sight to witness a solemn conclave of these decent and respectable people, seated in a semi-circle on their mats, assembled together in anxious conference with grave and earnest faces, intent looks, and placid demeanour, with their small metal pipes and huge clam shells for braziers and spittoons, debating among themselves some knotty point of interest or policy.

"Their dwellings are surrounded with stone walls, moss-grown, or covered with creeping plants, and numerous shady trees springing up from among the houses. These latter are of wood and cane, neatly thatched, and constructed with very considerable pretensions to domestic comfort. They are of one story, and the floors, a little elevated from the ground, are covered with well-made mats. We rested several nights in the temples of this people, for though suspicious of strangers and jealously inclined on other points, they scrupled not to offer us even the sacred vessels of the shrine for vulgar uses, and seemed ignorant of such a crime as sacrilege. Our profanity, in using these Joss-Houses as dining rooms and dormitories, was entirely the result of their own free will and invitation. In every village, near the temple, are small stone mausolea, where the edicts of the Emperor they bow to are carefully consumed with fire, in order that the precious relics may not be desecrated by strewing the common ground.

"The soil of these islands is arable, and troops of half-wild horses scamper over the grassy plains, whils herds of large black oxen browse on the hill sides. They plough their Batata fields with a single ox, rudely and superficially, cultivate a few paddy fields, weave a kind of cloth with a frame and shuttle, and manufacture seines and other fishing gear.

"The variety and beauty of the vegetation clothing the sides of the mountains of Pa-tchung-san, and its neighbour Koo-kien-san, is very striking. The light glaucous foliage of a species of *Spondias*, mingled with the leaves of the *Pandanus* and broad fronds of the Palmyra Palm, varied with masses of the dark green Cycas, and here and there the feathery sprays of elegant Acacias, with large-flowered *Hibisci*, *Convolvuli*, Climbing plants and Creepers, interspersed with broad patches of Norwegian Pines, rising from beds of tall grass and gigantic reeds, formed together a scene of singular botanical interest.

"For places of sepulture, they most frequently select the more picturesque and beautiful spots in the island, in sunny glades, or shady dells, or by the side of some tall tree. Often the tombs are single, but more frequently they are placed in groups. They are mostly long, low domes, surrounded by rude walls of old and moss-grown stones, arched over, and terminating in a loose pile; in front there is a small recess, before which are placed two tiles or tablets to record the name and virtues of the deceased. Oblations, in the form of flowers and vessels of water, are offered at the tombs, and, among other curious items to assist the departed on their pilgrimage, I have even seen an old umbrella carefully deposited by the side of the grave. They likewise bury their dead in caves and caverns near the sea, conveying the body to the spot in covered hand-barrows; and, carefully closing up the entrance, they place the memorials of the dead man on tiles against the rock.

"With reference to their modes of religious belief I am unable to offer anything of a satisfactory nature, but am of opinion that they are perfect idolaters. Their temples, in many instances, were adorned with moral maxims, and sometimes with an image of the god of China, and, on one occasion, I made a copy of a very gorgeous painting of some hideous deity, between a man and a bull. This ox-god of the Meïa-co-shimahs cannot fail to bring to the recollection of many of my readers the celebrated Apis of the Egyptians, the most important of those deities which spring out of the fetish-worship, that so peculiarly distinguished the religious system of those remarkable people. The outline of this painting is gold, and the horns are yellow. Herodotus has recorded the existence of a sacred heifer-mummy, cased in gold; and the golden calf, which seduced the Israelites from their allegiance to the God of their fathers, is an off-shoot from the same superstition.

"Of the diseases noticed, the most prominent were those arising chiefly from personal neglect. Of these, opthalmia, in rather a severe form, attacks the eyes, frequently producing total loss of vision; many of them, moreover, are blear-eyed, from the tarsi being the part affected. From the same cause, exanthematous eruptions, particularly scabies, psoriasis, acne, impetigo, and lepra, attack their surface; whilst a species of large plague boil sometimes breaks out in the neck, groin, and axilla, leaving very troublesome ulcers. Elephantiasis, in its several stages, is frequently developed. In the wintry months they suffer from influenza and catarrhal affections, and during the summer the small pox occasionally commits terrible ravages. Very few cases of malformation came under my notice, and still fewer of any congenital deformity of the limbs; in one case

Ox God

of Méia-co-shimas

I performed the operation of dividing the hamstring tendons for contraction of the lower extremity, with a favourable result."

On the 4th of February, much to our regret, we quitted Ty-pin-san, when it was satisfactory to notice that the people expressed themselves pleased with our visit and were equally anxious for our return; our feelings were not, however, so much interested here as at the Pa-tchung-san group. It was my intention to have sighted Y-na-koo, and, if practicable, to have landed for the purpose of obtaining astronomical data for fixing its position; for this object we revisited the northern coast-line of Koo-kien-san, and procured sand from one of its bays. The morning was beautifully fine, but before noon we were visited by thick rainy weather, and compelled to relinquish any further acquaintance, for the present, with these dangerous shores. Our course was now shaped for Batan, in order to re-connect the meridians of both groups with Hong-Kong.

On the morning of the 7th of February, 1844, we dropped anchor in the Bay of San Domingo, Batan, and were fortunate enough to secure our astronomical observations without delay. Our crew had been some time on short allowance of bread, and we now had an opportunity of indulging them with pigs and yams, galore, being cheap as well as excellent; several fine bullocks were also killed and embarked, and a stock of vegetables laid in. The Batan islands produce everything needful, not only in abundance, but also of the finest quality. For the benefit of future visitors, I obtained from the Alcalde the

H

following stipulated prices, at which supplies may be obtained, the dollar being valued at 4*s.* 4*d.*:—

Bullocks (1st Class)	10 dollars.	
„ (2nd „)	8 „	
„ (3rd „)	4 „	Enough for one
Goats (1 large)	1 „	day's supply.
Small ditto	1 to 2 reals.	
Fowls (per dozen)	2 dollars.	Not plentiful.
Pullets (per dozen)	1 „	
Pigs (large size)	6 „	
„ (second)	3 „	
„ (young)	2 to 4 reals.	
Eggs (one hundred)	1 dollar.	

VEGETABLES.

Yams (per 100)	1½ dollars.
Ducais (per 100)	6 reals.
Sweet Potato, large (per 100)	4 „
Onions (per cwt.)..........	5 dollars.
Pumpkins (per 100)	3 „
Cocos (per 100)...........	2 reals.
Cocoa-nuts (per dozen)	2 „

(Eight Reals are equal to one Dollar.)

Potatoes, Turnips, Carrots, Radishes, and Cabbages may be shortly added to the above, but not for sale within a year. The Alcalde Villalba is a very energetic, active man, and a good farmer; he deserves encouragement and assistance from all who may visit the Batanes; good potatoes, and seeds of various vegetables grown in China, would be truly acceptable.

Leaving Batan on the 10th of February, we shaped our course for rounding the northern Lema Islands, near Hong-Kong, and upon nearing them on the 12th observed a Junk coming down before the wind, steering very wild, her sails lowered, and evidently in distress. At this time it blew very fresh; and having steered for her, Lieut. Inglefield succeeded in boarding her, in our second cutter, a boat of the life boat-build, constructed purposely for us, after the model of the catraïas of the coast of Portugal. At the time we boarded her the crew were in the act of cutting away her mast; we succeeded in attaching a hawser to her, and she was eventually secured by our stream cable. I had intended towing her into Hong-Kong, but on her coming alongside, the crew eagerly quitted her, and meeting with further concussion from the ship, she dropped astern, broke her tow-rope, and within a few minutes settled in the water and disappeared. By the accounts received from her crew, we learned that she was from Chin-chew, one of the northern provinces of China, with a cargo of trifling value, bound to one of the southern ports, aud that she had been for some time in a sinking state.

On the 13th of February we returned to our anchorage at Hong-Kong, where we met Rear Admiral Sir Thomas Cochrane, in the 'Agincourt', upon whom the chief command in China had now devolved. Nothing worthy of note occurred during the present visit to Hong-Kong. Having refitted and provisioned, and completed our term-day observations, we departed, on the 6th of March, for Macao, where we anchored on the day following.

Having obtained the necessary observations for our Chronometers, and quitted Macao on the 10th, we passed to the southward of the Pratas, and reached the entrance of the bay of Manila on the morning of the 16th of March. Here we observed the U.S. Frigate 'Brandywine' working in, but by keeping closer to the land, and taking advantage of currents, we contrived to pass her, and by half-past five that evening were safely moored off the city of Manila; our friend the 'Brandywine', reached about noon the following day.

I immediately paid my respects to His Excellency General Alcala, the Captain General of the Philippines, who received me very kindly, and offered every assistance which the port could afford. Being anxious to obtain a complete suite of Magnetic observations, I procured his sanction to pitching our tent upon the exercising ground, situated to the southward of the city lines; and a dragoon guard was posted to keep off the people, as it was feared, from the fearfully superstitious character of the natives, that some mischief might result from our being taken for necromancers. This may be readily conceived, when the reader is informed that one of our countrymen travelling in the interior, nearly lost his life from the circumstance of his being found possessed of some bottles of beer, which it was declared, were destined to poison the population.

By some mistake, the party landing to clear the ground, and erect the Magnetic tents, mistook the locality intended, and deliberately commenced upon a green spot within the southern Bastion. As the Governor had allowed me to make my own selection, the Spanish officer, commanding the Engineers, would no doubt have considered any objection to be inconsistent with the Governor's sanction; fortunately I had an opportunity of explaining the mistake, but he persisted in saying, that if it were necessary we might remain. We moved to another spot, for I had before heard it urged, as a Spanish law, that no occupation of ground could be made within a prescribed distance of lines of fortification, I think sixty yards, and an instance occurred to me in 1838, at Acapulco, in which I was ordered to decamp, after my transit was placed, and in the meridian!

After the completion of our observations, on the term-day, the General and suite paid a visit to the tents, and appeared to be much gratified by viewing the instruments, as well as by an explanation of the portable Magnetometers, Fox's needle, &c.; we were also visited by many other scientific persons in the town, all of whom seemed to take much interest in us, and our proceedings. After experiencing great kinduess and attention from the authorities, I proceeded to take my leave of the worthy Governor, and having fully explained to him the nature of our intended operations within his government, and the advantages which would result to the civilized world in general, he, in the same spirit which had actuated him on our first reception, acquainted me, that in every place under his jurisdiction orders would be given permitting us to make any observations that might be thought desirable. On my requesting a letter to the Governor of Samboanga, in Mindañao, he informed me that a gentleman then present, and of English extraction, was about to proceed there on duty, and that he had instructed him to explain his wishes in that quarter. The Port Captain, Salomon, very kindly supplied me with copies of all the charts they possessed, with all reported as well as newly determined, dangers inserted in red ink, and having embarked our instruments, we left our friends at Manila, with much reluctance, this being one of the first resting-places where we could be said to have been free from official restraint.

"Manila Bay offers a scene of quiet beauty and repose on a hot, calm day, which I have seldom noticed in any other part of the world. The numerous shipping lie perfectly motionless at their anchorage; light, airy canoes catch the faint, passing land-breeze, and glide along in the blue distance, their white sails looking like birds upon the water; the Cavitè passage-boats, with their strange out-riggers and enormous lateen sails, press along towards the cigar-famed city; the gay "banca" comes sweeping by, perhaps the bearer of some gaily dressed Mestiza *blanchisseuse*; while the swarthy Luzon boatmen propel their ponderous barges by means of long poles, which they press against their shoulders, inclining their bodies almost parallel to the sea, as they walk along the platforms on the outside of their craft. Beautiful striped and banded water-snakes play around the vessel, raising occasionally their scaly heads, and gliding along the smooth surface of the bay in graceful undulations. The white porpoise 'rolls his graceless form', as he gambols merrily with his awkward companions; while clouds of noisy, screaming tern hover above the tide-ripple, quarrelling for scraps thrown overboard from the shipping.

"Should you chance to approach Manila early in the morning, you may observe the stone steps leading down into the river, crowded with persons of all ages, and of both sexes, nearly in a state of nudity, enjoying the luxury of a cool and healthy ablution before the labours of the day commence, and many a female form, of perfect symmetry, may there be seen crouching gracefully, as 'with nectar pure her oozy locks she laves'. It is very singular, however, to perceive, now and then, black, warty snakes make their appearance among the bathers, who neither exhibit alarm, nor appear to evince the slightest notice of their presence. These reptiles (*Chersydrus granulatus*), which swarm in the river, although not very attractive in their aspect, are perfectly harmless."

On the evening of the 1st of April we quitted the Bay of Manila and shortly before noon on the following day, neared the island of Cabras, situated off the western end of Luban. As much unnecessary precaution about approaching this island, is inserted in the sailing directions, and I knew from my own experience, by grazing it very closely in 1840, that no extensive reef lies off its western end, I determined on ascertaining the correctness of my friend the Captain of the Port's information as to the passage between it and Luban. The day was beautifully clear, we could see some distance from our mast-heads, and we steered a course for mid-channel, passing through without obtaining bottom with 150 fathoms. The deepest water is on the Cabras side, and its shores may be grazed at the reef-line in twenty fathoms; a ledge extends from Luban, but the reef-line is well defined. The position of Cabras I found to be more easterly than placed on the charts: but of this hereafter. Passing Cabras, we found ourselves suddenly becalmed under the lee of Luban; I would therefore advise persons selecting this channel, to preserve a course westerly of south, until well to the southward, by which means the breeze will be retained. We now proceeded to look after the Panagatan reef, or Camden shoal, which although known for years, has not found a place on any of the charts; the track of the Aetrevida and Descubierta in 1792, leads immediately over the spot; but it is not improbable that, by the assumption of a different meridian between that and the present period, they passed to the eastward, and by night. The reef patch extends five miles, east and west, and three miles, north and south, on which there is about five fathoms at the extreme edge, and about three feet, average, over the mass; upon it rise three small islets, covered with trees, they are all coralline, and probably upheaved; that to the westward is the highest, rising sixteen feet above the mean tide level, or twelve feet above the highest spring tides, and is covered with timber trees. The others merely produce *Pandanus*, wild pines, and shrubby grass.

Panagatan appears to be the Bisayan, or corrupted Malay name for large shells, chiefly *Tridacna*, which are supposed to abound on this reef. By day there can be no fear of approaching it, as all dangers are clearly visible, and the extreme boundary of the reef itself is well defined by its peculiar whiteness, independent of the islands upon it; the water is deep all round. The islands in the neighbourhood easterly, are termed the Semirara group, but this is incorrect, the island of Semirara is far to the N.E., barely in sight; those immediately to the east* have not yet obtained decided names, not being inhabited by any persons in communication with the Spanish authorities, and by the accounts received of them, from officers of the Spanish gun boats, it is probable

* Named Pirate Island by us.

that they are the resorts of the pirates which infest these seas. Although there is a large salt lagoon in the largest Panagatan island, we did not succeed in finding fresh water upon any of the group; it is, however, evidently visited by fishermen from the neighbourhing islands; its position will be found in the Appendix.

Quitting Panagatan, we passed along the western coast of Panay, running over several spots where dangers had been reported without meeting any signs calling for further search, and on the evening of the 7th found ourselves off the Island of Mindañao, or Magindanão of the old charts. On the following morning we had a fine view of this very picturesque and lofty island; the light airs prevented our making much progress through the water, but a strong southerly current swept us quietly along, disclosing at every irregularity of the coast-line, inviting spots in the valleys apparently cleared for cultivation by the hand of man, and what is always deeply interesting to wanderers like ourselves, occasional symptoms of rills of clear water, where this important necessary of life could be procured free from the customary contaminations occasioned by the proximity of a town.

The lofty heights of Mindañao appeared to afford more than ordinary interest to our contemplation at the present moment; frequently bright yellow spots of cleared land presented themselves on the gentle swellings of the hills immediately below the lofty ranges, and already aware of the wild and independent character of the natives of the interior, our glasses were not unfrequently directed in search of the abodes of the Aborigines; the stock, probably, from whence the lawless and much dreaded tribe of the Illañons, crossed by the Malay, had descended. These people take their name from the Bay of Illañon, situated to the S.E. of Samboanga, the capital being the city of Mindañao. They are at peace with the Spanish authorities.

Shortly after noon we rounded the south western point of Mindañao, and opened the Santa Cruz Islands, situated about two miles to the southward of the town of Samboanga, and on passing the Fort and Bay of Calderas on our left, got sight of the Spanish colours on the Fort of Samboanga. Vessels passing this strait, and more particularly if intended to anchor off Samboanga, should keep close to the Mindañao shore, not only to avoid the dangerous patches which lie off the Santa Cruz Islands, but also to ensure anchorage in those cases, which failure of wind and strong currents render advisable. There are no dangers on the north side of the channel but what are well beaconed by the outer fishing stakes; these, in almost every place in the eastern seas frequented by the Malay, will be found to be placed in three or more fathoms.

About 4 o'clock in the evening we dropped anchor off the town of Samboanga, in seventeen fathoms, and by advice received at Manila, moored, to prevent fouling the cables amongst the rocks, which the eddies, resulting from the strong currents of this strait, frequently produce. I immediately paid a visit to Colonel Figueroa, the Commandant or Governor, by whom I was received with all the hearty cordiality which I had been informed at Manila, was the type of his character. The gentleman before alluded to, had arrived, and being now present, repeated the wishes of the Governor of Manila; to these the Colonel gave his hearty acquiescence, desiring me to select any position for my observatory, I should think most advantageous, and tendering all the assistance his authority could command to further the objects of our mission. After passing a few agreeable hours, I returned to the ship, and on the following morning, before the sun was available for our purpose, we pitched our tents near the nearest western Vigia, or watch-house, and conveyed thither the instruments necessary for obtaining the requisite observations. As my presence was strictly required for this duty, I was unable to pay that attention at the Casa Real, which, probably, some official about the person of the Governor, thought indispensable; all appeared to be progressing with ease and regularity, when, on the afternoon of the second day a very abrupt verbal message arrived by a naval officer intimating, "that our boats were to cease sounding instantly." Suspecting that this could not proceed from the Governor, I requested him to return to the person from whom it emanated, and say that when the Governor intimated his wish in writing it should be obeyed, but as he must be aware that sounding was the most important part of our duty, I felt satisfied there must be some misconception. At the same time I despatched the First Lieutenant in order to explain my views to the Governor; and, on his return, I arranged matters so as to meet any objections which might be urged by the superior authorities of Manila. My Lieutenant acquainted me that the Governor was just on the point of starting upon an expedition with the gun-boats and troops to the eastward, to arrange some little disputes with the native authorities, and that I should have no opportunity of visiting him personally that evening, as intended; in proof, however, of his kindness and consideration, he begged to present me with a handsome Malay Kris. This present was entrusted to the Midshipman in charge of the tent, who for security placed it under his pillow, but ere long it was dexterously abstracted during his slumbers. The present remonstrance originated in the law to which I have already referred, relative to carrying on any operations within a certain distance of the Forts, as the second in command thought that our sounding boats carried their lines too abruptly, and, I must confess, somewhat too openly, up to their defences.

This arranged, all went on smoothly, two boats were despatched to carry out the easterly survey, and, taking two others with myself, I proceeded to the examination of the western, making our bivouac the first evening on the beach at Calderas, and indulging our boats' crews with wild hogs which we had been fortunate to procure from the people residing in that neighbourhood. The name Calderas implies the presence of thermal springs, but none could be found, nor were the residents aware of any having existed. Some of our party amused themselves in their inland rambles shooting birds, monkeys, &c., of which the following from Mr. Adams furnishes an account.

"As we landed in the boats on this our first visit, the scenery had a very pleasing appearance. The dark mountains of Mindañao, covered, nearly to the summits, with dense forests, with richly-wooded eminences placed beneath their feet, formed a grand, imposing background; while before us, covered with villages, lay stretched in calm and sunny beauty, the fertile plain of Samboanga, watered by a meandering stream which flowed into the sea near our observatory. Samboanga, although a place of banishment for criminals, is a very pleasant, lively little village; it is surrounded by green groves of graceful cocoa-nuts, which here attain a very great elevation, and, as you wander under their refreshing shade, you will be amused by numbers of paroquets, clinging in fantastic attitudes to the great petioles of the leaves, while various other birds hover continually around their spreading tops. As you penetrate more deeply the scenery grows far more wild, and, emerging from some lonely hut, the Indian may be seen proceeding to climb the tall, cylindric trunks, to hang his primitive, bamboo pitchers on the new-cut footstalks of the leaves, for the purpose of collecting toddy. The ground beneath is covered with the fallen nuts, which are greedily devoured by the land-crabs, which here perforate the soil in every direction. The natives set ingenious traps for these 'nati consumere frugos', formed of the internodes of large bamboos, provided with a valve, which allows the animal to enter, but forbids his voluntary exit. Numbers of monkeys are heard chattering and wailing in the distant forest; and in one of our rambles near Calderas, a large species was shot as he sat, unconscious of his fate, munching berries in a lofty tree-top, and I well remember the piteous expression of his brown and wrinkled face, as I drew him from the undergrowth where he had fallen.

"In these woodland haunts, you will see the native

light his fire by the primitive mode of rubbing together two pieces of stick. Lucretius alludes to the probable mode of thus obtaining fire, in his poem 'De natura Rerum'.*

"'Et ramosa tamen quom, ventis pulsa, vacillans
Æstuat, in ramos incumbens arboris, arbor,
Exprimitur validis extritus viribus, ignis:
Emicat interdum flammäi fervidus ardor,
Mutua dum inter se ramei, stipesque, teruntur.'

"On one occasion we came suddenly upon a small hamlet, named Dumalon, and were invited, in the true spirit of hospitality, to enter one of the dwellings of these simple people. There we saw a complete picture of a Bisayan family. Two old wrinkled crones bustled about the nibon floor, engaged in culinary and household cares; young girls were busy making mats, the men were lazily smoking, and chewing betel, whilst a mother was carefully rocking her tender new-born, infant in a cradle of very original construction. A bamboo, suspended horizontally by a rope at each end, from the rafters, supported two strings, to which the cross-piece of the cradle was attached near its centre. By gently pressing on the margin of the crib, the elasticity of the apparatus caused an up and down movement, serving as a pleasant lullaby to the small, brown, dozing suckling.

"On our return, we came suddenly upon a group of natives, who had just succeeded in killing a wild-boar, and who very willingly, for a trifling consideration, parted with a choice morsel for our consumption; and upon experiment, we found it tolerably palatable, although, of course somewhat tough, and lean."

* Lib. v. 1095–1099.

On regaining the sea-side, where our tent was pitched for the bivouack on the loose dry sand, sentinels were placed for fear of the pirates, who are very numerous and daring along this coast. To guard against these, small look-out houses, or vigias are erected on poles at the height of thirty feet above the ground, and are in communication with the Gun-Boat Establishment. Some have arms, but the one I visited had a wooden swivel, which the guard informed me, "was to break the head of the assailant." They are also furnished with a formidable defence on the plan of the battering ram, being a piece of heavy timber about four feet long, and five in diameter, suspended at its centre by a rattan to the roof. It is easily managed by hand, and driven end-on, would deal a deadly blow. The beach is lined with forest trees of great size and beauty, extending as far as the water's edge, and at distant intervals along the shore, fishing weirs are placed, The fish penetrate the labyrinths of these preserves, and eventually enter the furthermost compartment, from which it is impossible to escape. The Indians showed themselves very dexterous in spearing the captive fish, and I have even seen them suddenly plunge into the enclosure, dive beneath their scaly prey, and stab them with a knife.

"Between Calderas and Samboanga are numerous ponds and small inland streams, abounding with large *Hydrosauri* (aquatic lizards), that splash about the water like young alligators. Fish, of good size and rare species, are numerous in the ponds, and capturing them with a drag-net afforded us much amusement. Along the margins of these small fresh-water lakes are thousands of shells, *Melaniæ*, *Neritinæ*, *Navicellæ*, and *Assimineæ*. It was here, also, I captured several specimens of that rare and singular fresh-water crustacean, the *Utica gracilipes*. During the evening, vast numbers of *Pteropi* (gigantic bats) pass over head, on slow flapping wing, from the islands in the distance, to pursue their wonted depredations on on the fruits of the forests beyond Samboanga."

No good fresh water is to be procured at Calderas Point, but it may be obtained from a small rivulet upon the opposite side of the bay within. About a mile beyond, to the N.W., I fell in with several streams running into the sea, and one so very convenient for the approach of the ship, and so very inviting, with its bright clear water gushing across the pebbly beach into the sea, that I determined to bring the 'Samarang' thither for water before proceeding to sea. Having completed our survey of this coast, we returned to Samboanga, and, after taking leave of the authorities, shaped our course for the Island of Sooloo, the residence of the Sultan of that Archipelago, as well as the legitimate ruler of part of the north-eastern coast of Borneo, Banguey, and islands adjacent.

CHAPTER IV.

SOOLOO, MANADO, TERNATE, AND GILOLO.

Arrive at the Island of Sooloo—Astronomical observations—Impertinent curiosity of the natives—Visit to the Sultan—Hall of Audience—Dress and appointments—Remonstrance on the subject of piracy—City of Sooloo—Means of defence—Celebes—Manado—Reception by the Governor—Ternate—Courteous Invitation from the Governor — Fix Observatory on a coral reef off Gilolo—Surprised by the natives — Fire musketry to frighten them—Attacked by five Prahus—Discomforture of the enemy—Vessels with the killed and wounded disabled and burnt—Second attack of five larger Prahus—Author knocked overboard by a ball from one of the Chief's brass guns—Severely wounded in the hip—Enemy put to flight—Further arrival of the natives—Ammunition expended, return to the ship—Boats recur to the scene of action under the command of Lieut. Heard—Destroy several of the enemy's Prahus with shot and Congreve rockets—Woman and child saved from a burning Prahu—Cessation of hostilities.

The Charts of the Sooloo Sea afford but very poor aid in the navigation of that region, the outer space having been very imperfectly examined, and abounding with dangers which render it necessary to be constantly on the alert; it is studded with rocky patches, which, being marked by overfalls, constantly give rise to anxiety, and which even by day are sufficiently annoying; but the ripplings of these eddies, rendered more distinct by the stillness and general calms prevailing at night, tend to cause greater uneasiness. Passing over, however, these inconveniences, we reached Sooloo on the 16th of April, having made our approach by the west, instead of the more certain channel from the north; and having been compelled to drop a kedge for the night, and despatch our boat to a schooner seen off the town, in order to show a light to lead us to the anchorage; but it was not until the ensuing dawn that the breeze enabled us to move, and before 8 o'clock we had reached our position. Shortly after, we were visited by Mr. Wyndham, the owner of the schooner 'Velocipede', which we had observed at anchor, and, as he had been long resident at Sooloo and conversant with their language, I was glad to accept of the tender of his services as Interpreter, and requesting him to make the necessary arrangements for my visit to the Sultan, I proceeded to the nearest rocky point in order to obtain the necessary astronomical observations for securing its position. I selected a spot distant from the town, in the hope of remaining unmolested by the prying multitude, but in this I was, as usual, disappointed; several small parties, armed with spears and krises, came around us; and as neither party understood Malay, nor we their language (Bisayan), explanation, or remonstrance, was impossible. The proximity of their weapons much disturbed our magnetic observations, and compelled me to surround my position with a body of men, under arms, before I could proceed. This manœuvre not being very palatable to

Sultan

MAHOMED PULALU

of Sooloo.

some of young blood present, and finding that I did not adopt such decisive measures as they themselves would probably have had recourse to, they became rather impertinent and troublesome; but an order "to load and fix bayonets" had, however, a most decided effect, convincing them that we were not to be trifled with. After this little manifestation of hostility, their conduct suddenly changed to one of more civil deportment, and finally, leaving their arms in the bush, we became on good terms.

The necessary arrangements for our visit to His Highness the Sultan having been made by Mr. Wyndham, I proceeded thither, accompanied by all the Officers who could be spared, attended by our boats fully equipped for service, from which, also, the complimentary salutes could be returned. On arriving at the landing place we were met by the Officers of the Sultan, and conducted to the house of the Prime Minister, Datu Muluk; he received us in state, and, after exchanging salutes of twenty-one guns, accompanied us on foot to the residence of the Sultan, about a quarter of a mile within the town. We found the place of reception, or Hall of Audience, a plain building raised upon posts about four feet above the ground, and about forty feet square; it had no throne, or raised chair of state, as at Brunai, but a carved high-backed arm-chair was placed for the Sultan, and a table, chairs, and benches for those of minor degree.

The Sultan was already seated, and surrounded by his Chiefs and Guards in their gorgeous dresses; he was himself clothed in a purple embroidered vest, with a rich flowing robe or mantle of green velvet with gold embroidery; and around his waist was a broad band of gold lace, attached in the centre by a large ornamental clasp of gold, set with stones. He rose, and, extending his hand to welcome me, motioned to be seated in the chair opposite to him. He appeared to be about five feet ten, very emaciated, with a heavy countenance exhibiting traces of imbecility; forehead narrow, face large, and evidently suffering under weakness arising from excessive indulgence in the use of opium. They affected to believe that I was a descendant of Dalrymple, to whose memory they appear to attach great respect. During his visit to Sooloo he acquired the friendship of the Sultan, Alimudin, about that period restored by the English to his Sovereignty over these islands, and pledged each other as brothers, by the ceremony of drawing blood from the arm of each and mixing it in glasses. By this solemn act Dalrymple became a sharer of the Sultan's power, and the Island of Toolyan, in the eastern bay, was ceded to him; even now they considered it so entirely British property, that the Sultan, learning my wish to visit it, offered to send a person with me to inspect it.

Beyond this our interview with the Sultan was limited to a communication I thought it necessary to make on the subject of the frequent resort of the Ballignini Pirates to his ports, and the facilities he afforded them of effecting the sale of their captured slaves in the markets of Sooloo. I further gave him to understand, that if it should be found that he furnished them shelter, under pursuit, it would entail severe retribution from the British Flag; he promised his attention to this subject, and that he would inquire into the facts which I then detailed to him, relative to recent visits of the pirates. After taking refreshment of chocolate, sherbet, &c., we retired. On our return to the boats, which, owing to the fall of tide, had been compelled to shift down to the outer pier on which the houses are constructed, we noticed three very suspicious-looking boats attached; these, Mr. Wyndham assured me, were pirates, and, moreover, that they had only a few days previously landed some captured women, chiefly taken amongst the Bisayas, or the coasts of the islands between Mindañao and Luzon, and exposed them for sale in the public market; we had not sufficient evidence to interpose our authority, and as the Datu Muluk was supposed to be a party interested in their proceedings, it was not likely that any remonstrance I might have made to the Sultan would be productive of any benefit; the natives in the boats were rather inclined to be impertinent and to resent the curiosity of one of our party, but fortunately it passed over.

The city of Sooloo is built much in the same manner as Brunai, running out in three lines into the sea, the piles of the outer houses being in four fathoms, and the intervals between the rows admitting of the 'Samarang' being secured in the mouth of the main street; one half of the town stands over the water, but the chiefs all reside on *terra firma*. There are two batteries, one on each side of the main water communication just alluded to. The mode of their construction is good, viz. by parallel lines of heavy piles driven closely together at a distance of ten feet between, the parallels cross tied, and the interval filled with earth; embrasures are fitted similar to the ports of a vessel, and would offer formidable resistance if the guns were served by Europeans; no more than five guns could, however, be mounted on each battery. On the chance of future hostilities, arising from their persisting in giving shelter to the pirates, I examined these batteries from the position where I would have placed the 'Samarang'. Not a gun from them could have told, and they would readily be driven from their works, by shells, whilst a force landed on either side, would take them in flank; in which direction they had omitted to provide any embrasures or defences.

After taking leave of our interpreter, Mr. Wyndham, who appears to possess much influence over these people, we proceeded to the westward with the intention of securing our southern passage by the eastern coast of Borneo. Shortly after clearing Sooloo the breeze failed, and, to avail myself of this delay, I visited the Island of Sooladdé, and obtained data for fixing its position. The calm continued the greater part of the day, and the Officer left in command, finding her drifting rapidly to the eastward, tried to anchor with the kedge; but the hawser snapped, and she was driven, with the loss of an anchor, a considerable distance before the contrary tide assisted her return, when, having recovered the edge of the bank, we dropped a bower anchor for the night, and at daylight, when the tide suited, made another effort to get southerly. On the 21st we were again becalmed, near an island which was not satisfactorily placed on the chart; we therefore anchored to secure its position. Many boats were noticed fishing, but one of a piratical complexion having anchored near my observing station, a boat was sent to reconnoitre him; he was inclined to resist, but, thinking probably that he would be punished by the ship, produced a pass, but it was neither signed nor dated, and as there was no cause for detention he was not molested further.

After the evening's observations were completed, we weighed, with a light favourable air, and were moving along very quietly when it was discovered that the channel a-head was barred by a reef, and before any measures could be adopted to haul off, she had taken the ground; kedges were instantly laid out, the ship hove into deep water, and in a very short time we were making a clear course.

On the 22nd we sighted the Island of Tawi-Tawi; a very high and extensive island, the southern and western great island of this Archipelago; the scenery was much diversified by clear green knolls, embellished here and there by clumps of trees, standing out clear on the profile. It is said to be one of the principal pirate establishments, but as it did not, at present, enter into my scheme of operations, I gave it a wide berth and stood on for Unsang, the nearest land of Borneo, now in sight. At 10 o'clock, on the morning of the 23rd, we anchored off Unsang, and landed for observations; and it being now near our Term-day, determined on completing the suite of magnetic observations on this eastern extremity of the Island of Borneo. We found three separate bars between us and the place selected for our Observatory; the outer, sand, the second, coral, and the third, (nearly a-wash) also coral, connected with the land; each had deep-water channels between them. This part of the coast of Borneo appeared very dreary although free from the Mangrove outline, and furnished solid ground upon which several varieties of useful and ornamental timber appeared to flourish; within the outer belt we found extensive swampy lagoons of brackish water, and one stream sufficiently fresh for consumption. This, no doubt, flows from the lofty mountains which may be seen in the rear when approaching the coast, and distant probably about ten or twelve miles. The only animals noticed were Hogs, Deer, and Monkeys; one gigantic individual of the last tribe presented himself to us whilst searching for hogs with one of my Lieutenants, who, having his rifle in readiness, was much inclined to shoot this impertinent approximation to the human species; he took his departure, however, with a hoarse cough, or what the sailors termed a 'horse laugh'. A humourous tar beside us intimated, 'that he took it so quietly that he thought he was going to offer the Lieutenant a cigar.' The seine was hauled with success, and much amusement was afforded to our sportsmen. About sunset we observed an immense flight of bats, migrating apparently towards the north, for the space of an hour, but although well peppered with ball and small shot, none were killed. This position on Unsang is situated in Lat. 5° 17′ 17″ N., and Long. 119° 12′ E., cutting off fifteen miles of the eastern coast as delineated on the charts.

Quitting Unsang on the 27th we passed on the western side of Tawi-Tawi, and cleared the intricacies of the Sooloo group, experiencing fresh breezes from the southward with an uneasy motion, which after our late cruize for some months in still water, became quite unpleasant; the currents were pressing us strong to the north-eastward, and the succeeding light breezes did not enable us to fetch to windward of Cape Rivers. My object was to endeavour to pass between Celebes and Borneo, touching at Macassar and thence to Singapore, but on the 5th of May we had merely fetched in with the land about fifteen miles to the eastward of Cape Rivers; the north-western extremity of Celebes. On the 6th we had beat up to the Cape, when I landed and obtained observations for fixing this important head-land. The position was selected upon the outer extreme islet, a high rocky pile of, apparently, upheaved grey basalt, about eighty feet above the sea level, and presenting the appearance of a pile of loose stones just deposited from a cart. The few shrubs or trees upon it were of the Fig tribe; and the whole island being coated and whitened by the dung of marine birds, it received the appellation of 'Slime Island'. Immediately within this, about 200 yards distant, was another islet of similar construction, but about 150 feet in height, and a space of half a mile, with a deep channel, intervened between it and the main island of Celebes, or Cape Rivers. The reefs extend southerly from these islets as far as the eye could reach from the summit of Slime Island, and the coast from the Cape, suddenly receding into deep and lonely bays, leaves a good channel or harbour within, where, had I been sure of obtaining water, I should have placed the 'Samarang'. Villages were noticed in the adjacent bays, and some few natives approached sufficiently near in their canoes to reconnoitre, but could not be induced to make our acquaintance. Knowing the jealousy of the Dutch Government, and not having time to spare for an experiment upon the courtesy of the Bugis, which is not unfrequently as doubtful as that of the Illaños, we endeavoured to beat along the coast to the southward. The position of Slime Island was found to be 1° 20′ 24″ N., and 120° 41′ 36″ E., rise of tide nine feet. Notwithstanding all our efforts to reach Cape Donda, for several days we gained nothing; twice we made attempts to approximate an island on which I wished to obtain further observations, with our two fastest pulling boats, but as our men became fagged, and it was impossible to reach in time to save the latitude, it was each time relinquished, the sailors asserting that they were " Fairy Islands, and glided away faster than we pulled." As our water began to run short, and I saw little prospect, with the prevailing light winds, of overcoming the strong northerly currents, being on the fifth day to leeward of our previous ground, I bore up and ran along the northern shore of Celebes in search of Manado.

In the present advanced state of Hydrographic knowledge, we are not prepared to understand how Manado, a Dutch position, established for many years, required searching after; to us, indeed, it would prove a discovery, for we had neither Latitude, Longitude, nor any Remarks calculated to afford the slightest information of its position or peculiarities; under these circumstances it could not be approached by night, and short as this run to leeward was, it occupied nine days. The richness of the mountainous regions of Celebes afford numerous interesting views; here the hand of cultivation has cleared away many spots both on hill and dale, which, with their bright grassy tints and contrasts of colour, exhibit an effect scarcely less interesting than that of more civilized regions.

On the 18th of May we found ourselves in the vicinity of Manado Tua, a very steep, conical, well-wooded island, apparently an old volcano, its elevation above the sea level being about 1500 feet. Calm enabled me to land and obtain sights, leaving orders for the ship to pass round its western side and pick me up in the afternoon. There was, however, little to interest, although the vegetation was most luxuriant, and would have afforded a rich treat to those interested in Orchidaceous plants, of which numerous varieties were collected. We met here a prahu employed in cutting the bamboo and rattan, which grew in great luxuriance, and by the description which I subsequently gave of her, as well as of the costume, and number of men and women for the size of the craft, was pronounced by the Governor to be a *pirate*. Had we not been armed, and accompanied by one of our cutters with her gun, we might possibly have discovered as much ourselves. They were civil and gave us water, but were disinclined to greater intimacy. The position, on the north face of Manado Tua, is in Lat. 1° 39′ 49″ N., 128° 35′ 7″ E.; the rock on the sea coast is composed of hornblende. Shortly after sunset we reached the ship just where I anticipated, and a light air favouring us, stood in for the land in the direction where we expected to find the town of Manado.

At 8 o'clock the following morning, we noticed a battery, situated in a deep bay on which the Dutch colours were flying, but from the absence of any town I suspected this could not be Manado. Lieut. Baugh was despatched in the gig to obtain the necessary information, which he very soon communicated by signal, and shaping our course to meet him, we found on his rejoining us, that we had to seek Manado in the deep bight to the eastward, and a brisk sea-breeze setting in soon after, enabled us to descry the colours on the Fort. On our approach, a canoe with a ragged black soldier, or Peon, came off to us, but as he could neither speak, nor make himself understood by any signs, he was not further noticed. As we approached the town, off which a barque under Dutch colours was at anchor, we were visited by her mate, an Englishman, who most kindly offered his assistance in piloting us into this most awkward port. It is, indeed, of so critical a character that, unassisted, we should have felt some difficulty about anchoring so completely under the face of a hill, and had it been two hours later, we could not have effected an entrance that night, as a land breeze commenced fresh off shore, before we were secured. The soundings decrease suddenly from sixty to thirty, fifteen, and five fathoms, so that it is necessary to approach the shore obliquely, or *alongshore*; and, in order to get bottom at thirty fathoms, the anchor must be dropped as soon as the cast of sixty is obtained; the stream anchor must be immediately placed inshore in one fathom, and the ship secured by it from the land-wind. By four o'clock this had been effected.

No officer, or messenger of any description, had visited Her Majesty's Ship 'Samarang' with her Colours and Pendant displayed, and I afterwards ascertained that the information given by Lieutenant Baugh of the Ship's name, and her destination, &c., had been duly conveyed from the first or Lower Fort before the 'Samarang' anchored. I, further, sent a message by the mate of the Dutch barque, stating my intention of calling upon the Resident or Governor. I was not received by any one on landing; the sentinels did not salute me in uniform; and it was only through the kindness of a countryman, Mr. Hart, who had been left behind, wounded in the 'Young Queen' in her affair, under the Hon. Mr. Murray, in the Coti River, that I found my way to the Resident's house.

Considering the object of my visit to be of importance as connected with scientific observation, I scarcely heeded these omissions of respect, beyond remarking to the Resident, in reply to his reiterated apologies of having no instructions how to proceed, "that the usages of civilized countries, such as Holland, needed no instructions for the reception of a ship of war; especially, as in the present instance, of one belonging to a nation in amity with his own"; and, declining to discuss the matter further, I intimated to him my intention of communicating this want of courtesy to my superior. I then requested to be informed, whether he had any instructions to prohibit my making the scientific observations for which I had come thither, and further told him, that his reply in the negative would oblige me to repair to the neighbouring Island of Ternate where I could rely upon a hearty reception. He affected to be displeased with my having so unceremoniously passed his Peon on approaching the harbour, but I gave him to understand, that the British Flag required that persons of my rank, commanding a Frigate, should be received on touching a foreign shore, by an Officer, in the same manner as that observed at Amboyna. Upon this he immediately summoned his advisers, and decided that every facility should be accorded; he, moreover, desired that his principal Surveyor, of Woods and Forests I suppose, should be in readiness at daylight, and accompany me to any spot which I might consider most suitable.

Before six o'clock the following morning, Papké Bulow, a well-informed gentleman who understood English, accompanied me to the beach north of the town, where I soon fixed upon a spot for the observatory. I was also fortunate in obtaining at a trifling rent a commodious cottage with every convenience, including the assistance of an intelligent, Spanish, Bisayan, to act as interpreter with the natives. This being the period for our May Term-day, the magnetic instruments were landed, exciting considerable curiosity among the garrison, whilst the natives kept at a more respectful distance, regarding us probably as some mysterious individuals dealing in arts of no trifling nature.

The town of Manado is situated in the bight of a deep bay, about nine miles south-easterly of Manado Tua, which being interpreted, is Old Manado. The position of the present town had formerly another name, but that of Manado has been substituted from the circumstance of one of the inhabitants of Manado Tua having been employed as Ambassador to Ternate, requesting the aid of the Dutch in settling their dissensions, and on being interrogated from whence he came, replied, 'Manado,' and upon the Dutch affording their advice (or taking possession), it assumed its present name. There are many absurd traditions as to their reasons for abandoning Manado Tua, which are not worth relation, but the fact to be inferred is, that they were compelled by an earthquake to seek a more secure position. The scarcity of fresh water may also have had some share in forming this determination. The neighbourhood of Manado is still subject to volcanic action; on the eastern side of the Peninsula, near Keema, a cone has been upheaved within a few years, and is at this moment a heap of cinders. Its crater, which may be overlooked from a conical mountain near it, is now in a state of activity, presenting the appearance of an iron pot, bottom upwards, with the lava bubbling through an orifice in its centre.

As a guide to seamen, the following is worthy of record:—The whole of the Bay of Manado is 'steep to', decreasing suddenly from one hundred and fifty fathoms, to sixty, ten, and one fathom; the anchorage should be approached *along the beach*, obliquely; let go the anchor when the line at the taffarel gives sixty, veer eight shackles and secure by stream anchor *on the reefs*. This will berth you in fifteen fathoms, and the operation must be completed before four P.M., or the land squalls may drive you off into one hundred and fifty fathoms.

On our arrival, we were informed that no bottom would be found beyond sixty fathoms, but having made our customary experiments, we ascertained, that after sixty, the bottom suddenly decreased to one hundred and fifty, and maintained this flat, more or less, for a considerable distance, a kedge therefore would safely retain a vessel until she could regain the bank. The holding ground off the mouth of the river is the best, and affords better scope. In the months of November, December, and January, the rollers are said to be terrific, but no instance has occurred of a vessel being wrecked, or driven ashore, that possessed decent ground tackle. It is impossible to escape from the bay to avoid them, as the rollers set in during calm, and are suddenly succeeded by heavy gusts and gales from N.W. By the Dutch ordinance, no national vessel belonging to their flag can drop anchor at Manado, but must proceed to Keema, on the eastern side of the Peninsula; where the whalers call frequently for supplies. There is an excellent road between it and Manado, constructed, I believe, as all the best in this region have been, by our friend Papké Bulow.

"During our stay at Manado, we spent some pleasant hours in the society of this old man, for many years resident there. At the time I saw him, Papké Bulow was an active, industrious, enterprising character, full of enthusiasm and zeal, and involved in various schemes and speculations; the following history of his life, from his own mouth, might probably prove interesting. He informed me that, about two years ago, his agricultural endeavours were all rendered fruitless by a severe drought; his crops entirely failed; his young trees perished before they yielded fruit; the labour of years was gone, and the capital of former savings expended; he was nearly ruined, a poor, desolate, and lonely man, no prattling children were around him now, to wean him from his sorrow; they were all laid low; nor had he any friends to sympathise in his grief. Turning to the faithful partner of his woes, he read encouragement in her looks, and determined to begin again. He had much to struggle with; the Dutch authorities deprived him of the office of Surveyor of the Roads, because, too honest in his heart, he scorned to harass and oppress the natives. His darling bridge (which he erected across the Manado river), the idol of his brain, broke down, his heart well nigh broke, too, for the mocking laugh of his enemies seemed ringing in his ears. A common mind might now have sunk in despair, but Papké bore nobly up against the stream that strove to drown his energies, and his heart grew firm within him. The bridge ere long was strengthened and repaired, his young plants thrived and grew apace; his wife regained her wonted smile, and Papké's home was now a cottage of contentment.

"One lovely evening, attended by his wife, he visited the spot where his children lay interred, his faithful Gertrude sat by his side, the parents' eyes were turned towards the graves, they pressed each others hands in silence, and tears stole down their cheeks. They may never have more children, but their lives will glide down peaceably and in affluence, to 'that bourne from which no traveller returns', the just reward of patient perseverence and mild endurance of misfortune." Subsequently we learned that this honest man had been patronized by the Government, and had been advanced to some station of importance under it.

"The Bugis women of Celebes are much better featured than the Malayan ladies of Borneo, although, like them, they spoil the appearance of their mouths by the odious practice of chewing the *sïrih* leaf; but as the custom of kissing is never indulged in by these Asiatics, perhaps it is not objected to by their husbands. The damsels of Manado dress their hair very frequently with a large knot curiously placed on the summit of the front part of the head; their forms are good, and voluptuous, though rather inclined to *embonpoint*, and some wear their hair long and flowing down the back. Among the female population are many half-castes, who are generally much better looking than their neighbours, and become the wives of Dutch merchants, or opulent Malay gentlemen. These carry their heads very high, and have numerous slaves under them, and I was sorry to observe that these female tyrants are commonly unjust and cruel in the extreme, visiting with their sore displeasure many of their defenceless female dependants, more particularly the younger and better-favoured among them, and should their suspicious jealousy once detect their husband's eye to linger upon the form of one, rather than that of another, the demon of revenge takes possession of their breasts, and unheard of brutality is sure to assail their victim. One lady I was introduced to has actually been known to have seized upon a poor suspected girl, dragged her to an obscure wood, and there having entirely stripped her naked, to have smeared her whole body with honey, and left her thus exposed bound to a tree, the prey of the wasps, and flies, and myriad ants, that would immediately be attracted to the spot."

Manado furnishes moderate supplies of Beef, Hogs, Poultry, Vegetables, Fruit, &c. Excellent water may be obtained at the river, but, if time permit, the boats should go well up the stream beyond the first fork, where it is much purer; the greatest inconvenience arises from the full boats being unable to get over the reef which bars the river at low water, and therefore can only obtain the turns between first quarter flood and the last half ebb.

The wood, unless specially contracted for, is too soft for fuel; other durable woods for ship building and ornamental purposes abound. The whole country in the vicinity of Manado is composed of lofty ranges surmounted by peaks, but the Klăbăt Mountain, which rises to the height of 6500 feet, and is nearer to the Keema or eastern shore of the Peninsula, is the most conspicuous. It has been clearly seen from Ternate and Meyo, and from sixty miles to the westward.

Manado Tua is also very lofty, and is an excellent guide for finding the way to Manado, which, as I have before remarked, is rather difficult. Our observations place the Fort of Manado in

Lat. 1° 30′ 23″ N.
Long. 124° 43′ 9″ E.
Dip. 1° 21′ 31″ S.

Rise of tide six feet, H.W. F. and C. nearly noon.

Quitting Manado on the 26th, we passed through Banca Strait, upon one point of which I landed, in order to fix the position of its eastern danger, which is situated in Lat. 1° 46′ 24″ N., Long. 124° 59′ 35″ E. Having rejoined the ship as she passed the island, we cleared Cape Coffin, the N.E. extremity of Celebes, and stood for the Island of Ternate, where our friends had prepared us to meet with a much more friendly reception than we had experienced at Manado.

On the morning of the 29th, having fallen towards Meyo, and calm succeeding, I landed, notwithstanding a heavy swell was running, and obtained its position. The northern rock on which we fixed our observatory was found to be in Lat. 1° 21′ 4″ Long. 126° 20′ 16″ E.

K 2

From this island we had a clear view of some of the most remarkable peaks in this neighbourhood, Klabat, Tyfore, Ternate and Tidore.

On the morning of the 1st of June, being becalmed off Ternate, I landed on the western side, and obtained observations, placing it in Lat. 0° 45′ 20″ N., and Long. 127° 10′ 57″; during the night we endeavoured to work through the strait between it and Tidore, but calm and currents eventually pressed us, broadside on, to a reef on Tidore, where we had to await the change of tide. With the morning breeze and fair tide, we worked up to the town of Ternate, where we were immediately visited by a guard boat, containing a pilot, and bringing offers of assistance from the Governor, accompanied by an invitation to stay at his house. I mention this circumstance more to show that the want of courtesy we experienced at Manado did not originate in any order from the Netherlands Government, as the same would have been in force at all their possessions in these seas, and having experienced the most flattering reception at Amboyna and Macassar, on my homeward route in the 'Sulphur', I feel confident that the conduct of the Resident at Manado cannot but be open to disapproval from the Dutch authorities, famed in these seas for their politeness to strangers, as well as for their efforts in the furtherance of every Scientific Expedition which has visited their ports.

"The Island of Ternate resembles a huge green mountain, covered with dense forest, with here and there large patches of tall grass. In some parts, where man has been at work, you will see the Durian (*Durio zibethinus*), and Limes (*Citrus limetta*), mixed up with the fantastically-formed stems of the *Pandanus candelabrum*, or Screw-Pine, the Cocoa-nut tree (*Cocos nucifera*), will be seen towering above the mild Nibon (*Areca tigillaria*), and the Plantains (*Musa paradisaica* and *sapientum*), mingling their broad green leaves with the dark feathery foliage of the Bamboo (*Arundo Bambu*). To these, the Jack, and Bread-fruit trees (*Artocarpus, nitegrifolia* and *incisa*), form a striking contrast, giving to the stranger a good idea of the splendour of tropical vegetation. Under the united foliage of these valuable trees, I noticed more than one member of the Parrot family, twisting themselves about the branches in every grotesque and awkward manner they could possibly devise. The black satin Grackle (*Graculus Indicus*), was also common among the Bamboo thickets. As I wandered along the shore, I noticed several woolly-headed Papoos, busily engaged in collecting coral, and heaping it up in stacks for the purpose of burning it into lime or *chunam*, to be used along with the betel-nut and sïrih-leaf, the favourite mascatory of the Malays; while numbers of indolent natives sat fishing in small canoes under the shade of gigantic cone-shaped hats, made from the fan-shaped leaves of the Palmyra Palm (*Borassus flabelliformis*). Down the sides of the mountain, run numerous fresh-water rivulets, abounding in an endless variety of shells (*Neritinæ*), while numbers of aquatic Saurians play and skip along the surface, or rest with their bellies on the trunks of prostrate trees that lie across the streamlets."

Not feeling sufficiently well to land at Ternate, and as my delay here was influenced by no other motive than that of determining its Latitude and Longitude, I decided on proceeding to the southward; I therefore despatched Lieut. Baugh to pay my respects to the Governor, and to inform him of our destination, with an offer to convey his despatches for Europe, or Java. On the return of Lieut. Baugh, I learned that the Governor was anxious that we should make some stay; and having heard the day before of my being on the western side of the island, had prepared a suite of rooms for my accommodation; he now entreated that I would postpone my departure, sending off the pilot to show us the most convenient anchorage. As Lieut. Baugh informed me that he had no wish to send any despatches, and as I was too unwell to land, I quitted Ternate somewhat reluctantly, and stood away to the southward, intending to pass through the Strait of Patientia, and connect our present meridian distances with those determined to Bouro, in 1840, it being one of my principal positions in the former voyage in the 'Sulphur'. Our progress was but slow, little better than drifting by the force of current, and on the morning of the 3rd, finding the ship still detained by calms, and had gained very little to the southward of the Island of Tidore, I determined upon making the most by our detention, by fixing the prominent points leading up to, and through, this Strait. The second barge and gig, were supplied with provisions for fourteen days, and Lieut. Baugh, appointed to the command of the former; Mr. Hooper, the Purser, volunteered as my amanuensis, and Mr. Adams, Assistant-Surgeon, was added, in the event of any illness happening to the party. I had left orders with the Senior Lieutenant, "to endeavour to keep close to us, and more particularly the following morning, as I wished to compare our boat chronometers with the rest. If the breeze favoured the ship, so as to take her to the Strait of Patientia, she was to anchor there and await my arrival."

Quitting the ship, about 7 o'clock, A.M., in the gig, with orders for the barge to follow me to the small island then in sight on the Gilolo shore, I proceeded to search for the nearest *terra firma* which would enable me to fix my instruments. On approaching the islet, I discovered that a reef, or coral flat, extended a considerable distance from it, and as it was then late, and gloomy weather prevailed, I feared losing the sun altogether by any further delay in seeking for more secure landing; it was therefore determined to *create* an islet for my instruments, by piling up coral slabs upon the reef. It proved to be very fragile, being as it were an underwood of coral trees into which we sunk, by our own weight, about eighteen inches; I succeeded, however, by pounding with crowbars, in effecting my purpose, and managed to secure the instruments firmly.

The forenoon observations having been taken, we strolled about the reef seeking shells and corallines, little apprehending the danger that was at hand. At noon I returned to the instruments, to obtain the meridian alt. of the sun, and had just completed this observation, when several natives, who had approached to satisfy their curiosity, suddenly stole away, and I heard them use terms signifying that they knew us to be Europeans. Shortly after, we heard yells from the bushes, and upon looking towards the island, distant about a quarter of a mile, we observed two divisions, consisting of about forty men, issuing from each flank, evidently with the intention of surrounding us; their leaders being dressed in tight scarlet clothes, and each man carrying a bundle of spears. During my conversation with the Resident of Manado, relative to the boat I had noticed at Manado Tua, he informed me, that the pirates only dress in scarlet, or gay dresses, and that the peaceable traders of these seas are invariably clothed in the dull plain colours which are manufactured amongst themselves; there could be little doubt, therefore, that we had now fallen in with a formidable party of these vagabond freebooters. They advanced in a hostile manner, capering and yelling, and on approaching, hurled their spears towards us, some of which fell very near the instruments.

Our party on the reef, consisting of three Officers and four seamen, were ordered to fall back on the gig, about thirty yards from the fixed instrument, the latter to load their muskets and fix bayonets, the barge at the same time was directed to close and cover us. A long period elapsed before any of the gig's muskets would go off, owing to bad percussion caps, so that the enemy, had they been at all expert, might have speared some of us before we could have repulsed them. Nor did this appear to result from any want of bravery on the part of our assailants, for the moment we commenced a discharge of musketry from the barge, as well as gig, they merely began to caper in defiance; subsequently, however, and as they found the balls flying very close to their heads, they hesitated in their advance, and decided upon a retreat. A great many of them might easily have been shot, but I directed our party to fire over their heads, merely to frighten them. Just as this fusilade opened, we observed a large prahu approaching suddenly from the rear of the island, evidently an accomplice, and endeavouring to cut off the barge, but on espying the muzzle of the brass six-pounder in her bow, they altered their intentions and sheered off. I waved them to keep away, but a man, speaking English intelligibly, and at the same time hoisting a dirty Dutch flag, hailed, saying, "that they belonged to Tidore", and merely wished to go to the river north of us, directly away from the island. He was directed to proceed, but having cleared, as he estimated, the range of the gun, he gradually changed his course, making a circuit, and using every effort to get behind the island and rejoin his companions in our rear. A warning shot was sent over him, and a rocket followed, but this only accelerated his motions, and he effected his purpose.

As I could not afford to lose my observations for securing this position, I waited for the afternoon sights and then packed up, with a view to retaliate this piece of treachery. On rounding the island I perceived two boats in the distance, which had made off, whilst the village from whence they had escaped remained apparently deserted. Mr. Hooper was despatched in the gig to destroy the huts and vessels on the beach, and rejoin us; which service he executed in his usual good style, annihilating, in addition to the village, six prahus, evidently designed for piratical pursuits. We chased the flying prahus in the barge, captured one, from which the crew had deserted, and came up with the other just in time to give them a dose of round and grape as they scrambled over the reef, leaving us in possession of their prahu, the very identical boat, with the Dutch flag, that had previously visited us. Both vessels were towed to sea and burned. About this time, nearly sunset, we were rejoined by Mr. Hooper, in the gig, and considering it unsafe to remain in the neighbourhood of this nest of pirates during the night, we made the best of our way, under canvas as well as oars, until midnight, when having reached a snug and lonely bay, distant about twenty miles from the scene of action, we anchored, as we thought, free from further molestation.

Our awnings were spread, and all but the watch had retired to rest, when about 2 o'clock, A.M., we were awakened by the sound of gongs and other instruments proceeding from the southward. Supposing this apparent merry-making to proceed from the shore, where the natives might be carousing, no notice was taken of it beyond warning the look-out-men; we soon discovered, however, that the sounds were rapidly approaching, and we had barely time to furl awnings and clear for action, before five large vessels were observed coming directly down upon us. The moon was just rising behind the hill in-shore of us, and by this fortuitous advantage we obtained a clear view of our enemy, without his being able to discern us; and as we had not time to weigh the anchor, and the cable might incommode the gun, I directed the latter to be given to the gig, by which we were prepared to meet the advancing force with more security. As the leader drew near, we could perceive that they were very large prahus, about ninety feet in length, with high stem and stern posts, prettily decorated with what, then, appeared to be long tufts of white feathers, but eventually proved to be long curled ribands of the bleached palmetto; above this were small triangular flags, surmounted by a large streamer on the mast. They were evidently on the look out for prey, being dressed in scarlet fighting accoutrements in the Illañon style, and were standing on the fighting stage above the rowers, ready for action. The foremost, having the light of the moon in his face, had passed without observing us amidst the gloom which reigned within the bay where we stationed ourselves, but on discovering his mistake, he hailed in Malay, as well as in broken English, demanding "Who are you?" Upon my reply "I am the Captain of a British Ship-of-war"! in both languages, he demanded, "Where is your ship?" "Outside!" was the return. This was the signal for action.

Considering us a secure prize, they instantly commenced capering, yelling, and hurling their spears, most of which fell beyond, and over us, but without inflicting any particular wounds. As we, in our barge and gig, had five of these huge vessels to contend with, decision was important, and from their extreme length we had the decided advantage, of rapidly turning, and of preventing their getting us directly a-head; had they accomplished this, they would have been able at one effort of their oars to run over and overwhelm us. It also enabled us to avoid their bow gun, which they had some difficulty in turning out of the direct line a-head. Four of the vessels were now outside of us, and further delay would be dangerous; commencing with their leader, then not more than twenty yards distant, we opened fire with our six-pounder gun, charged with round and canister, this was repeated on the second and third prahu with great rapidity, giving them four rounds each. The fourth retired, and the first, second, and third made for the reef, heeling over very much as their crews endeavoured to escape at one side. The musketry was reserved for particular objects on the reef, some who, on gaining the beach, had the audacity to turn round and hurl spears and stones. As it was important to secure the first three vessels, the gig was directed to weigh the barge's anchor, and attach the cable to the prahus in succession; these were towed off by the barge, and anchored by their own geer, sufficiently off shore to prevent their being re-captured by the enemy swimming off.

During our detention on this service, the fourth and fifth prahu had pulled to the reefs, and those who had escaped unwounded, embarking quickly, made off. I therefore left Mr. Hooper with the gig, to prevent the re-capture of our prizes, and went in pursuit of the other two. They had gained about a mile in advance, but as a proof of our greater velocity, even with their increased crews, we succeeded in coming up with them in a bay about two miles off. They did not wait after our second discharge, but fled to the jungle severely handled by our musketry; in the prahus which they had vacated were several dead and wounded, the latter were left in one of the vessels which we entirely disabled, whilst the other, containing the dead, was towed well to seaward and set on fire. About dawn, just as this skirmish was over, we noticed another division of five larger prahus, which, unperceived, had taken up their position in line abreast, completely cutting off the possibility of our rejoining the

gig; indeed, we fancied that we could observe some of our party confined as prisoners on the fighting stage of the Chief's vessel. All the vessels of this division were larger, and even more highly decorated than the first we had engaged, and were evidently bent on more decided resistance.

Inspired with the determination to rescue, what we had deemed to be our unfortunate shipmates, from the gripe of such an enemy, we advanced. The Chief, in the largest and outermost vessel, was most gorgeously attired, and he and his party capering amidst yells and antics, enough to confound the most determined, seemed to consider us as certain prey. Strict injunctions were given not to fire musketry until after the discharge of our long gun, and then onlyat such objects as were clearlydiscerned. After a rapid discharge of Shot, Canister and Rockets, they made for the reef, and one or two of the vessels appeared to be sinking, so much did they heel by the escape of the natives from one side.

The prahu that had occupied the van continued firing,and I was just aiming a rocket at the Chief, who was waving his kris aloft in defiance, when a well-directed shot from his brass gun struck my rocket-frame from beneath, and glancing upon my thigh, knocked me overboard, wounding me severely. Fortunately, I had sufficient presence of mind to hold on by the gunwale of the boat and thus supported myself until assisted into her by the Assistant-Surgeon Mr. Adams, and Mr. Joseph H. Marryat. The crew assert that the natives yelled lustily when they saw me fall, this was, however, their last effort, they fled precipitately to the reefs, and abandoned their vessels. Five others were now advancing, and one came within musket shot, but on examining the state of our ammunition it was reported that all the percussion caps were expended, and that but one round shot for the six-pounder remained. The rocket-frame was also knocked overboard with me.

As the enemy appeared to thicken from different quarters, and as all advantage on our side would cease with the discharge of the six-pounder, I was obliged to give up the idea of taking out our prizes; and as the gig had not been discovered amongst them, I reckoned upon the well-tried zeal and discretion of Mr. Hooper to rejoin, particularly as I knew my gig to be much fleeter than the barge, which had already proved to be superior in this respect to their heavy prahus. Lieut. Baugh was therefore directed to search for the ship, which he shortly after discovered, at about fifteen miles distance, in the offing. One large prahu appeared inclined to try her luck with us, but I was not displeased to observe her change her course and join those which we had left, as I considered the fresh force which would follow up this matter upon my reaching the ship, would like to have their share in the amusement.

About 10 o'clock, A.M., we reached the ship, when Lieut. Heard, supported by Lieut. Baugh and Mr. Loney, Master, was despatched in command of the barge, first and second cutters, with orders to seek Mr. Hooper, on meeting him, to retain his services, and act to the best of his judgment, in destroying the remaining pirates, but on no account to land, or risk the lives of the men under his command, by bush fighting.

By the report of Lieut. Heard, he proceeded to the

place where our last action had occurred; here he found about twelve or fourteen prahus, similarly ornamented to those which had attacked us, hauled into, and moored within a creek behind a village, but then inaccessible by reason of low water, which laid bare a reef, preventing approach within four hundred yards. The boats immediately opened fire upon the prahus, which they endeavoured to destroy, at least sixty round shot, beside Congreve Rockets having entered them. This was not effected without opposition; their fire was instantly responded to from a masked entrenched battery, in which was one heavy gun, apparently iron, and several smaller of brass, the latter no doubt withdrawn from their prahus for defence. Finding nothing further could be done, they pulled round the Peninsula, where they suspected a communication to be open in rear of the village; here they found two small prahus, evidently despatch boats, which they towed to sea and burned.

Mr. Hooper, finding that we did not return to him at daylight, towed his three prizes to sea and burned them. The largest was well stored with arms and gunpowder, and blew up at five separate explosions; all were supplied with swivels, and English muskets with the Tower mark; the brass gun of the largest was too heavy to embark in the gig, and Mr. Hooper also feared to encumber her in the event of being chased. Before setting fire to these prahus, a woman and child were taken out and landed on the rocks, and from her frequent exclamations of "Papua!" "Papua!" she was no doubt a slave captured from the coast of New Guinea, or some island adjacent. Having met and communicated with Lieut.

Heard, he was despatched by him to relieve my mind, but although her crew had been constantly engaged under oars, and with trifling intermission since the previous noon, and had just put forth their energies to the utmost, under a broiling sun, they begged so hard to be allowed to rejoin their companions, for the sake of avenging my misfortune, that I consented. The same may be said of the crew of the second barge; indeed, but one feeling appeared to animate Officers and crew. After sunset Lieut. Heard, and the division returned without accident,* and with a light air we began at length to make some progress towards the Strait of Patientia.

To what this strait owes its name I am at a loss to conjecture; if, however, it is from the fact of being a very tedious navigation, trying both to mind and body, and calling for perseverence, it certainly deserves the appellation. During our beat through, we were compelled to anchor to avoid being driven upon a reef, and in weighing, broke the stock of our pet anchor, one of 13 cwt., by Porter, which we had hitherto used in preference to the customary heavy bower of 30 cwt. In proof of our estimation of its qualities, I may safely say, that no particular regret would have been expressed for any other piece of iron in the ship, but this had so often performed its duty in times of need, and proved itself so trustworthy, that its loss, by merely this accident to the stock, was *felt* and reported to me with due solemnity, low as I was in my cot. Before reaching the southern end of the strait, we fell in with a schooner, under Dutch colours, endea-

* *Vide* Appendix.

vouring to beat through; the master of her came on board, and without letting him know that I was wounded, I questioned him very closely about the pirates which might be expected to frequent this neighbourhood. He spoke English well, and may have been of English extraction for aught I could tell; his information confirmed my opinion of their being Illañons, he distinctly declared that no vessel of such size, or armed for war, but the Illañons, could be in this neighbourhood; and upon my drawing one on paper, he stated, "that no vessel so large, or so equipped for war, belonged to any of the petty authorities of the neighbouring states." The impression which he left upon my mind was, that it was the remainder of the Illañon fleet which had been beaten on the eastward of Java, by the Dutch squadron, and that they were on their return from their customary expedition to the coast of New Guinea, the Papuan woman found on board the prahu, indicated their course to be from that island, or the Geby Group, situated between Gilolo and New Guinea. He informed us further that one Dutch gun-boat was stationed at Ternate, but the pirates cared little for her, nor was she of sufficient force, or sufficiently swift to contend with them. I mention these facts particularly, as in a document, subsequently sent to me, his deposition varied upon this matter.

L

CHAPTER V.

SINGAPORE AND BRUNAI.

Singapore—Occupy Recorder's house—Assemblage of Vessels of War —Opinion respecting site of Horsburgh Testimonial—Romania Islands — Samarang rejoins Dido at Saräwak — Letters from Europe—Mr. D'Aeth of the Dido capsized—Intrepidity of Mr. Brooke—Excursion up the River Linga in pursuit of Seriff Sahib —Town of Bunting—Assistance of the Balow Dyaks—Captain Keppel's account of the conference to which Seriff Jaffer was summoned—Mr. Brooke's address to the Balow Dyaks—Visit their habitations—Explore River Lundee—Return to Santubon entrance—Town of Tundong—Entertainment of Seguga, the Orang Kaya—Continue Survey of the Bay to Tanjong Datu—Return to Singapore—Expedition to rescue an European Female supposed to be living in captivity at Amboon, north coast of Borneo—Documents relative thereto—Mr. Presgrave's account—Statement of Haggee Hassan, a Lascar—Return to Saräwak—Embarkation of the Rajah Muda Hassim with his brothers and twenty-four wives—Brunai—Interview with the Sultan—Address to Queen Victoria—Brunai coal-district—Excursion with Mr. Brooke—Island of Cherimon—Port Victoria.

As my wound precluded the possibility of landing to obtain observations for the determinations of Meridian distances, I gave up all thoughts of calling at Bouro. On the 14th we passed that island; on the 18th ared the Straits of Salayer; on the 20th sighted and at Solombo, and on the 28th reached Singa- oming from the eastward, either from the northward or southward of Borneo, should endeavour to make Bintang Peaks, on a W.N.W. bearing, and not attempt to cross the straits current until within five miles of the N.E. end of the Bintang Island. We found ourselves set as far north as Pulo Aor, and lost a day in regaining the entrance of the strait. Here we met with the East India Company's Steamer, 'Phlegethon', towing a distressed junk.

Arrangements were now made for landing me at the Recorder's house, usually allotted to the Senior Naval Officer, when not occupied by the Recorder, and on the evening of the 29th, I was comfortably lodged, free from the noise and routine duties of the ship. We found here H.M. brig 'Harlequin', with my kind friend Captain the Honourable F. Hastings, and the French corvette 'Sabine', shortly increased by H.M. brig 'Serpent', 'Driver' steamer; 'Alligator' Troop Ship, the French frigate 'Siréne' and corvette, 'Victorieuse', the former having on board Monsieur Lagréne, Ambassador and Plenipotentiary to the Court of China. M. Lagréne most kindly paid me a visit, and was followed by the Commanders of the different French vessels in port.

On the 10th of July, H.M.S. 'Iris', Capt. Mundy, arrived from England; and on the 13th, Commodore Chads, in H.M.S. 'Cambrian', from China, thus rendering the place unusually gay. On the 16th, our numbers were diminished by the departure of the French squadron and the 'Iris' for China; but again increased by the addition of my good friends, Captain the Honourable H. Keppel, in 'Dido', and Giffard, in 'Vixen.' 'Cambrian' quitted as for Trincomalee, on the 20th, where

L 2

Commodore Chads would assume the post of second in command in India, commencing from the western points of the Straits of Malacca.

About this period I received a communication from the Governor, Lieut. Col. Butterworth, requesting an opinion as to the proper site for the Horsburgh Testimonial, intended to be erected as a Lighthouse, in some part of the Strait of Singapore. The sum of 6,400 dollars was already subscribed for this purpose. A surveying party, under the command of Lieut. Baugh was despatched to examine the Romania Islands and shoals adjacent, and upon the completion of the plan, executed by Mr. Richards, second master, my opinion was given in favour of placing it upon the outer and southern Romania Island; not only as calculated to guide vessels safely in and out of the straits, but as a better lead to ships approaching from the eastern side. Vessels could graze the island on which the Lighthouse would be erected, could anchor to await tide, and would always be in condition to make progress, without any attendant danger.

This would not, however, be the case if placed upon Pedro Branca; it is true that it would then point out where the dangers, so well described by Horsburgh, exist, and enable a vessel, if she had sufficient breeze, to avoid them, but more than this it would not effect; but if Romania Island *invites* approach and *securely* clears Pedro Branca, there can be no solid reason for putting a light in a spot where it would only partly serve one purpose. The Romania shoals are not dangerous, even if a vessel ground there, and she must then draw above eighteen feet; and the position at Romania would afford facilities of communication as well as of forwarding letters to Singapore, without detention. There are many other reasons for preferring this spot for a Lighthouse, one of which, and the most important, is, that the light will carry a vessel clear of Johore shoal as long as it is kept in sight, and the same outwards. No light in any other place could effect this desirable object.

On the 25th, the 'Dido' attended by the 'Phlegethon' steamer, lent by the Governor to assist in the suppression of piracy, sailed from Singapore for the Sarãwak, to organise an expedition to be undertaken by the boats up one of the neighbouring rivers. My friend Keppel wished us much to accompany him, and every endeavour was made to expedite the 'Samarang' in order to lend her powerful boat force: I fully expected, moreover, to have reached in time to have been included myself, as I had already commenced travelling with some expedition on crutches.

On the 5th August we quitted Singapore and anchored on the 11th off the Santubon entrance, where I quitted the ship with the barge and gig for Kuching; on my arrival there I learned that the boat expedition under Keppel, and accompanied by Mr. Brooke, had been warmly engaged, and that my former first lieutenant, Wade, as well as Mr. Stuart (of the 'Ariel'), and the Patinga Ali, had been killed; the 'Dido' remained at Kuching. As this report gave tidings of harder work than had been expected, not a moment was lost in adding the force which the 'Samarang' could afford, and despatching our barge for provisions, we started at nine o'clock the following morning for the Batang Lupar, which river we entered about sunset, and about 10, o'clock, P.M., anchored to await the tide. The bore at the mouth of this river is considered dangerous, but did not incommode us beyond the troubled water which followed, and kept us for a long period rolling heavily. Before dawn we were again advancing, but found our boats much impeded by the shoals over which the tide did not yet afford sufficient water. At dark we fired guns and several rockets, in order to make Phlegethon shew us her position, but heavy rain probably prevented this being noticed; about 8 o'clock we discovered lights and suddenly found ourselves alongside the 'Phlegethon', where I soon rejoined my friends Keppel and Brooke.

To render our visit the more welcome, I had brought with me their letters from Europe; these soon engrossed their attenion, and occupied them for the rest of the night with a degree of interest, known only to those who are subject to such a rambling life as ourselves. One incident, however, occurred to throw a gloom around our meeting, and was very nearly attended with fatal consequences. Mr. D'Aeth commanding the Dido's cutter, in his anxiety to get his despatches, had made an attempt to reach the steamer in a light canoe which capsized; a very rapid tide was running and it was pitch dark, but fortunately Mr. D'Aeth was a good swimmer and managed to sustain himself until the arrival of assistance; the cry of 'all right' soon relieved our fears. Mr. Brooke with his usual intrepidity, had been the foremost in rendering assistance; immediatelyon hearing cries of distress among the natives, he hastened to relieve them, and having done this with ccess returned equally drenched with Mr. D'Aeth, e he had been instrumental in saving.

The narrative of the attack on Patusan, by the Dido's boats preceding my arrival, is already well told by my friend Keppel; we were too late to bear a part in it, and had only the satisfaction of examining the still smoking ruins of the stockades, which they had so very gallantly stormed and carried; stockades which were strong in themselves, from their mere position, and being so admirably placed for supporting each other compelled him to divide his attacking force.

Nothing remaining unexecuted in this branch of the river, Phlegethon towed us to the mouth of the Linga, in order to communicate with the Chief at Bunting, and thence to Sarãwak, where, from fresh information obtained relative to Seriff Sahib having taken refuge in the Linga, a new expedition was planned up that river.

The Linga is a branch of the Batang Lupar river, forking southerly immediately within its mouth. Orders were quickly despatched to prepare the boat force of the 'Samarang' by midnight, at which hour I reached the ship and started for the *rendezvous* at the entrance of the Moratabas, where we all assembled by 8 o'clock on the following morning. Our force thus added, amounted to two heavy barges, two large cutters and three gigs; comprehending two six-pounders, two three-pounders, brass field guns, three rocket-tubes, and seventy men and officers. We reached the Linga on the night of the 28th, and anchored in its mouth about midnight, so arranging our flotilla as to prevent any chance of ingress or egress without our knowledge.

On the following morning some of the parties which had escaped from the Sakarran, and sought refuge in the jungle near this river, found themselves completely in our power, and had the question remained for the decision of our Malay Chief, it is probable their fate, particularly of the women, would not have been so mild. Mr. Brooke with his usual kindness, not only released these poor half famished creatures and prevented molestation, but also forwarded them to their homes, with supplies of provision.

We were soon visited by numerous canoes from the town of Bunting, bringing presents, and assurances of friendship from the authorities, with a promise that Seriff Sahib should not find refuge amongst them; at the same time giving us information of his having reached Pontranini, one of the tributary streams about fifty miles above Bunting. Pursuit was immediately decided upon, in which the Dyaks of this region unfavorable to Serif Sahib, were equally willing to join and act as pilots; it was also discovered that Makota, known by the soubriquet of the 'Serpent' with the remnant of his followers, was hourly expected in the mouth of this river, into which he had been driven during the fight on the Undop heights, (as described by Captain Keppel). Knowing that it would fare badly with this treacherous and cunning, although now harmless Chief, should he fall into the hands of any of our native followers, two boats were despatched to look out for, and bring him alive. After some little search they secured him in a deep muddy jungle, into which he had thrown himself upon perceiving the approach of our men: leaving him a prisoner on board the Phlegethon, we pushed on with the flood tide in pursuit of the Seriff Sahib.

For two days we continued forcing our boats for a

distance up this intricate creek, at times affording space for the oars, but generally compelling the heavy boats to pole, and the gigs to use their paddles ; until at length further advance, even in the canoe, which was ahead of my gig, and which had been almost carried by the natives for some distance, was impracticable. Here, however, we found the last bivouac of the fugitives, consisting of rapidly formed huts, over which they had doubtless spread their kedjangs, and the embers of their fires still alive. Keppel's bugle informed us that further pursuit was abandoned, and that fighting was to be superseded by feasting, a measure, under present fatigue, not likely to find many dissentients.

Keppel observes : "But this pursuit had the desired effect, proving to the natives what determination could achieve, in accomplishing our object even beyond the hopes of our sanguine Balow Dyak guides. The consequence was, that Seriff Sahib made a final and precipitate retreat across the mountains, in the direction of the Pontianak River ; so close were we on his rear, harassed as he was by the Balow Dyaks, who had refused him even the common means of subsistence, that he threw away his sword, and left behind him a child, whom he had hitherto carried in the jungle ; and this once dreaded chief was now driven, single and unattended, out of the reach of doing any further mischief."

On our return to Bunting in the evening, the boats drew up in fighting order before that town, and a display of guns and rockets at night was arranged, in order to exhibit to these people, who could now calmly view it, the force which, at a very short warning, could be brought to punish their misdeeds.

In the morning Seriff Jaffer was summoned to a conference. "To this," says Keppel, "he was obliged to attend, as the natives had learnt that we were not to be trifled with, and would have forced him on board rather than have permitted their village to have been destroyed. With Pangeran Budrudeen, as the representative of the Sultan, Seriff Jaffer was obliged to resign all pretensions to the government of the province, over which he had hitherto held sway; since it was considered from his being a Malay, and from his relationship to Seriff Sahib, that he was an unsafe person to be entrusted with so important a post. A second conference took place on shore, at which the chiefs of all the surrounding country attended, when the above sentence was confirmed. On this occasion I had the satisfaction of witnessing what must have been—from the effect I observed it to have produced on the hearers—a splendid piece of oratory delivered by Mr. Brooke, in the native tongue, with a degree of fluency I had never witnessed before, even in a Malay. The purport of it, as I understood, was, to point out emphatically the horrors of piracy on the one hand, which it was the determination of the British Government to suppress, and on the other hand, the blessings arising from peace and trade, which it was equally our wish to cultivate; and it concluded by fully explaining, that the measures lately adopted by us against piracy, were for the protection of all the peaceful communities along the coast; so great was the attention bestowed during the delivery of this speech, that the dropping of a pin might be heard. From these people many assurances were received of their anxiety and willingness to co-operate with us in our laudable undertaking; and one and all were alike urgent that the government of their river should be transferred to the English."

This affair completed, we examined their habitations, which although not projecting over the river, are constructed on piles in the Malay style, and evidently adapted for defence as well as accomodation. The principal residence which we visited was elevated about fourteen feet above the ground, and consisted of a building about 250 feet long by fifty wide. One third, running the entire length, appeared to be devoted as a terrace, to general convenience, upon which were noticed their nets and implements, and many were seated at their occupations, chiefly women, who were busy weaving their Sarongs. The remaining two-thirds were devoted to their cabins, which only the married are allowed to occupy. The ascent to this stage, of what may be termed cages, is by a log, notched deep enough for the foot to hold securely, when dry, but, even to a seaman, does not afford a pleasant ascent. The number of persons occupying one of these stages, was said to be three hundred. The whole space beneath was a complete slough, and we were only able to approach it by pieces of timber, laid in connection, and frequently sinking far enough to place the walker ankle deep in the mud. In this filth and mire revel the hogs and ducks, which in some measure checked our anxiety to purchase these species of stock. The dress of the Balow Dyaks differs little from that of the Dyaks noticed at Serambo.

During our detention here I witnessed the coming in of the Bore. As it was just low water we drew up in line within the entrance of the creek leading to Bunting, and came to anchor, but just atrip. The Bore came in as a roller, about three feet above the level, and passed up the main river; and one of our gigs being rather without the angle of the point, was carried completely up the bank, and lodged in the mud where she had to wait until the tide flowed sufficiently for her to float out. Had the boats been at anchor in the main stream and at slack tide been caught "broadside on", they must have been swamped.

On the morning of the 4th of September, the force quitted the Batang Lupar, and towed by the 'Phlegethon' entered the Santubon branch, where, by previous arrangement, wood had been cut by the natives for the use of the steamer, and where she was to await our despatches for England. The 'Samarang' was brought into the river, and the Surveys of the coast towards Tanjong Datu completed.

During our sojourn here, we were visited by a severe thunder-storm, attended with very vivid forked lightning, by which one of our carpenters was killed; the lightning struck one of the largest Casuarinas by which the beach is fringed, and cutting it in twain caused it to fall across the tent in which the carpenter and his crew were sleeping, crushing the thigh and spine of the poor fellow, of which he died immediately.

As our Survey included the mouth of the Lundu, and the 'Phlegethon' had left with our despatches, I started in company with Captain Keppel and Mr. Brooke, on a visit to the Orang Kaya, of that river. The Lundu is considered as a barred river to vessels, but boats may pass at dead low water, by keeping on its western bank, following out the curvature of the sand, which is then laid bare on either side. After passing these flats and reaching the first sandy point on the right, the river suddenly bends westerly, and preserves an even depth between four and six fathoms; the deepest water being here, as in most rivers, on the concave side. On approaching the town of Tundong, which is situated about nine miles from the mouth of the river, we found two very substantial booms, which were so neatly jointed below water that no axe would have separated the lashings, but it could be effected easily by a saw, unless the fastenings were of chain. The trees of which these were composed, were about two feet in diameter, and the holes through which the lashings, connecting, or jointing them, were passed, were so deeply grooved as to admit of their being completely imbedded. The lengths were about twenty feet each, and these wooden necklaces formed two very deep curves, or sacs, in the direction of the tide, at about 800 feet asunder. On the left, an indifferent wooden stockade, having three embrasures below, was intended to cover these booms; and if well served, might do some mischief before it could be stormed. But in this case they had foolishly placed their battery so near, that the guns of a Boat Expedition would scarcely permit them a chance of reloading.

The town of Tundong consists merely of a scattered collection of huts along the bank of the river, the principal one being constructed much after the manner of that noticed at Bunting. As this chief, or Orang Kaya (literally headman) was a particular friend of Mr. Brooke's we were entertained in his best style, in the terrace apartment; a very profuse display of Rice, Sugar and vegetable confectionary assuming a very imposing *coup d'oeil*, was spread in large brass embossed salvers and waiters, around which we were all seated, *à la Turque*, and to gratify our host, compelled to make some show of enjoyment. This finished, the apartment was cleared for dancing, and two performers went through the head dance with great *eclat*, if we may judge from the occasional yells of approbation which greeted certain parts of the exhibition. The great feat, which appeared to be particularly aimed at, was the turning slowly upon the ball of the great toe and heel of the right foot, whilst both knees were bent, and the left toe just clear of the ground, exhibiting the great muscular power of the calf and instep, accompanying the music by appropriate contortions of the head and arms, now viewing the skull, (suspended by a strap, and hanging beneath the left arm just at the hip,) over the right shoulder, behind, and now in front. The music consisting of four gongs, of different note, and two drums, was occasionally assisted by the shrill notes of some of the men as well as women. This was succeeded by a sword and shield dance, of which we were soon tired. In the hope of securing a comfortable nap, I had my cot suspended between two of the outer beams, but as they had tasted of wine, as well as rum, they deemed it a high compliment to keep us all awake the greater part of the night, singing, as we were informed, their late exploits, with the addition of some complimentary odes to our friend the Tuan Besar (Brooke), who heartily wished them as far off as the Batang Lupar.

On our return a party now accompanied us to the sea,

with their hunting dogs, to seek deer and wild hogs. The dogs used for these purposes are a very diminutive species terrier, not so large as the Scotch otter dogs, but they are very noisy, and manage to track the wild hog and confuse him, until he falls under the spear of the Dyak. My pursuits led me to other work, but on the return of the party to our boats, after sunset, they brought several wild hogs, on which our boat's crews had no disinclination to sup, added to quantities of fine oysters, which were procured in great profusion from the rocks, bared by low water, on the Island of Sampadien, where our bivouac was pitched for the night. On our return to the ship, the day following, my friends, Keppel and Brooke, returned to Kuching, the former to make preparations for the return of the 'Dido' to Singapore. Before parting, we had many discussions upon the present and future prospects of this settlement rising in the scale of importance. Mr. Brooke seemed to be strongly impressed with the expediency of removing the Rajah Muda Hassim, with his thirteen brothers, to Borneo Proper. They were considered as at present a dead clog on the advancement of the Dyak interests; and although the Rajah Muda, and one or two of his brothers, might feel disposed to further the views of Mr. Brooke respecting them, still there existed that latent feeling, on the part of the Malay, to consider the Dyak subservient to his purposes, and to oppress him by petty and troublesome inflictions. So long as this existed, Malay Pangerans, relatives of the Sultan of Brunai, remained at Kuching, the Dyak tribes would continue to doubt the power of Mr. Brooke to control them. It was from such feelings that offers of adhesion, to the cause of Mr. Brooke and his objects in view, were made, and several powerful Dyak Chiefs were induced to tender their alliance, upon the *bona fide* withdrawal of the Rajah Muda and family.

In the event of the 'Dido' not being able to assist in carrying out these views, and as my route would carry me along that coast, I volunteered the services of the 'Samarang', to afford convoy, and carry with me Mr. Brooke, and probably some of the unmarried brothers. At all events, it was decided, that the necessary preparations should be made, and Mr. Brooke's schooner, the 'Julia', was to be tendered for the conveyance of the Rajah and the women of his immediate family.

Our work carried us along the great Bay, formed by the bight between Tanjong Sipang and Tanjong Datu, and containing westerly, from Lundu, the rivers Samatan and Siru. The depth of the bay is free from danger between Satang and Talantalan Islands, as far as five fathoms, but within that depth a vessel should not enter without a good cause, as there are many sunken rocks. Between the Talantalan Islands and Tanjong Datu, it is very dangerous, as the whole sweep of that side of the bay up to Tanjong Datu is little better than a nest of dangers, which, at low water, show very distinctly to the southward of Pirate Island; and as rocks have lately been discovered, four or five miles off Sipang and Datu, on ground pretty closely examined, and where their existence was considered improbable, I think that this caution is particularly called for, where we suspect them within the limit I have assigned

The Talantalan Islands are remarkable for the resort of Turtle to a small sandy delta on its southern side, inhabited by a Malay family, who hold it of Mr. Brooke, on account of the eggs of these reptiles. On our several visits we obtained live turtle from them, at first, by courtesy (although paid for), but latterly, fearing that their capture might deter others from visiting the delta, and thus injure the sale of their eggs, they solicited the interference of Mr. Brooke to persuade us to discontinue our visits.

Having extended our survey as far as Tanjong Api I examined that position for fresh water, which I had been informed was not only good, but abundant. The information proved correct; Tanjong Api is a low rocky formation, on which the sea forces up the sand by its great exposure to westerly swell, and closes the mouth of a small river which would otherwise flow to the sea. It is probably a wise provision of nature that it is not permitted to flow with the accustomed freedom, as the water would, probably, be soon drained off and fail to afford that assistance either to the native or the traveller, which it now offers. The main stream thus dammed up by the sand, forms a dark deep-coloured pool of a reddish tint, resulting from the infusion of dead leaves and decayed vegetable matter which are constantly thrown into it, and would probably deter many from making use of this deeply-tinted water. But nature has again, with a view to purify her supply of this invaluable article, interposed a reservoir, by placing a small strip of pond, running parallel to the beach, containing about 100 tons of pure water which is filtered through the barrier of sand, and thus furnishes to the passing traveller that inestimable gift for which we wayfaring wanderers are so grateful. It is needless to talk of the beauty of tint or form to the seaman, unless it be enlivened by the cascade or pure fresh stream. The facility for watering is also great, unless, indeed, at such times when the surf renders all open beaches dangerous. But the beach at Tanjong Api is in a great measure protected: first, by an outer bank distant about half a mile, and running parallel to the curvature of the point; and secondly, by large beds of rock which stud out westerly. Between these rocks there is safe admission, but an anchor should be dropped outside and the boat hauled in stern foremost, as, even in calm, frequent little curls endanger wetting, if not swamping, from the constant roll which prevails about this point; the best landing is about sixty fathoms to the southward of the northernmost large black rock at the Point. Quitting Api, we called at a reef situated to the southward of the Islands of St. Pierre, which is not correctly laid down in the charts. This reef, which is given as a rock "a-wash", or covered at high water, is about seventy feet long by thirty wide, is perpetually eight feet above the level, and has very deep water all round; it is about one mile and a half to the southward of the two St. Pierre Islands, and is situated in Lat. 1° 51′ 44″ N., Long. 108° 38′ 33″ E.

On our arrival at Singapore, I found orders from Sir Thos. Cochrane to forward communications to Captain Keppel with all possible dispatch, directing the immediate return of the Dido to England. We met here the following vessels of war: 'Wolverine', Capt. Morris;

'Driver', Capt. Hayes; 'Vixen', Captain Giffard: and, as the orders were so imperative, I despatched the 'Wolverine' to seek the 'Dido' at Sarăwak; 'Driver' upon the same service; and directed Capt. Giffard of the 'Vixen', in his route to Hong-kong, to so far diverge from his course as to apprize him of the Admiral's intentions, should the currents have pressed him northerly. During the night, 'Dido' anchored, and 'Vixen' was detained to send Capt. Keppel's replies by that vessel. The Governor, Lieut. Col. Butterworth, having returned to this place, I had the pleasure of making his acquaintance; and the short period of our delay in port, refitting and provisioning, was agreeably occupied by interchanges of civility, and the arrangement of matters between Keppel and myself relative to the still unfinished affairs of Borneo.

At this period a question had arisen relative to the reported existence of an European female, said to have been seen somewhere about Ambong, and as the relatives of the late Mr. Presgrave, formerly Resident Councillor at Singapore, had some faint suspicion that it might be his widow, application had been made to the Supreme Government at Calcutta to have the matter satisfactorily enquired into. After a verbal conference with the Governor upon the subject, it was intimated to me, that if I would consent to conduct this investigation the 'Phlegethon' should be placed at my disposal; and foreseeing the important advantages which would necessarily result from the searching examination such an enquiry would entail, into the practices of the pirates on the north coast of Borneo, causing, with the aid of Mr. Brooke

M 2

through the Sultan of Brunai, a complete death-blow to the Slavery question, I gladly accepted the proposition which was followed by the following Official communication :—

"No. 199 of 1844.

"*From the* GOVERNOR *of* P. W. ISLAND, SINGAPORE, *and* MALACCA, *to* CAPTAIN SIR EDWARD BELCHER, C.B., *H.M.S.* '*Samarang.*' *Dated Singapore, 2nd October*, 1844.

"SIR,

"With reference to the personal communication I had the honor of holding with you this morning relative to the supposed detention of an European female at Amboon or Malloodoo, when you graciously volunteered to make the necessary enquiries concerning her during your visit to the coast of Borneo, I beg to solicit your attention to the enclosed documents on the subject.

"No. 1 is the Deposition of a Lascar, named Haggee Honsain, who touched at Amboon for water, remained there two days, and distinctly declares that he corroborated what he had previously heard, by visiting the said female, and that he could not be mistaken as to her being of European extraction.

"This Deposition appeared in the Singapore Free Press, under date the 30th September, 1841, and led to the Document marked No. 2, received in a communication from the Secretary to the Government of India, under date 30th March, 1842. I cannot find that anything was done on the occasion, with a view of identifying the person in question, or of ascertaining if there was any foundation for the statement made by Haggee Honsain, but Mr. Bonham appears to have satisfied the parties concerned that it could not possibly have been "Mrs. Presgrave" consequent on the prevailing winds at the season of the year at which (28th December, 1819) the 'Guilford' left Singapore on her voyage to England, subsequently to which she has never been heard of.

"The latest information that I can offer you, is the extract of a letter from Mr. Brooke of Borneo to the address of the Resident Councillor at Singapore, under date the 6th November last, which is also annexed, marked No. 3. From the former gentleman it is possible you may obtain more minute particulars.

"I shall be obliged by your delivering the accompanying two letters addressed to the Chieftains at Maloodoo and Amboon, which I think will assist in effecting the object in view, and probably tend to facilitate the trading intercourse between that part of the coast of Borneo and Singapore. A copy of these letters is also enclosed, No. 4.

"In conclusion I beg to acquaint you that I have given instructions for the steamer 'Phlegethon' to be placed under your orders for the projected trip to the coast of Borneo, and have directed her Commander to wait upon you for further instructions. On parting from the 'Phlegethon' I request that you will do me the favor to give positive orders to her Commander to return to Singapore, with the replies from the Chieftains at Amboon and Mulloodoo to my letters to their address, and such communication as you may be pleased to favor me with touching the result of your expedition.

"I have the honor to be, Sir, your most obedient servant,

"J. W. BUTTERWORTH, *Governor*.

"*Singapore*,
"*2nd October*, 1844."

(No. 1.)

"Hadjee Hassan, a Lascar of the late ship 'Sultana, states: I was one of the party in the cutter which landed at Maloodoo; I cannot say how long I remained at that place; but I had been at Brunai ten days when the steamer arrived; when at Maloodoo, I lived at the house of a Syed, and was treated very well. About three days after leaving Maloodoo for Brunai we touched at a place called Amboon, for water, where there is a good harbour; there were about forty houses on the beach. I had previously heard when on board the boat, from the crew, that there was an European female residing at Amboon. The house was pointed out to me, which induced me to enter; it was raised on poles about six feet high, and situated in the centre of the village. On entering, I saw, seated on a mat, an European female; she was dressed in the Malay costume, there was a Malay woman seated near her, and five or six children were playing about the house. I remained about a minute, the European female did not attempt to leave or did she say a word; she looked at me for a moment, and then hung down her head. I am most positive she was an European female, and about forty years of age, fair, with blue eyes and light hair. We remained at Amboon two days, but I did not see the female save on the occasion just stated. I heard that about fifteen years since, the female alluded to had been taken to Amboon, but whether a vessel had been wrecked or captured, about the time, I did not learn. Tampassook is inland of Amboon."

"No. 556 of 1842.

"*From* J. H. MADDOCK, Esq., *Secretary to the Government of India, To the* HON. S. G. BONHAM, Esq., *Governor of the Eastern Settlement. Dated Fort William*, 30*th March*, 1844.

"Political Department.

"SIR,

"By direction of the Governor General in Council I have the honor to transmit for your information and guidance the accompanying copy of the correspondence, noted in the margin,* with Mr. Presgrave of this City, relative to an European female said to be in confinement in the Island of Borneo, and believed to be his sister-in-law.

"I have the honor to be, Sir, your most obedient servant,

"(Sd.) T. H. MADDOCK, *Secretary to the Government of India.*

"*Fort William*,

"30*th March*, 1842."

(*Copies.*)

"*Calcutta*, 29*th March*, 1842.

"*From* R. PRESGRAVE, Esq., *To* T. H. MADDOCK, Esq., *Secretary to the Government of India, &c.*

(No. 2.)

"SIR,

"May I request that you will do me the honor to lay this letter before the Right Honourable the Governor General, in the hope that under the circumstances stated, his Lordship will graciously be pleased to afford such assistance as it may be in the power of Government to give towards ascertaining the identity of an European female, supposed to be now a captive at Amboon in the Island of Borneo,

* From Mr. Presgrave, D. 29th March, 1843. To do. D. 30th do.

with the widow of my late brother, Mr. Edward Presgrave, who, as you are aware, was the Resident Councillor at Singapore for several years.

"In the Singapore Free Press Price Current, under date 30th September last, a statement appeared regarding the detention of an European female at Borneo, a copy of which I have the honor to annex to this letter.

"This statement was copied into the Indian newspapers, but did not at the time attract my attention. It seems, however, that a copy of a Bombay journal, containing the statement referred to, reached my brother-in-law, Mr. Cooper, in London, in January last, who upon perusing it was immediately struck with the circumstances which seemed to him to render it at least not impossible that the unfortunate female detained at Borneo, might be no other than the widow of my late brother, Mr. Edward Presgrave. Mr. Cooper addressed me on the subject by the Mail which has just arrived, and although the evidence on which his conjectures are founded does not appear to be very conclusive, I feel urged by every sentiment of natural affection to exert myself to the utmost to ascertain who the female in question is, and I am confident that, for such an object, I shall not apply in vain for the kind assistance of Government, as far as it can be afforded.

"In 1830, my brother died at Penang, and his widow shortly after took her passage in the 'Guilford', bound from China to England, which touched at Singapore on her homeward voyage; no tidings have ever reached England or this country of the fate of the 'Guilford' or of her crew and passengers. It is obvious that in her homeward course she might have been lost in the neighbourhood of Borneo. The female alluded to in the statement of the Singapore paper is stated to have been about fifteen years on the island; this is certainly a longer period than has elapsed since the loss of the 'Guilford', but from the very loose manner in which natives speak in regard to dates, the discrepancy is not of any great importance. The female is described as being about forty years of age, fair, with light air and blue eyes, a description which would exactly correspond with that of my sister-in-law, supposing her to be now alive.

"I feel strongly the slightness of these grounds, but at the same time, as the idea of the possibility that the widow of my late brother may be a captive in the Island of Borneo, has occurred to my relatives in England as well as to myself, I cannot forbear making every exertion to arrive at the truth. It would ill become me to endeavour to point out in what mode the Government might most easily ascertain whether, in point of fact, there is any female captive at Borneo, but for any instructions His Lordship may be pleased to deliver on the subject either to the local Government in the Straits or to the Commanders of Her Majesty's and the Hon. Company's vessels, I shall be most truly grateful.

" *Extract from the Bombay paper which arrived in London the 7th January*, 1842.

" ' EUROPEAN FEMALE AT BORNEO.

" 'The mention by Capt. Page that some of the Lascars of the 'Sultana', who had found their way to Maludu (northern extremity of Borneo), had therein seen an European female, led to some enquiry on the subject by the local authorities, and the following is a copy of the deposition of one of the Sultana's crew, taken here in the course of the investigation:—Haggee Hassan, a Lascar, states that, 'I was one of the party in the cutter which landed at Maludu, I cannot say how long I remained at this place, but I had been at Borneo ten days when the steamer arrived. When at Maludu, I lived at the house of a Syed, and was treated very well. About three days after leaving Maludu, we touched at a place called Amboon, for water, where there is a good harbour, there were about forty houses on the beach. I had previously heard when on board the boat, from the crew, that there was an European female residing at Amboon. The house was pointed out to me which induced me to enter, it was raised on poles about six feet high, and situated in the centre of the village. On entering I saw, seated on a mat, an European female; she was dressed in the Malay costume, there was a Malay woman seated near her, and five or six children were playing about the house. I did not see any man in the house. I remained about a minute. The European female did not attempt to leave, nor did she say a word; she looked at me for a moment and then hung down her head. I am most positive she was an European, and about forty years of age, fair, with blue eyes and light hair. We remained at Amboon two days, but I did not see the female save on the occasion just stated. I heard that about fifteen years since, the female alluded to had been taken to Amboon, but whether a vessel had been wrecked or captured, I did not learn. Tampassook is inland of Amboon.'

"This is all the testimony that has been elicited, but there seems no reason to question its truth, for what could have prompted the Lascar to invent any story of the kind. There is also to countenance his statement, the fact of missionaries and others who have of late years visited Borneo, having often heard mention made of an European female being still in that neighbourhood. When our Government adopts means, as it no doubt will, to effect the release of the twelve Lascars of the 'Sultana' who are still detained at Maludu, some clue may be discovered to the identity of the female in question, and means taken to release her.'

"(True extract.)

(Sd.) "R. PRESGRAVE."

"*From* T. H. Maddock, Esq., *Secretary to the Government of India,*
To R. Presgrave, Esq. *Dated Fort William, 30th March,* 1842.

"Sir,

"I am directed to acknowledge the receipt of your letter, dated 29th instant, relative to a female captive in Borneo whom you believe to be your sister-in-law, and in reply to inform you that a copy of your letter will be communicated to the Governor of the Straits Settlements with an expression of the wish of this Government that he will avail himself of the best and earliest opportunity of ascertaining the correctness of the statement which has appeared in a Singapore newspaper respecting the European female said to be residing at Maludu, in the Island of Borneo, and of rescuing her if she desires to leave her present place of residence.

"I have the honor to be, Sir, yours &c.

"(Sd.) T. H. MADDOCK,

"*Fort William,* "*Secretary to the Government of India.*"
"*30th March,* 1842."

"*Extract from Mr. Brooke's letter. Dated 6th November,* 1843.

(No. 3.)

"When in Borneo I became acquainted with an Arab (who has been long resident there) who told me that an European woman a short time since was at Amboon, I have commissioned him to liberate her, if possible, or, at any rate, to gain certain information of her condition and country."

(True copies.)

"J. W. BUTTERWORTH."

No. 1 of 1844.

"*From* The Honourable Colonel Butterworth, *Companion of the Most Honorable the Military Order of the Bath, Governor of Prince of Wales Island, Singapore, and Malacca, To* The Rajah of Maloodoo, *Coast of Borneo. Dated Singapore, 4th October,* 1844.

" (After Compliments.)

(No. 4.)

"It having been brought to my notice that an European female is residing in my friend's country, I have sent my steamer, accompanied by a man-of-war under Captain Sir Edward Belcher, C.B., in the full assurance, that should such a person be at Amboon or Maloodoo, my friend will do me the favor to allow her to come to Singapore on my vessel.

"Should any trading boats belonging to my friend wish to come to Singapore, I shall be happy to afford them every assistance in my power.

(True Copy.)

"J. W. BUTTERWORTH, *Governor of Prince of Wales Island,*
" *Singapore, and Malacca.*"

Mr. Brooke having ordered a gun boat to be constructed here for defence against the pirates, and her builder being anxious that we should test her abilities, before she proceeded to Sarãwak, I took advantage of one of our exercising days, with the guns in our boats, to try her; after this, she was directed to precede us to Sarãwak, under the command of Lieut. Baugh; hoping, also, that we should be able to derive some advantage from her aid in surveying the coast contained between Sarãwak and Borneo Proper.

On the evening of the 5th of October, 'Phlegethon' was despatched with information to Mr. Brooke, at Sarãwak, requesting his co-operation, and urging the necessity of embarking his friends the Rajah Muda Hassim, and followers, so as not to delay us when we reached the mouth of the river. It was highly important to the success of our mission that we should have the full influence of the Rajah Muda Hassim, at Brunai, or we might otherwise have been over-reached by the duplicity of the Prime Minister Pangeran Usop, whom we well knew to be the staunch friend of the pirates, and who would use his utmost endeavours to frustrate any scheme, having for its object an investigation into any piratical manœuvres, in which he might probably be remotely, if not directly, implicated.

On the 6th of October, the 'Samarang' quitted Singapore, and reaching the mouth of the Moratabas on the 13th, we found the 'Phlegethon' anchored, and her people cutting firewood.

The following morning, we moved on to Kuching and joined our friend, Mr. Brooke, whom I found very busy making the necessary arrangements for the embarkation of the Rajah's family. As it would materially curtail the delay, it was kindly arranged by Captain Scott, commanding the 'Phlegethon', that he would receive them on board that vessel, giving up his cabin to the wives of the Rajah, and his brothers, amounting together to twenty-four. Any description of the fuss and ceremony of their embarkation would be tedious. As one important feature, it was imperative that no inferior eye should behold these fair creatures, and to obviate any such profanation, the awnings were spread, the after part of the vessel screened off with heavy canvas, and the people kept in the fore part of the vessel. Late at night, the Royal barge came alongside by torch-light, and each precious individual, carefully concealed by a mantle, was smuggled singly into the vessel, and carried below. Twenty-four of these poor creatures were thus crammed into a space not sufficient for half the number; and at the moment of their embarkation, a special request was made "to look another way." Any disregard of such an intimation, to their own people, would have entailed instant visitation of the kris, and we noticed that all the crew of the Rajah's vessel not immediately concerned in their removal, kneeled, stooping with their heads to the bow of his barge. Mr. Brooke and myself, were seated abaft the gun on the stern of the vessel, and I observed that he not only abstained most punctiliously from looking in the proscribed direction, but earnestly enjoined me to obedience. The embarkation being completed, about midnight, we were compelled to await the dawn for our progress down the river, reaching the Moratabas entrance about eight. Here Mr. Brooke embarked with me in the 'Samarang' and after a deal of parade on the part of the native vessels, which thus far accompanied us, in compliment to the Rajahs, Brooke and Muda Hassim, we took our departure, the 'Phlegethon' having orders, "to proceed direct to the Island of Moarra, and there await our arrival."

On the 22nd, the 'Samarang' anchored amongst the Labuan group, situated about fifteen miles north of Moarra, and having made the necessary arrangements for executing the survey of those islands during my absence at Brunai, I proceeded with a barge and the gig, with such officers as could be spared, and joined the 'Phlegethon,' where I found matters in a state far from pleasant. A boat had been despatched from the 'Phlegethon,' containing Budduruddin, the half brother of the Rajah, and Mr. Williamson, Mr. Brooke's intelligent and energetic interpreter, to acquaint the Sultan of the arrival of his uncle the Rajah Muda Hassim and to request the immediate assistance of the state barges to take out the ladies, one of whom had actually died of exhaustion in the confined air below; all had suffered severely and the Rajah himself was covered with a fine rash, similar to *miliary*, as well as those children which they now ventured to expose to the air. Although at the moment of their greatest state of exhaustion, it had been urged upon the Rajah to shield the women from notice by screens on deck, still he would not consent to their removal to purer air.

It appeared that a report had reached Brunai of an intention, on the part of Great Britain, to send a force of sixteen or seventeen vessels to attack and reduce them to subjection, and every measure had been taken by Pangeran Usop to put the batteries into a state for defence. The party in the boat, containing Budduruddin, were therefore hailed, from the battery on Pulo Cherimon, "to keep off," and very offensive language made use of, highly insulting to the British Flag, of which, fortunately, only Budduruddin and Mr. Williamson were cognizant.

Fortunately, it did not occur to our boat, or instant punishment would necessarily have ensued; nor was the *extent* of the insult ever communicated to me. The boat, after a short parley, was permitted to proceed to the city, where, upon it becoming known that the Rajah and his suite had arrived in the mouth of the river, a panic arose amongst the war party, and the Sultan being half an idiot, and merely the tool of Pangeran Usop, the latter began to look about him for support at this crisis, but without success. This delayed the arrival of the boats for taking out the Rajah's family, and as further delay was dangerous, not only to the party embarked, but also to the health of the crew of the steamer, I caused her to weigh with the flood and move up the river. We found the river much narrowed, by stones, since our previous visit, and in order to pass through the very narrow passage left open between the battery at Cherimon and Areng, we had to graze the battery of the former within one hundred yards, but we did not notice any symptoms of resistance, and shortly after 8 o'clock, P.M., the 'Phlegethon' was securely moored in the main street of the city of Brunai! within pistol shot of the house of the Rajah, and within musket shot of that of the Sultan. We met the state barges very gorgeously decorated, a little above Cherimon, and as they came alongside shortly after anchoring, before midnight we were freed from the Rajah's family.

On the day following, I embarked the Rajah in our barge, attended by the armed boats of the 'Phlegethon', and landed him in state at the Sultan's Palace, where he was duly presented, and favourably received; Pangeran Usop not venturing to approach with the privileged circle, and evidently quite *au desespoir* at the Rajah's influence over his nephew.

In my address to the Sultan, expressive of the pleasure I felt at re-visiting Borneo, and of returning to him the Rajah Muda Hassim, I did not fail to remark upon the Treaty which he had executed only the last year, and to express my great surprise that any foolish reports, or distrust of such a powerful nation as Great Britain, could have induced him to assume such a hostile position, and one in which the slightest misconception, or accident, might have entailed the most deplorable consequences.

A direct, or immediate reply, in these cases, is not considered as complimentary; a serious charge requires due deliberation: no want of courtesy was exhibited, on the contrary, the Sultan regretted that anything should have occurred to displease, and after some interchanges of compliments on our renewed acquaintance, we retired, with more formality than pleased me. I was rather disappointed at not finding the Rajah immediately invested with full powers, and publicly received as next in authority to thc Sultan. But, as Mr. Brooke observed, " still water runs deep, leave them to their own course." One or two private meetings followed, and at length his expression was most fully verified. A state evening meeting was arranged, on which occasion the Rajah and his brothers occupied their usual places in the circle. The Rajah, addressing the Sultan, commenced by pointing out to him the danger of the councils and proceedings of Pangeran Usop, and dwelt particularly on the late act of defiance, by which he had endangered the peace of the country. Pangeran Usop replied, but as all this was carried on in the most courteous manner, I could not, from my then imperfect knowledge of the Malay language, but believe that mere matters of courtesy were passing, until Mr. Brooke observed, "how beautiful! how beautifully he is dissecting that rascal, and how neatly he replies, every word, on both sides, is in the highest strain of courtesy, and yet they are cutting each other's throats!"

At length the Sultan, motioning the Rajah to him, said, "my father enjoined me at his death to be guided by your counsel, and I intend to do so;" and feeling suddenly ill, retired, desiring Mr. Brooke "to consider the Rajah as conducting affairs." On the retirement of the Sultan, the Rajah immediately assumed the power, and arraigning Pangeran Usop with his impolitic acts, sent the remaining Ministers to the Sultan, accompanied by Pangeran Usop, to propose the immediate razing of the batteries, in order that no further offence should, by possibility, be offered, from this source, to Great Britain. Upon the return of the Ministers, with the formal assent of the Sultan thereto, orders were forthwith issued for "their demolition before dawn." Pangeran Usop was mildly treated, and permitted to act in an inferior station; he was evidently much pleased that he did not fare worse, and it is highly probable that the presence of Mr. Brooke tended much to this desirable end. Affairs having been thus arranged, a document, addressed to the Queen of England, was duly completed, and the seals of the Sultan and Pangerans formally attached, requesting the friendship of Great Britain, and offering aid in the suppression of piracy; and, as a further proof of their anxiety for the advantages of commercial relations, offering to cede the Island of Labuan, and its dependencies, upon terms to be hereafter agreed upon.

THE SULTAN OF BRUNAI TO THE QUEEN OF ENGLAND.

"THIS Document is addressed by the Sultan, and the Rajah Muda Hassim, as Rulers of the territory of Borneo, to the Queen of England. The Sultan, and the Rajah Muda Hassim, desire to gain the friendship and aid of the Queen of England, for the suppression of piracy, and the encouragement and extension of trade; and to assist in forwarding these objects, they are willing to cede, to the Queen of England, the Island of Labuan, and its islets, on such terms as may hereafter be arranged by any person appointed by Her Majesty. The Sultan, and the Rajah Muda Hassim, consider that an English Settlement on Labuan, will be of great service to the natives of the coast, and will draw a considerable trade from the northward, and from China; and should Her Majesty the Queen of England decide upon the measure, the Sultan, and the Rajah Muda Hassim, promise to afford every assistance to the English Authorities."

As we had obtained information from the authorities, as well as from the notes of Mr. Lay (formerly naturalist, and my companion, in the 'Blossom's' voyage), who had visited this region, that coal abounded on the south and western bases of the Kianggi hill, we procured the necessary guides, and accompanied by Mr. Brooke, proceeded thither, taking with us a small canoe to facilitate our examination, on arriving at the creek or stream, which we were informed we should have to traverse.

The Kianggi is a moderately elevated rise, probably about fifty feet above the river level, is the southern hillock of the high range overlooking the left bank of the river, and runs continuous from the point nearly opposite to the Island of Moarra, exhibiting, to the eye, strong indications throughout its entire length, of being charged with coal. The Island of Areng, examined by us in 1843, is situated about one third down the river, which, together with Cherimon, which we know to contain coal, are probably merely dismembered portions of this range, and from the fragments of coal collected by Mr. Brooke, on the nearest point of Moarra, in our visit of 1843, I think that we shall not be wrong in infering that the whole

N

range is carboniferous. Nearly opposite to the city of Brunai, this range bends to the south west, and the knoll or hummock of land, termed Bukit Kianggi, well clothed with timber and rather luxuriant vegetation, terminates the range in a still more westerly direction, fronting the city to the north. At the base of this hill a clear spring gushes out, to which the natives may be constantly observed pursuing their course, with canoes laden with Bamboos, which serve them the purpose of water-vessels, and generally consist of three joints, which contain about as many gallons, or thirty lbs., a load under which you may frequently notice naked little urchins of four or five years old, staggering from the canoes up and along the stages to their houses; this, although among their household duties, is considered to belong to the department of the women. As all the water used in the town appears to be derived from this source, its supply is of course abundant; and as the rivulet which runs behind the hill is also bright and fresh, and supplied from this hill, it leads us to a geological inference, at which we were not otherwise able to arrive during so rapid an examination, viz., that the inclination of the sandstone beds on the southern face of this hill is favourable to a south-westerly dip; and as this also coincides with the denuded parts at Areng and Cherimon, and was subsequently found to correspond as far as the northern extremity of Labuan, we may not be presumed to travel much out of bounds in assuming, that the entire line between these extremes, probably thirty miles in a N.E. direction, would afford, at certain depths below the surface, a fair prospect of meeting with good coal. Our examination up the Kianggi rivulet did not

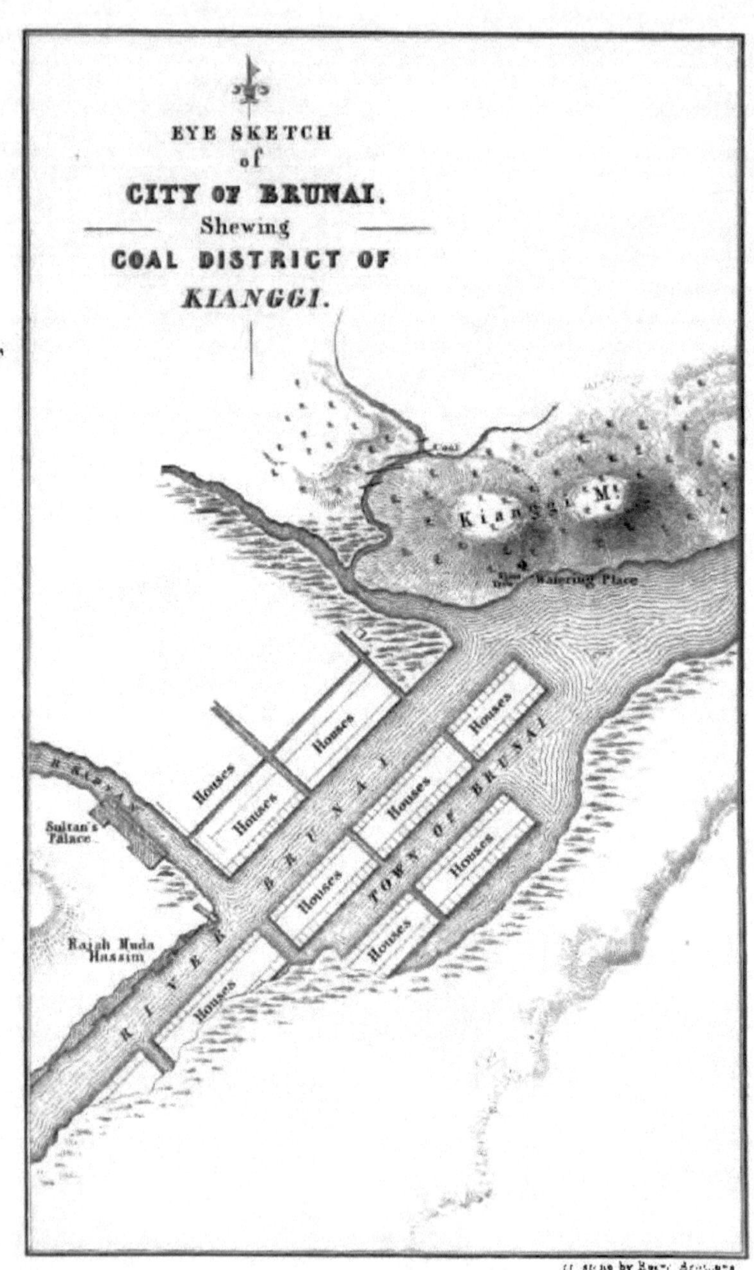

EYE SKETCH
of
CITY OF BRUNAI.
Shewing
COAL DISTRICT OF
KIANGGI.
Coal
Kiangsi Mt
Watering Place
Houses
Houses
Houses
Houses
Houses
Houses
Houses
Houses
Houses
Houses
RIVER BRUNAI
TOWN OF BRUNAI
Sultan's Palace
Rajah Muda Hassim

afford any large seams, but simply sufficient to prove that a vein of very excellent coal existed, and traversed the bed of the stream in a south-west direction, from the base of Kianggi; the accompanying strata were of a light blueish grey, and very friable sandstone, but the sides of the rivulet were so muddy, and covered with thick underwood, that no satisfactory examination could be pursued without detention. During the period in which we were employed examining the bed of the stream, one of our guides waded up a branch leading to the northern base of the hill, and returned with some large lumps of coal, apparently obtained from a spot where it had been worked free from water. It was of entirely different composition to that obtained in the narrow seams; the latter approaching nearly to Cannel coal, whilst the block brought from above was similar to that of the Newcastle districts in England.

On the day following, Mr. Brooke and a party, which went to the spring to bathe and examine a noted Upas tree in the vicinity, travelled over the summit of Kianggi, and found a pit or cavity on the northern base of the hill from whence, as the specimens produced agreed in composition, it is probable that our guide of the previous day obtained his lump.

In the eye sketch, which accompanies this, the position of Kianggi and the points from whence the coal was obtained, will be better understood;—*a* is the point where the seam of Cannel coal crosses the rivulet; *b*, the spot where Mr. Brooke found it *in situ*; and *c*, the watering bay where they landed; the dotted line showing the path across the hill.

N 2

As Mr. Adams accompanied the party on this visit to the Upas tree, I will let him tell his own tale of the excursion.

"While staying at Brunai, I attended Mr. Brooke and the brothers of Muda Hassim, in a little inland trip, to examine into the nature of the coal mines, reported to exist among the hills in the vicinity. We landed in the Rajah's boat at the watering place, near the Upas tree, and climbing up the acclivity of a hill, descended among the richly cultivated vallies of the Kianggi, an agricultural race, who cultivate the Pepper-vines on the hill-sides, and rear the Plaintain, and the Sago in the sunny dells. These poor tillers of the soil would appear to belong to the aboriginal, or Idaan race of Borneo. They are a timid, and inoffensive people, supplying the indolent Malays with Rice and Sago, for which they receive in return but a very inadequate reward. Living in the closest vicinity and friendship with the Brunese, they would seem to have forgotten the use of arms, totally unlike the tribes called Muruts, who likewise inhabit Borneo proper, and who are considered among the bravest of the Dyak tribes. The path we took, called by the Malays "*jalan subuk,*" passing over the hills to the coal measures of Kianggi, was said to lead to the haunts of the fierce and war-like Muruts.

"The houses of the Kianggis are rude, but romantically shrouded in dense masses of evergreen trees. Both men and women are almost in a state of nudity, the former wearing the simple perineal band and waist-cloth, and the latter short sarongs, which, however, leave the breasts and legs exposed. The ladies are by no means ugly, but want that agreeable *embonpoint*, and voluptuous grace of outline that characterize many of the Dyak women.

"In the course of our progress we had to wade across a rapid stream, which was effected by our seizing on a long pole, held above the steep banks of the rushing rivulet by the Rajah's attendants, in order to prevent our being carried away by the force of the current. After threading several shady woods, and meeting here and there with traces of coal, we came at length to a cavity hollowed out in the banks of the Kianggi stream, where the natives had formed a rude shaft. A diver went into the water and brought up large masses of excellent, though somewhat bituminous, coal from the river's bed, and the ground was strewn with the same mineral in all directions. Dripping wet, and somewhat weary, we again retraced our steps, well pleased with the success of our expedition. In returning to Rajah Brooke's house, we passed through the middle of the floating market, and had a capital opportunity of seeing the flower of Brunese beauty. The young girls are plump and well-formed, with rather agreeable features, and beautifully long black, though somewhat coarse hair, hanging down their backs.

"Among the curiosities noticed on this excursion may be mentioned an isolated Upas tree (*Antiaris toxicaria*). It is situated at the bend of the river near the watering-place, and stands nearly forty feet high, its trunk is almost straight, and covered with a somewhat smooth bark, of a reddish tan colour, and its head consists of a dense mass of dark green, glossy foliage. There are numerous incisions around the base of the stem, made by the natives for the purpose of procuring the poisonous juice for tipping the arrows of their sumpitans.

"Although, ominously, the Brunese have selected the supposed deadly shade of the poison-tree as a place of interment, and the ground beneath is crowded with tombs, yet vegetation flourishes luxuriantly around its roots, and clings to its base to such a degree that I experienced some little difficulty in approaching the stem for the purpose of tapping it for a portion of sap. On approaching the tree, I experienced no ill effects from the effluvium which it is asserted by Leschenault de la Tour, and others, is frequently sufficient to produce nausea, vertigo, and vomiting. The Malays, however, that accompanied us, viewed the tree with evident suspicion. In order to prove, by experiment, the effect of the Upas-poisoned sumpit or arrow, it was tried on a troublesome cat near our house, but it had not the rapid effect we were led to imagine. A little while after the receipt of the wound there was foaming at the mouth, followed by spasmodic contractions of the limbs, ending in exhaustion and frequent convulsions, which caused the animal to tumble into the river, and thus terminated the life of the unfortunate feline victim of experimental science. The Upas does not, then, after all, appear to be nearly so poisonous in its properties as the Manchineel (*Hippomane Mancinella*) of the West Indies, the dew that falls from the leaves of which blisters the skin, and many people are reported to have died by simply sleeping under its branches. In Java, there is a plant called Tjettek, or *Upas Rajah*, from the roots of which, one of the most dangerous of known vegetable poisons is prepared, acting like *Nux vomica*.

"This must not be confounded with the real Upas or *Antiaris*, as it is a true *Strychnos*, (the *S. Tiente*) and belongs to the same genus as the St. Ignatius' beans of the Philippines (*S. Ignatia*), and the plant (*S. toxifera*) which furnishes the basis of the Wourali poison, which the intrepid and enthusiastic Mr. Waterton brought from Guayana. The Upas, Hippo, Antsjar, or Upo, is found in Java, Bali, and Celebes, as well as in Borneo, and it is a curious fact, that the wholesome and useful Bread-fruit tree, the delicious Mulberry, nay, even the famous Cow tree of South America, which supplies the Indians with milk, and the common Fig, should, with their luxuriant properties, belong to the same natural order of plants which includes the deadly Upas."

One exception to the above proved, I think, that the effluvium from the Upas is not altogether harmless; a separate visit was made by Dr. Lawson, the Surgeon of the 'Phlegethon', accompanied by one of the mates. On this occasion, they went prepared to obtain a large portion of the wood, bark, and juice, and the mate, a powerful person and of a strong constitution, felt so much stupified as to be compelled to withdraw from his position on the tree. The only method of solving this point satisfactorily, would be to try the effect of confining an animal under glass, with a portion of the juice with the bark, exposed sufficiently to the rays of the sun as to cause the diffusion of the vapour.

"Darwin, in his 'Botanic Garden', misled by the fabulous account of N. P. Foersch, has given us the following exaggerated, though certainly poetical description of the Bohon Upar :—

"'Fierce in dead silence on the blasted heath,
Fell Upas sits, the Hydra-Tree of death ;
Lo ! from one root th' envenomed soil below,
A thousand vegetative serpents grow ;
In shining rays, the scaly-monster spreads,
O'er ten square leagues his far-diverging heads ;
Or in one trunk entwists his tangled form,
Looks o'er the clouds, and hisses in the storm ;
Steep'd in fell poison, as his sharp teeth part,
A thousand tongues in quick vibration dart,
Snatch the proud Eagle towering o'er the heath,
Or pounce the Lion, as he stalks beneath ;
Or strew, as marshall'd hosts contend in vain,
With human skeletons the whitened plain.'"

Having satisfactorily terminated our affairs with the Sultan, and obtained from the Rajah the best information relative to our communications with Ambong, which is within his particular domains ; having consulted, also, with Seriff Sahé, one of the Arab merchants, well versed in all the affairs of the Chiefs to the eastward, relative to the possibility of any European female being known, we quitted Brunai, taking with us a pilot, and kinsman of the Rajah, to assist us. Our leave-taking with the Rajah Muda Hassim, and Pangeran Budruddin was, in some degree, affecting : we had not, it is true, seen much of each other, but when the moment for parting arrived, I was pleased to find they were extremely grateful for the little we had done for them. The parting between Brooke and Budruddin, in particular, showed that the Malay and English can be warmly attached.

Running the steamer well up the river, so as not to

produce too much concussion to their fragile dwellings, we gave our parting salute of twenty-one guns. The river was in a state of great animation with canoes, and some so frail, that the undulations caused by our paddles swamped them. Many tried their speed alongside of us, but steam prevailed, and by the time we had reached the end of the main street, we were alone in our black cloud. On passing the Island of Cherimon, I really felt, much as the compliment was flattering to our Flag, that the utter demolition of the batteries, which presented rather a pleasing feature in the landscape, was almost too great an exhibition of humility. We reached the 'Samarang' off Labuan, the same evening, and having executed the necessary details of the southern face of this group, before sunset, the ship was moved to the passage between the islands leading northerly, and before dark safely anchored in the new harbour, which, in honour to our Gracious Queen, and under the impression that ere long the Flag of Great Britain would proudly wave over it as her territory, I named, "Port Victoria."*

Great exertion was now in force to complete this channel, and make the necessary search for coal; accompanied by Mr. Brooke, we traced the eastern side of Labuan, and discovered seams at one or two of its north eastern extremities, which promised a more abundant supply beneath. These seams amounted to eight and ten inches in thickness, the dip of the main ones inclined at angles of twenty to forty degrees southerly, or towards the

* This has at length been realized, Capt. Mundy, of the 'Iris', having formally taken possion of it. Vide Newspaper reports, and letter at p. 34.

body of the island, (and I have subsequently ascertained again crops out on the west,) it may therefore be inferred that good coal underlies to the southward, the upper beds being but the precursor of our English coal districts. Specimens of the coal from Brunai, as well as from the different positions on Labuan, with the rocks composing the accompanying strata, were forwarded to the Lords Commissioners of the Admiralty, and from a special examination made upon them, at their request, by Sir H. De la Beche, the talented Director of the Ordnance Geological Survey of Great Britain, the coal was pronounced to be "of a quality quite equal to our best Newcastle."

I am still of opinion that coal could at all times be landed direct from England at less than the cost of raising it, either here or at Brunai, independent of the almost insurmountable difficulty of obtaining labourers: and I am perfectly satisfied that it would prove advantageous to load vessels, intended for any settlement formed here, with coal as ballast, to which may be added the very small tonnage of dry goods, which might be required; and having delivered here, take in timber for Hong-Kong, which could readily be procured either at Labuan or the adjacent land, and would prove a valuable article at that colony.

The land on the northern part of Labuan is elevated about forty feet above the level of the sea, covered with a rich black loam highly charged with oxide of iron, on which there are good timber trees; whilst the vegetation, generally, flourishes luxuriantly: water is also abundant, but more particularly on the low lands to the south-westward, where several vigorous streams flow into the sea. Near Port Victoria, where the land is marshy, fresh water is scarce, and, in the event of selecting it as the site for a town, it must either be conducted thither, or obtained by digging wells. The approaches to Port Victoria are deep, but have patches of rock near the surface, which are easily avoided. In the N.E. or bad monsoon, (if the latter term be applicable at all,) there is safe harbour for several vessels, and during the fine season, for any number which would frequent these regions. Although the native pilots were doubtful of a passage to the northward, we found it to be perfectly safe, and were towed through by the 'Phlegethon'; it was fortunate we determined on maintaining the off shore course during the night, for very dangerous reefs, some above water, were subsequently discovered off Pulo Tiga.

CHAPTER VI.

AMBONG, MANILA AND EASTERN BORNEO.

Reach the Bay of Ambong—Peaks of Kini Balu—Town of Ambong and adjacent scenery—Value of stock and provisions—Tampassook River—Sultan of Tampassook—His predilection for spirits—Depart for Manila—Pass Balabac and Balambangan—Monkey Conchologists—Fishing Boats—Island of Dumaran—Pursuit of a Pirate—Reach Manila—Kindness of the Governor—Arrival of six Lascars, bringing information of the wreck of the 'Premier'—Depart to rescue her crew—Arrival at Sooloo—Entertainment to the Ministers on board the 'Samarang'—Pulo Panjang—Marine Observatory of novel construction—Remains of villages destroyed by fire—Town of Gunung Taboor—Ambassador from the Sultan—Fire salutes—Procession and music—Loss of the 'Premier'—Statement of the Sultan—Execution of a Treaty with Great Britain—Departure for Bulungan.

On the 3rd of November, towed by the 'Phlegethon', we reached the entrance of the Bay of Ambong, and the charts of the coast, affording no clue as to the navigation, we were obliged to trust entirely to the native pilot, on board the 'Phlegethon', who very soon contrived to ground us upon a detached reef, lying off the western point of entrance. Had they given us notice of less than three fathoms, and slipped the tow-ropes, we could easily have avoided it, as we saw the danger in time, but too late for us to slip. The effort to alter course made it worse. This is one of the difficulties attending being *towed*; a steamer can back off, but the vessel towed would, in all probability, run over her before her course could be changed. After a short delay, she towed us clear, and, with the boat's leading, we dropped our anchor in this snug little port about sunset. The Rajah's friends landed, and arranged for our visit on the following morning.

The whole of this territory eastward to Maludu Bay, is considered to be within the jurisdiction of the Rajah Muda Hassim, and to facilitate our operations here, and prevent any possible doubt, relative to the release of this female, if traced, his near kinsman, a Pangeran of high caste, would exert his authority. At first, he appeared to doubt the reception he would meet with, but on returning, after his first communication with these people, he made up his mind to remain here altogether.

A very slight examination of the place, and of the neighbouring people, the Bajows and Dusons, satisfied me that we should not find the female, of whom we were in quest, at Ambong. In the first place, it did not contain a single house in which she could have been concealed from the view or knowledge of the neighbouring people; in the second, there were not four of these huts habitable, or inhabited, and they belonged to parties who resort here solely for the purpose of making salt; finally, had such a person been in the possession of any of the higher powers, they were, evidently, too eager to find cause of complaint against those whom they term their oppressors, and would instantly have given the desired information;

the place, moreover, was too insignificant to contain such a rarity as an European woman, without their knowledge, and they informed us, that the Sultan of Tampassook alone could possess her, if she existed at all.

Ambong is situated in the extreme depth of a deep sac, surrounded by lofty hills, of smooth undulating surfaces, and of gentle ascent; the alternations of wood and cleared land affording a most beautiful landscape, not inferior to any I have seen. Immediately behind Ambong a very high range forms an amphitheatre, embracing two-thirds of this interesting scenery, and from our anchorage, about half a mile from the town, this is again surmounted by the imposing peaks of Kini Balu, towering over our heads in great majesty, and appearing, from its deep blue tints, almost in the immediate vicinity, though in reality, many miles distant. Our observations from several positions, afford the mean height of its peak to be 13,698 feet.

The harbour of Ambong abounds in beautifully sheltered little bays, but barred by coral patches, which rise exactly upon the spots where they disturb the utility of these snug retreats. I am satisfied, however, that if necessary, the greater number of these obstacles could be removed, as they are mostly situated upon sandy beds. During the course of our survey of the port, I ascended two hills exceeding 2,000 feet in elevation above the sea, and from thence enjoyed most magnificent views of the surrounding scenery, embracing the whole line of coast for thirty miles northerly, and overlooking the rivers of Abai and Tampassook, with their park-like scenery. To seaward, I noticed the Group of Mantanani, but to the southward, the view was obstructed by the mountain ranges. The summit of Kini Balu was shrouded in mist, but I could sufficiently trace the outline and surrounding scenery to judge of the difficulty which would attend its ascent. On my return to the town of Ambong, I found a brisk traffic going on for fowls, bullocks, cocoanuts, and other articles; quantities of wax were brought down, but did not find purchasers. At first, a glass bottle was eagerly taken for a fine fowl, sometimes less, but before the evening they had fallen much in value, and on the close of the market the rate of exchange terminated with three bottles for two fowls. Bullocks, of the Bramin breed, about thirteen hands high, with humps, very sleek and fat, and weighing about three cwt., commenced at twenty yards of calico, but the closing price had increased to forty; on a later visit, a prize animal, a perfect picture, fetched sixty. The calico cost in England 9*s*. per piece of forty yards, or not quite 2¾*d*. per yard, making the value to range between five and fifteen shillings per animal.

A great drawback to this port is the want of a sufficient supply of water; small runs, just adequate to the wants of the population, abound, but at no particular spot could we meet with enough to supply shipping. The people residing at the beach are of the Bajow race, frequently termed, "the wandering Bajows, or Sea-gipsies", their pursuits are those of fishermen, or probably pirates, when opportunity offers. An Orang Kaya, or (head man,) with half a dozen Malays, comprise the entire residency of Ambong, and upon the tops of the surrounding cultivated hills, the huts of the Dusuns (pronounced Doosoon) are seen through the thick foliage of Banana, capped by the cocoa-nut. This latter fruit, of which we purchased large supplies, was not only of great importance in maintaining the health of our crew, but its milk furnished the boat's crews with a most grateful beverage when fatigued at the oar.

We quitted Ambong on the 10th, at dawn, and at 9 o'clock anchored off the mouth of the river Tampassook, in six fathoms; the shoalness of the water, under our present knowledge of the coast, preventing the approach of the 'Samarang' nearer than two miles. We, therefore, advanced in the 'Phlegethon', and with our boat force in tow, anchored within a quarter of a mile of the rivers mouth. We clearly perceived from the decks of the steamer, that the people upon the tongue on the left bank were not *peaceable* Bajows; bright muskets, swords, spears, shields, &c., were the principal objects in the hands of those seen moving about the beach, and the scarlet dresses of some of the parties soon assured us that they were Illaňons. Accompanied by Mr. Brooke, we started with our force, entering the river against a strong current, which caused the sea to curl astern of us, at times topping rather ominously; we arrived, however, safe within the tongue of land, and pitched our instruments for obtaining the necessary observations. We were soon visited by the Illaňons, whom we found to consist of five parties, having as many Rajahs, with an entire force of about two hundred persons; they occupied six or seven strongly built houses within the sandy tongue, and were evidently prepared for defence. At first, they were inclined to be rather free and impertinent, but, after casting a few glances at the brazen ornaments in the bows of our boats, they withdrew towards their houses, leaving one or two of the most daring, dressed out in bits of armour, and one with a mail shirt, to watch our movements. Ere long we noticed a move in their camp, and surmising, probably, that our force had not entered the river, from mere motives of curiosity, commenced stealing off with much precipitation, conveying their goods into the jungle. Shortly after, some horsemen came down to the opposite bank of the river, and were ferried across; these proved to be messengers from the Sultan of Tampassook, to inform us that that personage was *en route* to visit us, and his arrival, shortly after, was so entirely void of ceremony, that he was amongst us before I became aware of his august presence. Mr. Brooke did not appear either to be pleased with his visit, or inclined to treat him as an important personage.

He was invited to enter our barge, where Mr. Brooke was seated, and upon conversing with him respecting the object of our search, he declared, that had any European female been landed upon any part of Borneo between Brunai and Maludu Bay, he must have been made acquainted with it. It was intimated to him that a large sum would be given if she could be produced, as much as 200 dollars, being nearly ten times the value they assign to a female of eighteen years of age; but they all persisted in asserting that the tale was entirely without foundation. Indeed, the sum realized by the redemption of Mrs. Page and her husband, lately wrecked upon this coast, would have caused overtures to be made long since, had any other white person remained captive. It is not improbable that the Lascar, who asserts that he saw an European female, might have mistaken a Malay woman for one, who might by chance have been travelling with her husband in that neighbourhood, possibly one of the wives of Seriff Hoosman, who has himself been in the Port of Ambong; and this is rendered still more probable, as he married into the Sooloo Royal Family, who are particularly fair, and it would require no stretch of imagination on the part of a Lascar to term one of that race European.

The people of Ambong complained very much of the oppression of Seriff Hoosman, and informed us that his extortions prevailed along the entire coast of Borneo, between Brunai and Maludu Bay, where his stronghold is situate, and that he had lately compelled them to provide a Prahu and a certain number of men to assist in completing his fleet, which to the amount of 200 sail were now about to make an Excursion to the northward, from the Islands of Banguey and Balabac, in order to enforce tribute of birds' nests, which the authorities of Palawan had refused to pay. They expressed themselves very anxious to see him punished, and offered their aid in boats and pilots, if we would pursue him. I very much question, however, if these people were not themselves the greater pirates; the offer of boats and men, where but few of the latter, and none of the former, were noticed, was in itself suspicious.

Our new ally, the Sultan of Tampassook, was very anxious that we should pay him a visit at his city, and I was much inclined to do so, but, as Mr. Brooke suggested, the probability of his influence being too weak to protect us from insult, and having already indulged too freely with wine at our tiffin, we declined the honour for the present. In all such cases I am of opinion, that the less distrust is exhibited, the more influence you obtain over the party into whose hands you give yourself; and by adopting this principle in my intercourse with the uncivilized regions of Africa, America and the Pacific, I have generally succeeded in gaining the confidence and friendship of the natives. Before quitting Tampassook, however, we had reason, in this instance, to approve of Mr. Brooke's judgment; the Sultan was not only too much inebriated to be respected by his own party, but his earnest entreaties for Rum to complete his debauchery, evinced to what a pitch of absurdity we might have been reduced; as once in his power, courtesy, or policy, might have induced us to accede to his request, which we now were in a condtition to decline; so leaving him in his glory, we bid adieu, and returned to the 'Phlegethon.'

The 'Samarang' having weighed by previous signal, was now taken in tow, and about 9 o'clock the same evening dropped anchor off the small group of Mantanani, where we employed our boats examining the dangers, and fixing their position during the time which we required to complete our several despatches for England. It was clear to the mind of Mr. Brooke, as well as myself, that the report of the European female was unfounded; but at the same time it afforded me great satisfaction to be able, in my despatch to the Governor of the Straits, to inform him, that the enquiry had been conducted under such favourable circumstances, the whole powers of Northern Borneo, English as well as Malay, having, by good fortune, been enlisted in the cause; and therefore the friends of the late Mr. Presgrave and his wife, might consider the question of her existence in a state of captivity, utterly without foundation. After a parting dinner to my kind friend Mr. Brooke, and the zealous and hospitable Commander of the 'Phlegethon', Capt. Scott,* they departed for Sarãwak and Singapore, leaving the 'Samarang' to pursue her voyage to Manila.

From the reports we obtained of this Seriff Housman, and his piratical fleet of Prahus, I determined to pass through the channel, between Balambangan and Balabac, and endeavour to ascertain the truth of their assertions, as well as the force he might have with him. I had further determined on making our way towards Manila by the Inner Passage, on the eastern coast of Palawan, a route formerly preferred, but now considered not so safe as that to the westward, probably on account of defective charts.

On the 15th November, the wind failing, and finding the current setting to the southward, we dropped our kedge anchor close to the eastern coast of Balabac, at the the entrance of a very deep and inviting bay, which I purposed exploring. In the morning I examined the landing, but found all access to the bay completely barred, and the extremity of the ledge, then dry, on which I landed for a short time, preventing the approach of a light gig within 500 yards of the coast. The scenery was wild; lofty ranges of mountainous land clothed with timber

* Since deceased.

from their summits to the sea, without a trace of grass or cleared spaces, and the coast receding into dark bays, gave to the whole an aspect of solitude and stillness, which one is frequently apt, in these regions, to associate with the pirate haunt. Not a sail was to be seen, in vain we sought the outline of a prahu or canoe, or even of any human being. Monkeys innumerable were busily occupied among the reefs searching for various marine objects, and with such intentness, that we almost fancied they were emulating us in our conchological pursuits.

About nine o'clock, favoured by light breezes from the southward, we weighed, or rather lost, our anchor in the coral reef, and aided by light airs, gently stole along the land, our glasses closely scanning every opening in this deeply indented coast, in expectation of discovering this reported pirate fleet. We at length observed a number of fishing boats employed upon the reefs, which extend several miles to seaward, but their shape, size, and number of persons belonging to them, clearly showed them to be simply fishermen, or those employed in quest of the *Béche de mer*, or Sea-slug, which, with the large Pearl Oyster (*Avicula margaritifera*), are articles of extensive commerce in these countries. After obtaining observations on the near reef of Nassabutta, we passed between it, and the small sandy Island Commiron, entering the Mindoro and Sooloo Seas. At this season strong north easterly winds are generally experienced, in what is termed the Palawan channel, or that lying parallel to the western coast line of Palawan, and at nearly the same period, (in the month of November, 1840,) in the 'Sulphur', we escaped a heavy gale, reaching Manila, whilst the French frigate 'Madagascar', not having cleared the shoals, was wrecked on the Bombay reef. On the eastern side, we endeavoured to keep just within the soundings, varying from seven to thirty fathoms; and until we reached the Island of Dumaran, in Lat. 10° 29′ 12″ N., had light favourable airs, enabling us to carry all possible canvass; our passage from Mantanani to this position was thus effected in the short period of eight days.

As I found the western extremity of Dumaran to disagree considerably with the position assigned to it upon our Admiralty charts, I determined upon landing and fixing the position of it, or of the nearest available *terra firma*. I had selected one of the small off-lying islets to the N.E., when I noticed through my telescope, several suspicious looking characters showing from among the trees, which fringed the western side, and immediately after discerned the hull of a vessel too large and rakish for fishing pursuits. As I did not then contemplate meeting an Illañon pirate in this unfrequented spot, I merely ordered the two cutters to be fully armed, and under the command of Lieuts. Anderson and Robertson, to accompany me; the former, on further noticing a move on the part of the people on shore to their vessel, being directed, "to join me by a circuit round the eastern end of the island."

We had scarcely quitted the ship, when the boat from the island, which we now discerned to be pulling a number of oars, made an attempt to escape to windward, but the fleetness of our boats rendering such a manœuvre in that direction impossible, he with great rapidity raised his tripod mast, and set an enormous sail, steering directly across our course. We soon noticed their huge Illañon swords, which glittered in the sun, and directions were given to the second cutter, which had her brass three-pounder ready, "to bring him to," followed by rockets from my gig, and some few random discharges of muskets. The ship now joined in the chase, and tried the range of the shell guns, but without effect; under sail and oars she distanced us, and rounding the Island of Dumaran, was lost to our sight. Giving up the chase, which had at least afforded our crew some little excitement, we landed upon the eastern extremity of Dumaran, and completed our observations. That this was an Illañon pirate, or one of their allies from Borneo, there could not be the slightest doubt; the prahu, masts, sails, and equipment, were sufficient to stamp her character, and although I had not decided evidence of any piratical act to constitute her *a pirate*, still, her being found armed, without sufficient plea for being in the track of the general trade passing through these seas, would have warranted her detention, and, if Illañon, I should have left her in the hands of her *allies*, the Spanish Authorities of Manila. Our fair wind deserted us at Dumaran point, which we found fifteen miles too far east on the chart, and clouds, with a short chopping sea, foretold stronger breezes than we had experienced for many months; before midnight, we had a sharp north-easter, and were reduced to double reefed topsails, stretching off to the southward of the Cujos Islands. Finding the current set us very rapidly to the southward, I endeavoured to regain my ground on the Palawan side, and fortunately fetched to windward of the S.W. Cujo rock, beyond which we noticed several other rocks and islets, during a beat up this channel, which are not inserted on the charts.

On the 24th, we reached the eastern Group of the Calamianes, and, having discovered our main-top-sail yard to be sprung, ran in and anchored between these islands to repair damages, arising from the late bad weather. About sunset, we again sailed, having secured the positions of several points, and passing between the Apo Islands, rounded Goat Island on the 25th, reaching our anchorage, off Manila, at 8 o'clock, P.M., on the 27th, just sixteen days from Mantanani.

Upon our arrival, we learned, that during the interval which had elapsed since quitting Mantanani, the inhabitants of Manila had experienced a severe hurricane, its greatest severity having been felt about the south-eastern extreme of Luzon, where considerable damage was sustained. H.M.S. 'Alligator', which we found here awaiting our arrival with supplies, met this gale at the mouth of Manila Bay, split all her sails, and was driven back five days; and it was evidently the same gale experienced by us, although in a less degree, off the Cujos, on the 22nd of November.

A great change had taken place in affairs at Manila since our last visit; the Governor-General had been succeeded by General Claveria, and Mr. Farren had been appointed Consul, to carry out the provisions of the agreement respecting sugar, the produce of free labour. My friend the Captain of the Port had also been succeeded by Captain Barcaistegui. The Governor received me with every demonstration of kindness, and upon my expressing a wish to possess some document which would facilitate future operations within his jurisdiction, it was immediately granted. In my communication with the General, in which I was most promptly assisted by my friend Mr. Otadui, whose kindness and hospitality is well known to our profession, indeed, to almost every English gentleman who visits Manila, I learned, that although the pirates had committed depredations far up the Mindoro Sea, yet the tale told by the people at Ambong, relative to the projected excursion to Palawan, by Seriff Housman, as related to the collection of tribute, was incorrect. His fleet of boats was occupied in clearing a Bremen brig, which had grounded on the reefs eastward of Banguey, and had been deserted by her crew, who made their escape to some of the Spanish settlements; but no act of piracy had been committed, as they merely took what they found deserted. Still, it is highly probable, that had the crew remained by their vessel, they would have been captured, and the question of piracy become established.

We had scarcely commenced our refit, when the following letters were forwarded to me by the Consul, from Mr. Wyndham, the gentleman before alluded to as resident at Sooloo; one addressed by him to Signor José Rogers, of Manila, the other received by him from the Master of the 'Premier', supposed to be living in captivity.

LETTER FROM MR. WYNDHAM TO MR. JOSEPH ROGERS.

Sooloo, October, 1844.

My dear Rogers,

Since writing my last letter, two of my prows have arrived from the north coast of Borneo, and brought me the melancholy tidings of the total loss of the British barque, 'Premier', on that inhospitable coast. Enclosed is a true copy of a letter, sent by the Captain, directed to any person into whose hands it may fall, wherein he states the perilous situation of himself, officers and the rest of the crew; six of the crew, Lascars, came here in the Soloo prow, brought by the Captain of her, from the Sultan of Curan; on arrival here of the prow, they immediately made known to me all the particulars, as they have been eye-witnesses to all the transactions of the damned treacherous thieves of Rajahs, who have robbed the poor fellows of all they had saved. As yet I do not know what ransom I have to pay for the six Lascars, but I suppose not less than seven hundred dollars for the whole. Had they been wrecked within the Sultan of Sooloo's dominions, or kidnapped by any of the Baugene pirates, I could demand them as British subjects, and, although myself a Briton, I am here considered as a Chief, and could demand their liberty, but they are a long way from here, and to rescue them it will be necessary to use force. I heartily wish our Government may take cognizance of this, which I consider a serious affair, and give them a good drubbing, which will teach them better manners in future. I do not know if I am acting right in ransoming these Lascars for so great a sum; however, they are British subjects, and to leave them here is consigning them to death, which humanity forbids, and although I have no security for the recovery of the money, poor as I am, I have not the heart to leave the poor fellows here.

If this reaches you in safety, forward the enclosed as quick as possible to some British Authority, and make it as public as you can. Within these three days my hopes have somewhat survived, as I am taking in pearl shell daily; according to recent news, I doubt not I shall take perhaps four or five hundred piculs, but not leave here till too late to meet your agreement with the Frenchman, the shell I am receiving is very nice shell, I am just going now to weigh forty piculs.

Yours truly,

WILLIAM WYNDHAM.

LETTER FROM THE MASTER OF THE 'PREMIER'.

(Given *verbatim et literatim.*)

Copy. Goonong Tabboo River, 10th Sept., 1844.

To the BRITISH CONSUL *or any European Merchant at Sooloo or Manila.*

Gentlemen,

I take this opportunity of informing you of the sad state we are now living in. On the 27th of July, 1844, the barque 'Premier' from Hong-Kong, bound to the Island of Bally, in ballast and Chinese cash, for Rice, was wrecked on Pulo Panjang, and was obliged to take to our boats, but next day after leaving the ship, was taken in tow by a proa, and enticed us to go to Sultan Gooning's, as he would send us to Macassar soon; but when we got there, he put us off from day to day, and made the excuse, that he would get all things from the ship, and send everything to Macassar with us in a proa.

We remained at his house five days, and was sent on board a proa in the river to live, where we had little to eat, and not a mat to lie upon. When he came from the wreck he had twenty or thirty proas loaded with all the iron and cash they could get; and it was agreed with the Rajah of Balongan to divide the ship's crew. So the Sultan kept six Lascars and us seven Europeans; the Lascars are all slaves, and we hear that he will sell us to the Sagi people, to be taken into the interior of Borneo, so as we will never be heard of more. Upon hearing this, I went to him to see if he would allow us to leave his island, and after some time he said we might take our own boats, he having the oars, rudder and sails, with our own provisions, and boats' rullocks; however, we made our escape in the night to Rajah Moody's, and there remain, but the Sultan is going to war with him if he does not give us up, and has told several people that he will murder us, so we are obliged to keep watch at night at the Rajah's house, and several attempts has been made to set fire to it. On the 12th (that is two days) they go to war, and we are to use the large guns.

We humbly beg, whoever may get these few lines, that he will use his power to take from this country any that may remain alive of us to tell the whole of our sad fate. The names of the Europeans are

W. Brownrigg,	*Master.*
J. Watson,	*Chief Mate.*
J. Mathers,	*Second Mate.*
F. Potina,	*Seaman.*
H. Mathers,	*Apprentice.*
W. Parken,	*Apprentice.*
S. Mc' Dowell,	*Apprentice.*

The two latter sick.

We poor seaman beg for relief with all possible speed, and will ever be your obedient servants.

(*Signed.*) Wm. Brownrigg,

Pulo Mantan.

P.S. Since I wrote, the Rajah came to me and said that he would send us to Coté in a fast pulling canoe this night (11th Sept.), so as to be out of the way of the Sultan, and to get to Macassar sooner.

We shall be obliged to fight our way down the river, and the Rajah has supplied us with muskets and amunition.

(*Signed.*) W. BROWNRIGG.

Such a communication did not admit of a moment's delay, and after taking the depositions of the Lascars, the 'Samarang' was, on the 10th December, making the best of her way to the relief of our countrymen, and reached Sooloo on the 15th. We had, before quitting Manila, received accounts of the murder of a Lieutenant, and the capture of two seamen belonging to the French corvette, 'Sabine', whilst engaged watering in the Bay of Maloza, on the western side of Basilan; they had gone up the river in a small boat in pursuit of game, or objects of natural history. As the captives had been carried into the jungle, and could not be recovered, application was made, for the intercession of the authorities of Samboangan, and after some days delay, they were ransomed, as we understood, for fifteen hundred dollars.

On arriving at Sooloo, I was informed by Mr. Wyndham, that the French squadron had touched there, and that the interference of the Sultan had been requested; that they had returned to Basilan to punish the pirates, and were expected back shortly to make further communications to the Sultan. I immediately waited upon the Sultan, and entered upon the business relative to our countrymen still in captivity at Curan, on the eastern coast of Borneo, and intimated to him my wish, that he would lend his powerful assistance in order to effect their recovery. I was much pleased at the frankness and cordiality with which he entered into my views, promising, without hesitation, not only his interference by letter, but that he would also despatch one of his own prahus with a Hadji, and proper officers to accompany us, and facilitate our operations. I took advantage at the same time, upon perceiving that his feelings were excited by the transit of the six Lascars through his territory, to intimate to him, that the British Government would not sanction anything in the shape of *ransom*, and that distressed subjects of Great Britain, upon reaching the territories of her allies were not only free, but entitled to the same kindness and attention as subjects of his, or those of any other foreign nation would meet with, on reaching any of Her possessions.

I was much gratified on finding not only a complete recognition of this principle, but an express denial of any right on the part of his subjects to require ransom for the six Lascars forwarded to Manila; it was decided, also, that the matter should be made one of special inquiry, and that the Nakoda of the prahu (Si-Dawut) who had brought them, should be punished, if he had exacted it without it being paid at Curan. He further remarked, that if the arrival of the six Lascars had been properly brought before him in the first instance, he would have directed their immediate release, as he had previously done, when Mr. Wyndham had claimed two Englishmen, and that the difference of colour had probably been the cause of mistake.

I found a great deal of jealousy and party-spirit existing

on either side of the *rivulet*, which divides the town; I had invited the Sultan and all the authorities to visit the 'Samarang', but as the former cannot, by usage, go afloat, the invitation was accepted only on the part of the Chiefs, by the Prime Minister Datoo Muluk Mandalya. On the day appointed, however, he postponed the visit until the following, and on that day sent a message, stating, "that the Sultan had forbidden him." I had contracted a friendship with the Datoo Danielle, and had visited him at his house in the country; he is about twenty-eight years of age, of the east river party, and nearly allied to the Sultan, a non-opium-consumer, and a very correct, independent, powerful character, and one of the heads of the independents. The Court party are, however, endeavouring to weaken his influence by cross marriages; namely, by his brother, with a sister of the Sultan, and by the son of the Prime Minister with his sister.

To understand this completely, it is necessary to observe that by their laws, the brother would, in the first instance, by his marriage with the Sultan's sister, have to cross the rivulet to his wife, she being of higher blood; and in the second, the sister would have to do likewise to the son of the Prime Minister, also by blood, nearer to the throne. These alliances being prejudicial to Datoo Danielle's politics, were therefore suspended. Datoo Danielle was not, however, to be blinded by the subterfuge of the Prime Minister; and, determined to act independently, came to Mr. Wyndham's house in state, and accompanied me with some of his friends to the 'Samarang.' I foresaw that this would create a sensation, and we had been but a few minutes seated at a cold collation, adapted to their tastes, when the officer of the watch reported, that the Prime Minister and all his satellites were alongside. As his refusal had been so *public* and *official*, I deemed it improper to wait upon him, and therefore directed the Lieutenant to receive him. He found his way, however, in a very short time, to my cabin, evidently endeavouring to conceal his chagrin, and to make himself at home. The ship was completely filled with his followers, all dressed out in their gorgeous finery, and proving that up to the last moment they were prepared for the visit. The scene that ensued, could only be compared to some of our theatrical representations of eastern pageantry; silk, gold, and velvet predominated, the dresses exhibiting the diversified taste of wives or sisters, who employ a large portion of their time on embroidery.

After inspecting the ship, and appearing much gratified, the Prime Minister and his party retired, leaving Datoo Danielle and his suite with me, who, after picking up some little mementos from my cabin, accompanied me to the shore, where I determined to await the issue of this affair, suspecting that our wily friend, the Prime Minister would not fail to try his weight with the Sultan. My suspicions proved correct; Datoo Danielle was summoned to the royal presence, and it was demanded "why he had presumed to visit the ship without the sanction of the Sultan"! He very boldly replied by reminding the Court of his position, "that he was not a slave, nor the son of a slave, and knew of no law which forbade him to return the civility he had received from the Captain of a British Ship-of-war." This had a very decided effect; they now changed their manner from intimidation to that of coaxing, inviting him to describe, fully, all that he had seen to the Sultan and others, who had not been so fortunate as himself, in viewing leisurely, and having all things clearly explained to him. Great fear prevailed amongst the ladies when the Chiefs were afloat, as a report gained credit, on shore, that their husbands had been made prisoners; and I was informed, that the principal female leaders were wo-manning their canoes to release them, trusting, doubtless, to our gallantry in yielding to their demands.

This diversion had a most salutary effect; it rendered all parties more civil, and while it expedited the prahu intended to accompany us, it gave us, also, much greater weight in the affairs of the island, and I may say, admitted me into their councils. Several suspicious prahus, supposed to be connected with the pirates, took their departure about this period, and from the several matters communicated to me, touching the pirates of Balligñini. (Bangene of the charts), I am satisfied that ample grounds could be adduced for their dispersion, or even annihilation. They assert, here, "that they have no connexion with them," but during our detention, several of these boats arrived, and I was informed that slaves captured amongst the Philippines were publicly sold in the market, and that others remained for sale in the island. I was offered sufficient proof of their connexion with their Chiefs here, and guides to their haunts, if I would act; but as our orders were imperative, not to interfere unless an act of piracy on a British vessel was proved, I could have no pretence for taking up the cause of the Spanish Government.

These pirates are a desperate race, and prefer self-destruction to submitting to capture. The honest party here would aid by giving information, and if the assertion of the Sultan and his party be sincere, that they have no interest or participation with the pirates, their punishment, or expulsion from the Island of Bang-ene, cannot but be satisfactory to him.

Mr. Wyndham had, in the most spirited manner, proffered his services to accompany me to Borneo, and act as interpreter; but taking into consideration the importance of his presence at this moment, at Sooloo, the unprotected state of his own property, and the earnest solicitation of the Sultan, as well as the better disposed Datoos, that I would not leave them without a friend, who could act between them and the French, as a confidential interpreter, I preferred his remaining, and after much delay for the prahu and party, quitted Sooloo on the morning of the 21st, taking the prahu in tow. Our pace, however, being too rapid for her to be towed, we passed two heavy spars, one over each quarter, as davits, and hoisted her up astern, her weight, although but little longer than one of our cutters, being greater than that of our barges. The crew, consisting of ten persons, were taken on board. The Nakoda, and one of his officers, proved intelligent pilots, and the Chargé, or Hadgi, the bearer of the letter for the Sultan of Curan, was a young priest, who had performed his pilgrimage to Mecca, but who, nevertheless, could not keep either the seventh or tenth commandment; and to avoid the necessity of passing a spear between his ribs, they essayed the *salt water* cure, considered in some cases to have a very decided effect. At first, I believe anything rather than love was uppermost in his thoughts; however, after, he had been a day on board the 'Samarang', he recovered the tone of his stomach, and would even venture to take wine, *medicinally* of course.

On the 25th of Dec., we sighted Pulo Panjang, on the north reef of which, the 'Premier' had been wrecked, and passing between it and Maratua, hauled in for the broad opening, in which the mouth of the Curan, called the Pantai, was to be sought. On nearing the Great Bay, we found ourselves, at ten miles off shore, in four fathoms, breeze, fresh and fair, and with but slight prospect of entering, particularly as our pilot did not appear either to be at home on the ground, or to like the risk of taking charge of so large a ship. Any delay incurred the risk of a long detention, or until a pilot could be procured from within; I, therefore, put the party into the prahu, hoisted out my boats, and despatching one barge, with Lieut. Baugh and the prahu, to seek for information, employed the others sounding for deeper water. About 5 o'clock, P.M., the several boats had signalled depths, not under two and a quarter fathoms, and after watching carefully the direction in which I noticed two and a half to prevail, and made a mental chart, we bore up under a press of canvas, determined to cut our own channel, the boats leading through two and a half, and two and a quarter, creamy mud, until 8, 50', when the depths increased, and we safely anchored in ten fathoms, within the mouth of the Pantai.

Lieut. Baugh returned about nine, having convoyed the prahu as far as the first bend of the river. The following day it was calm until long after high water, and as it eventually proved that the night tide rose higher than that of the morning, it was fortunate that we had taken advantage of the strong breeze, as our entry might otherwise have been delayed some days, and incurred much labour and exposure during the heat of the forenoon. As the receding tide bared the surrounding banks, nothing presented but very loose mud, and we were therefore rather at loss for a spot to obtain observations, for securing the position of the mouth of this almost unknown river. I have had but too much reason to admit, that necessity sharpens our wits, and as in this case we were successful, and it may afford a useful hint to others similarly situated, I will mention the method by which we overcame this difficulty. The mangrove trees which stud the coast-line, were very large, and grew well out in a depth of three feet at ordinary low water: having selected the largest tree, the trunk was sawed off horizontally, at such a convenient height above high water as to serve for the Azimuth circle; whilst another near it was treated in a similar manner, for the artificial horizon, and the surrounding trees being cleared away, to prevent the vibration arising from the wind on their branches and leaves affecting us, their trunks were lashed horizontally above high-water mark, as rests for the platform, which was composed of heavy planks brought from the ship. The surface of the trunk allotted for the artificial horizon did not, however, afford the space, as well as solidity, required; three large spike nails were therefore driven in *obliquely on its circumference*, and on these three points one of our observing slates (twelve inches square, by three inches in thick-

P 2

ness), was brought to a true level. By this method we founded on an almost inaccessible marine position, a dry, comfortable, and efficient observatory.

Having obtained all the data which we required at this point of the river, we shifted the 'Samarang' about eight miles higher up, until we met a fork of the stream which afforded solid landing, and beyond which the shoal water for the present interrupted the further advance of the ship; she was therefore secured here, and as no tidings of our envoy, nor any human beings were discerned to be moving in this region, preparations were made for further exploration in the boats. The northern arm was first explored, but on the report of the Officers, that it did not appear to offer a probable course to the main river, we started on the 26th with the whole boat division, on the western branch. After an unsuccessful trip of two days, we returned, under the impression that no river existed on that line of coast, it being throughout salt, to its creeks; we however determined to make a second attempt on the east, and provisioning for the extended period of fourteen days, again started for a more minute investigation of the rejected line. We soon found that it conducted us into a fine broad, and magnificent river, and the fact of its being barely brackish, was satisfactory evidence of our having gained the main stream. As we advanced beyond the influence of salt water, the scenery became more inviting, presenting clear grassy meadow land, varied with gentle hills and knolls, covered to their summits with the rich foliage peculiar to the inland parts of Borneo. About 9, A.M., on the 30th of December, we noticed what at first sight appeared to be a Malay battery, or stockade, constructed upon the summit of a hill which completely commanded the whole reach of the river below this place, extending above a mile in a direct line; preparations were made for action, if necessary, but upon a nearer approach it turned out to be a tomb, and we soon discovered that the place was not only without inhabitants, but that the town which had been near it, had been lately burned. A large state prahu was hauled up in the creek and left to decay, and the plantain and other fruit trees lately cut down, exhibited indubitable symptoms of recent war. We remained at this spot to afford the boat's crew a run on shore, to cook, and rest until the afternoon.

The building which we had surmised to be a battery, proved to be the tomb of a chief, probably the head man of the village; some of the most inquisitive of the party had commenced digging, in the expectation of finding arms or other curiosities, an act of profanation I should certainly not have permitted had I been present when it commenced; as, however, they had proceeded to some depth, and the ground was too much disturbed for further concealment, I directed tools to be brought, to complete the examination. The first aperture was about three feet wide, six long, and five deep, and perpendicular, as in our graves; at the bottom an excavation about the size of a small coffin was made laterally, into which the body, wrapped in cloths, was placed; short boards were then placed diagonally to the opening, and the tomb was completely sealed by the pressure of the earth from above. Having replaced the earth, and reduced it to a level, the boats were again put in motion, and as we advanced we noticed the remains of two other villages on our right, which had apparently shared the same fate. These symptoms at any other time would probably have been deemed favourable omens to many of our party intent on war, but as our present object was the recovery of our countrymen, it was requisite to adopt peaceable measures before we had recourse to any more severe. Owing to the strength of the tide, we had not made much progress before dark, when we anchored for the night, placing the boats in a position for mutual support. As we had been rather taken by surprise at Gilolo, we were perhaps unusually sensitive of alarm; about midnight, the sound of gongs in the distance set our flotilla in motion, and in a few moments we were ready for friend or foe.

The first impression, resulting from a guilty conscience, was that of having disturbed the bones of the poor chief at the village, which, if discovered by the natives, might have roused them to punish the desecration; the sounds, however, died away, and after cautioning the sentinels to be on the alert, we were soon in the arms of Morpheus, though not perhaps so composedly as if we had been free from any chance of disturbance. In the morning we again moved forward, still without any signs of human beings, although every mile that we advanced the cleared condition of the land, and other objects, satisfied us that we could not be far distant from their dwellings. Shortly before eight, we discovered the first inhabited house, and immediately afterwards the outskirts of the town of Gunung Taboor.

The boats being in a condition for work, with all useless lumber stowed below, we advanced towards the town; it was found to be closely stockaded, each of the timbers being about a foot in thickness, and about twenty feet in height; and at distances of about fifty yards asunder, strong houses were built into it, evidently intended for batteries, although they had but one circular hole for the muzzle of a gun to be pointed through, and fitting so closely as scarcely to admit of any correct aim. On the range of stockade, numbers of small Dutch flags were displayed. On our approach, an ambassador was sent to convey the welcome of the Sultan, and to inquire with what number of guns we would salute. My reply was, "that until I knew whom I was to salute, I must decline giving an answer." This somewhat discomposed my new friend, but upon my observing to him, that as I saw nothing but Dutch colours I was at a loss how to act, until I knew what power held the place; he immediately rejoined, that there were no Dutch here, and the Dutch had nothing to do with them. This caused me to enquire where their own colours were, and why the Dutch colours predominated. His reply was: "the colours you see are Bugis, from Celebes, excepting that large Dutch flag, which was a present from the Governor of Macassar." To prevent further discussion I informed the ambassador, that in order to prove the good faith of the Sultan of Gunung Taboor, I would engage to return his royal salute of twenty-one guns to the colours of our most gracious Majesty, upon his displaying his own flag. This was immediately acquiesced in, and upon hearing their final gun, our boats commenced a salute, completing our return-fire, without a single failure, in 210 seconds, or ten seconds per gun. The effect upon the ambassador, and our new friends, who remained on board, was amusing in the extreme, they clapped their hands in raptures of astonishment, exclaiming, well done English! well done English! English brothers, Gunung Taboor!

This ended, we had now to land, and pay our formal visit to the Sultan, who had sent his state canopy, attended by officers of the court to conduct us. It is important to be somewhat minute in a first introduction to one of the Eastern potentates of Borneo. A huge log of about two feet diameter, smoothed on the upper surface, with its inner end well lodged in the mud, formed our main path, or landing, to the entrance of the stockade, where it was succeeded by a raised platform, on which were arranged the Prime Minister, and the rest of the administration; the state canopy, a huge scarlet silken umbrella fringed with gold; the state musicians, dressed in scarlet, and furnished with two squeaking tabors; two drummers, in the same uniform, with English brass drums (pilfered from us at Balambangan), furnished the guard of reception. The Prime Minister placing himself on my left side, taking my left hand in his, and passing his right hand under my right arm, conducted me under the said canopy; the other officers, similarly supported, following in the same order, to the sound of the squeaking tabors and drums, until we reached the hall of audience; a large building, on the right of the palace enclosure, open on all sides, whilst the flooring was covered with neat mats, and gaily painted chinese chests, the latter, furnished with small yellow cloths, with scarlet patterns embroidered with gold, serving as seats.

The Sultan, a fine, well-shaped, intelligent young man, of about five feet eleven, and thirty years of age, most

State Procession of the Sultan of Gunung Taboor

elegantly habited in scarlet and gold embroidery, advanced to meet me, and with an affectionate embrace, bid me welcome to his territory of Gunung Taboor. He informed me, that he had received my Ambassador, the Hadji, from Sooloo, and had sent his own messenger with him to conduct us up; they had, however, unfortunately, missed us.

We now entered upon the business of our visit, but before relating any discussion with the Sultan, it will be as well to state the amount of evidence deposed to by the six Lascars which had arrived at Manila, as it was upon their depositions that my investigation was conducted, and I am bound to acknowledge that the replies of the Sultan to every point enquired into, were perfect; I found, indeed, that he had kept a journal, in which was entered the receipt or delivery of every article saved from the wreck, as well as the conversations had with the Captain of the 'Premier.' There could be no doubt as to the genuine cordiality of our reception, it was *eagerly kind*, and the anxiety of the Sultan to prove his friendship was manifested in every possible manner.

EXTRACT FROM NOTES TAKEN AT EXAMINATION OF LASCARS.

"The 'Premier' struck at 11 o'clock at night; they got one anchor out astern, the cable parted; they continued to work until 10 o'clock the next day: the Captain then fired guns, went round and examined the ship, there was a hole in the bow, and the water poured in fast. At this time no prahus were seen. The boats were got out, and such things as could be saved put into them. At 3 o'clock, P.M., they quitted her, and landed on the nearest island.

"The Captain, Chief-mate, Carpenter, and three boys, stayed to set fire to the ship, they made use of a dammer (resin) butt, which they placed on the main-deck, near the main-mast, between decks, and strewed the dammer about, placing sticks on it to burn. The galley was upon the upper deck, near the fore-mast. There were no pirate boats in sight, when the Captain set fire to her. The Captain was known as *Captain Milne*. No rock passed through her, her main keel was not gone. The three boats which left her were the long-boat, cutter, and gig. The long-boat had two casks of water, two small casks of beer, carpenter's chest, chief-mate's chest, and Lascar's bags. The cutter took one cask of rum, the Chinese copper cash, Captain's things, arms, &c.; she was swamped; think that the plug was not in, there was not much sea, although the wind was fresh.

The crew of the cutter got into the long-boat, and lightened her to make her safe. All night and day at sea, and got to Pulo Derawan the next night. Crew were summoned. The Captain said that he was going back to Samboanga, the Lascars refused to go there, but wished to go to Macassar. The Serang said that he would remain with his people. The Captain shoved off, and said, those who wished to come, might. No one would go.

After remaining eight days, a prahu came from Pulo Panjang with eight Malay men, who took us, eighteen in number, to Raboo Raboo, where the Sultan of Curan, and the Hadji Kuning of Bulungan, were. We were separated, the Sultan of Curan took six, and the Hadji Kuning twelve. Previous to this, or about four days after we had been on the island, four Lascars built a catamaran (or raft), and put to sea; they are supposed to have perished."

These statements having been recited to the Sultan, he asserted, in the first place, that the Captain did not give his name *Brownrigg*, but that he was known by his crew, as well as the people here, as *Milne*. He informed me that all the Europeans had been taken away from Sambiliong, the fortified position on the heights, on the opposite side of the river, distant three miles, on the 26th of October last, by a Dutch schooner-of-war, and he produced a Dutch document to that effect. He also produced several papers purporting to be Commercial Treaties and Correspondence with the Dutch Authorities at Banjarmassin, as well as a gold-headed cane, and a flag presented to him from the same quarter.

This business terminated, the Sultan was anxious to know why I declined saluting him under the Dutch flag, which, upon being explained, he requested that I would give him an English one. I then explained to him, that he could not, legally, show any but his own colours, unless subject to a particular State, and in such case, the power whose flag was shown would send a force to cause it to be respected; and that Great Britain never permitted her flag to be displayed where it might, by any possibility, be insulted. After obtaining from the Sultan full information respecting the treatment of the Europeans, as well as the Lascars, the latter of whom, he declared, that he had sent to Sooloo, without ransom; that he was still in *debt* to the Nakoda Si-Dawut for the goods he had left behind, amounting only to one hundred and eighty dollars; and he further informed me, that he should write fully to the Sultan of Sooloo upon these matters.

He further stated, that the English became very troublesome, and although better fed than themselves, were sullen and discontented; that they leagued with the Rajah Muda, his cousin, who had rebelled, and, as he required their aid to work his guns, had seduced them to escape to him, under the promise of sending them safely to Kotai,* the Sultan of which was his uncle, and that they would in all probability have been murdered had they reached that river, in retaliation for

* Generally by Englishmen written Coti, but in Malay pronounced and written Kotai.

the affair of Mr. Murray, the preceding year; at all events, that if they survived, they would require a heavy ransom for them. But by keeping a close blockade upon Sambiliong, this had been prevented. He complained bitterly of the ungenerous conduct of *Captain Milne,* as he termed him, for demanding a desk with pens, knives, and other articles which he had presented him on their first acquaintance, and by papers which were read, as well as receipts left behind, they had delivered up to them everything which could be found. The final observation of the Sultan was very complete:—"Everything I could find to restore, I was glad to send away, because it reminded us of bad men; but the iron of the vessel, which the natives cut out of the wood, where the fire had bared it, and had been worked into spears and kris blades, I was unable to recover. But I am so happy that you have come to give us better thoughts of your countrymen; we must be friends; I must have an English flag." As this was a convenient moment, I urged the propriety of officially making known to our Government his friendly disposition and anxiety for alliance with Great Britain, but before I could receive anything of this nature, I must clearly understand on what footing he stood with other nations. He produced all his papers, and solemnly denied any agreement with other nations which bound him to more than friendly reception, and permission to trade. Upon this, I drew up a Treaty, which was duly completed, and the Sultan standing up before his people with our right thumbs locked, declared us "Brothers"; a royal salute was then fired from our boats to complete this ceremony, the Sultan and his suite coming down to the beach to witness this operation, as well as the exhibition of some Congreve rockets, an engine of war totally unknown to them. Our good luck on such occasions was not wanting; the second rocket fired, entered a large dead tree at about eight hundred yards distance, and setting it on fire, astonished them greatly. On our return to the Palace the Sultan informed me that the remaining twelve Lascars were probably still at Bulungan, I therefore requested his assistance in their recovery, which he most promptly acceded to, ordering his Admiral, or chief naval Officer, a near relative, and also a Hadji, to prepare a prahu immediately and accompany us, although at war with that Sultan as well as with the Rajah Muda, at Sambiliong, all resulting from disputes about the 'Premier' and her people.

Taking temporary leave of our friends, the Sultan and Prime Minister, and accompanied by his prahu, commanded by Tuan Hadji, we dropped down to the ship, and shortly moved to the mouth of the Pantai river. The spring tides were now on, and by keeping an E.S.E. course, or the opposite to that by which we had entered, we reached the sea about midnight. Here we hove to, hoisted our boats up, and placed the prahu, a boat of forty-three feet in length, upon our decks, which much astonished the Malays, as well as some of our own establishment. About noon we passed the reef on which the wreck of the 'Premier' was noticed, and about 4, P.M., dropped our anchor in four fathoms, about four miles off the entrance of the Sãbãnoon, one of the mouths of the Bulungan. About 5 o'clock, the boats being duly equipped, and provisioned for ten days, we quitted the ship with the same force as before, comprising five boats, four guns, three rocket frames, with seventy-two men and officers; and, having some doubt as to our reception in this river, the addition of the prahu, a fleet boat, and well armed, were important as well as imposing

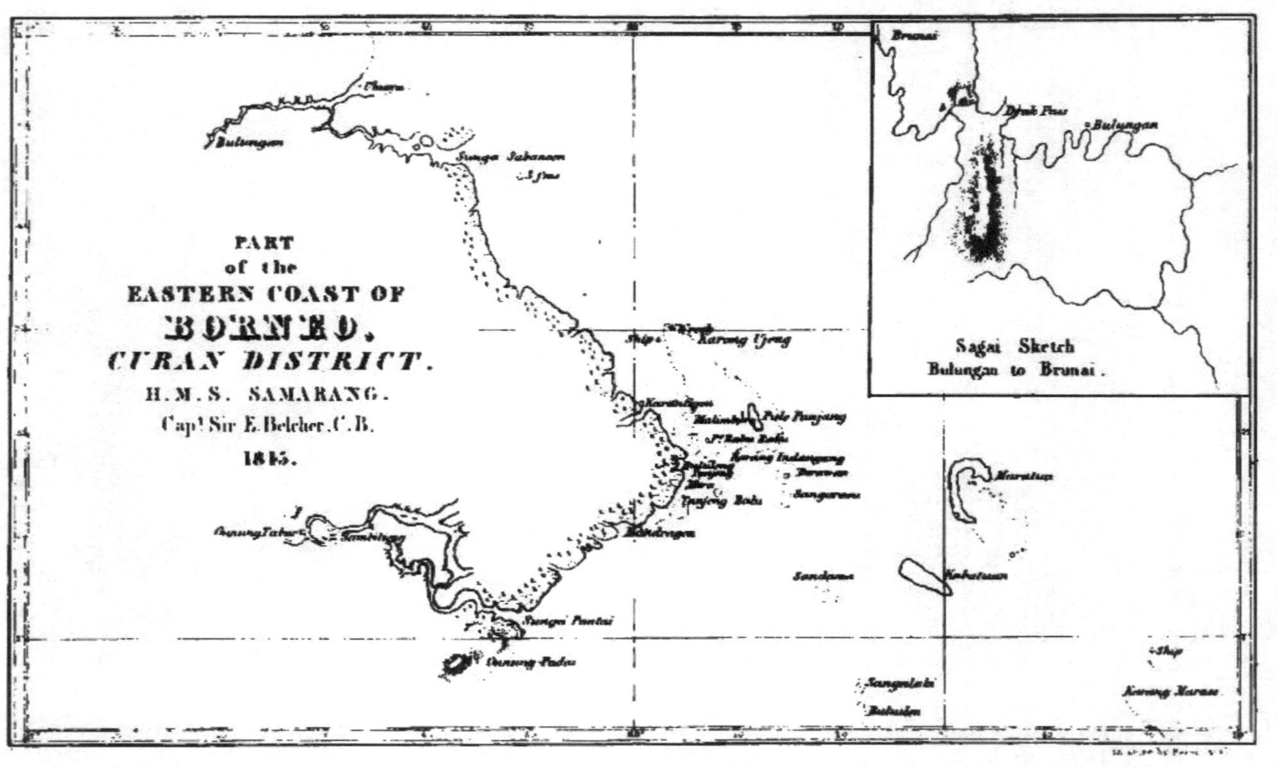
PART
of the
EASTERN COAST OF
BORNEO,
CURAN DISTRICT.
H.M.S. SAMARANG.
Capt. Sir E. Belcher, C.B.
1845.
Bulungan
Sunga Sabanan
Karang Ujeng
Pulo Panjang
Karang Indangang
Tanjong Batu
Muratua
Kabatuan
Sandama
Sungai Pantai
Karang Marasa
Brunai
Djeuh Pass
Bulungan
Sagai Sketch
Bulungan to Brunai.

CHAPTER VII.

EASTERN COAST OF BORNEO.

River Bulungan — Ceremonial visit —Exchange of salutes — Interview with the Sultan — Sagai tribes — Friendship of their Chief — Release of the Lascars — Treaty with the Sultan of Bulungan — Quit Bulungan, and return to Gunung Taboor—Complete terms of friendly agreement with Sultan—Offer of the Island of Maratua—Quit the position off Premier Reef—Examine the Island of Maratua—Escape of 'Samarang' from a most dangerous extremity—Approach the Coast—Anchor to avoid danger—Beauty of Corallines observed beneath us—Enter the Reefs and find a safe anchorage within—Ligitan Group—Conflict of one of the boats with an Illanon Pirate—Prahu burned—Curious instrument found on board her for capturing slaves—Arrival at Sooloo—Meet French Squadron—Exchange civilities with Mons. Lagréne and Admiral Cecile—Friendly relations with Sultan of Sooloo—February Magnetic Term-Day—Kindness of Datoo Danielle.

After many difficulties, arising from groping our way through sand-banks, &c., we reached the mouth of the Săbănoon about nine, and anchored for the night. At dawn on the 3rd of January, 1845, we moved forward, the river wide and uninteresting, the banks being fringed with either Mangrove or Nipa. It is a curious fact, and one well worthy the attention of those who navigate these parts, that the deep water in all the rivers which we have visited in Borneo, is always to be found on that side where the Nipa palm abounds; shoals being almost the constant attendant of the Mangrove.

Having advanced fifteen miles within this archipelago, we arrived at another branch of the Bulungan, called the Oomara, which is here open to the sea, and the water of which, still fresh, clearly proved that some very extensive river, or lake, must feed these numerous mouths of the Bulungan. Pursuing our coarse up the Oomara, about two in the afternoon we descried a canoe, and sent one of our fleetest boats with the interpreter to bring her to us. The people in the canoe were much alarmed, and disposed to resist, but upon their recognising our interpreter Tuan Hadji, as a friend, they were soon upon good terms: they belonged, and were bound, to Curan, but having been several days absent from Bulungan, could not furnish us with any intelligence. Shortly after dark, however, lights were noticed on the river above us, and Tuan Hadji had now an opportunity of showing his address. Giving orders to his own people in the prahu to play a particular tune on the gongs and drums, &c., he advanced in the bow of my gig, singing a song or hymn, which, he observed, would soon be answered. He was successful, and not long afterwards we were visited by several canoes, in one of which was a principal chief, whom he requested to despatch a swift canoe to Bulungan to desire them "not to be afraid, that we were on a friendly visit"; for we learned that they were much frightened, and were sending away their women and children and dismantling their houses, in fact, preparing for either war or retreat, and any panic might entirely frustrate the recovery of the Lascars.

We anchored for the night, and at dawn moved forward. The river now became more interesting, although

not exhibiting the picturesque lake scenery of the Curan district; large patches of cleared land, and the huts of the Sagai people (*Idaan* or *Sagai* of this region) were scattered along the banks, and many of the natives, now no longer influenced by fear, kept pace in their canoes abreast of our boats: in some cases, where they contained men of importance, and known to Tuan Hadji, who was now in my boat, they were permitted to come on board and chat with him. About 10 o'clock, some of the Sagai canoes, containing Chiefs dressed in the most fantastic manner, and standing, or slightly stooping, in their paddling action, began to thicken and form our escort; their curiosity being evidently much excited, whilst some of the principal betrayed great anxiety to get on board of our boats. This, however, could not be allowed, as our men were already sufficiently fatigued without being further impeded by the additional strain of towing their canoes. At noon we anchored to dine, and dress in white, and shortly after moved on for Bulungan. Some of my readers may smile at the idea of our dressing just at the moment that we might be expected to become engaged; but such points of etiquette, coolly and formally carried out, serve to reduce a force into a proper condition of discipline; a well-dressed orderly body of men adds, moreover, very materially to semblance of power, exhibiting a degree of coolness and determination; and further, without orders being issued, intimates to them, in terms generally understood, that action may be looked for. It will now be seen that I had not adopted these measures inconsiderately.

We were shortly met by a canoe containing some of

Q

the state officers, one of whom, the Laksimana, or Lord High Admiral, the brother, I believe, of the Sultan, came on board, and was very civil, until, on our reaching the lower end of the town, he imperiously *ordered* us "to anchor immediately." As I began to notice some little confusion this was not attended to; a dispatch boat then came off from the shore with a similar order, which we also disregarded. By this opportunity I sent a message to the Sultan, informing him "that as my visit was to him, I should anchor in the most convenient spot for that purpose." Considerable alarm prevailed, until ranging up within twenty yards of the muzzles of his guns, which had no protection of any kind, we dropped our anchors. These guns, about ten in number (two heavy iron ship guns, and the remainder brass Leilas *), were loosely mounted on the bank, and any attempt either to fire or re-load them, would have entailed death from our musketry.

The Prime Minister, an Arab priest, a fine commanding person, about sixty years of age, came off to arrange about the salutes, which they would willingly have foregone, but having been informed by the envoy from the Sultan of Gunung Taboor, of the etiquette observed there, their pride could not submit to less. It was arranged that they should, as a token of friendship, salute Her Majesty's flag with twenty-one guns, which should be duly returned from the boats. My reason for insisting upon the *previous* salute from them, was the doubt of their returning a similar number of guns, and

* A Leila varies from a one to a twenty-four pounder; they are longer in proportion than other guns, and are bell-mouthed.

thus giving cause for further discussion, perhaps at the twentieth discharge.

We now witnessed the absurdity of all this parade of their guns, not one of them was loaded! and it was some time before they could collect their amunition, part of which was obtained from the Bugis merchants, residing at the extreme end of the town; one reason, perhaps, for their wishing us to anchor off that position. They had, moreover, but *one rammer*, and having no cartridges made, were compelled to raise the guns in their arms at an elevation of thirty or forty degrees, to put the powder in. Of shot they had none; musketry none, but of sumpitans with poisoned arrows, with Sagais expert in their use, an abundance. It occupied exactly twenty-five minutes to fire twenty-one guns; it was returned by one of our barges, without a failure of a tube, in two and a half minutes, followed by a congreve rocket, which lost itself at full range in the mountain opposite to the town; very much to the astonishment of the Sagais, who naturally enough termed the rocket a *fire sumpitan*, or as named by our Malay friends at Sarãwak and Borneo, a *sumpitan api*.

These ceremonies completed, we landed, and proceeded to the palace, but not attended with any of the state observed at Gunung Taboor. The reception room here, which was in the palace of the Sultan, was, although large, and exhibiting more state in its trappings, dismal and dark; it was furnished with an imposing throne, surrounded by steps, and hung with heavy crimson curtains, behind which we frequently detected the bright inquisitive eyes and white foreheads of the ladies of the court. Seats were prepared as at Gunung Taboor, upon the open area, one chest, covered with what might have been intended for a table-cover, of a yellow ground, with scarlet patterns, being devoted to myself and the Sultan, who received me with as much warmth as I judged to be in his constitution. He is a heavy, rather corpulent and indolent person, about fifty-five years of age, of mild demeanour, and exhibited his disposition to be on good terms by hooking our thumbs and holding them up in public, professing himself my firm friend. As this was a repetition of the scene at Gunung Taboor, I suspect it to be a state ceremony, implying to his subjects friendly alliance; I had no doubt of his being favourably disposed towards us, but whilst retaining my hand in his I detected a certain nervous trembling, which suggested to me that he had not the vigour requisite for command, and that my measures must be guided accordingly.

Upon opening the business relative to the Lascars, this weakness, upon his part, was manifestly beginning to operate, and after urging the unexpected nature of my demand, he requested a few minutes deliberation with his chiefs before he could give a decided answer. He then observed, but evidently by dictation from a scowling chief near him whose *tout ensemble* was anything but prepossessing, "that some of the Lascars could be produced in two days, possibly less, but that the production of two who were three days' journey in the interior, could not be promised under a detention of less than six days." As I suspected some intention on the part of the ministers, to tire or elude our patience by this six days delay, and I had fortunately still enough provision to last us for ten days longer, I was quite prepared for them, and very coolly told them "*that having come thus far for these people, I determined to remain until they were all produced*"; I reminded them at the same time that my detention would entail on them the expense of supporting our men, and accompanied this intelligence with a hint, that Fowls, Bullocks, or wild Hogs would be esteemed useful for that purpose.

This had a most decided effect, and produced an engagement to deliver up ten of the Lascars in two days, and the remaining two in six days. These affairs being arranged, one of the houses overlooking the river, and vacated during this panic, was allotted to me, and the Sultan apparently much relieved, took leave with great *empressement*, promising to interest the Sagais in procuring us supplies of wild Hogs, which, as a Mahommedan, his own people could not interfere with. In his endeavours to explain his feelings he observed, "that our friendship was like his two fingers, joined together at the hand, that he was father, and myself his son." Provisions of all kinds we found ridiculously dear, and as our Gunung Taboor friends had not brought with them sufficient rice, we had to purchase it for them from the Bugis traders, at the rate of half a dollar per gallon.

I had an excellent opportunity of looking narrowly into the character of this Sagai tribe. They are a much finer and larger built race than the *Dyaks* of Sarãwak, or the *Kadyans* or *Dusuns* of northern Borneo; their skin is fairer and softer, with eyes occasionally blue; the hair is lighter, and in one particular individual whom I noticed at Gunung Taboor, a fine athletic and jovial character, the blue eye, sandy hair and freckled complexion, reminded me much of our Scottish Highlanders. They are very fond of ornament, and in most cases seem to regard them as shielding some part of the frame from injury in battle, they are therefore useful as well as ornamental.

Of these, the ear-rings occupy a prominent feature; they are large rings of white metal, apparently lead or tin, generally four through the lobe in each ear, being about an inch and a half in diameter, and about $\frac{3}{16}$ths in thickness. The upper part of the ear is also perforated, and a tiger's tooth passed through it, hangs down to cover the rings. They explained that by turning two rings up above the ear and toggling, or keying, it with the Tiger's tooth, it would resist the blow of a *parang*, and save loss of life. The head-dress is usually composed of monkey skin, capped by a brazen ridge with about three inches side projections, forming altogether a picturesque helmet, surmounted by feathers of the Argus Pheasant, Toucan, or other birds. The fighting dress is composed of a quilted scarlet jacket occasionally trimmed with yellow tape. The loins are protected by a thickly matted tail-piece which corresponds to the skirts of a fashionable coat, and serve to protect that region from the arrows of the sumpitan; add to this the shield, sumpitan, and parang, and you have, with the athletic form within, the Sagai or Idaan of this region, estimated to amount in number, on the banks of the Bulungan, to sixty thousand men.

The *parang* of Eastern Borneo differs very materially from the *kris;* it is very slender at the handle, which is

Crung Sagai Drak

formed of deer bone, and very neatly carved, the blade runs broad and thick at its point, to which, in giving a blow, it carries its whole weight, it is slightly hollowed on one side, and bevelled like a chisel on the opposite, by which it becomes useful in felling trees or obstacles in the way of advance, it seldom exceeds two feet in length. The scabbard, which is of red wood, is very tastefully carved, and has a small knife attached to it, similar to the Scottish knife and fork. With the chief of this tribe, an intelligent, although compact little fellow, very similar to our friend *Meta*, of the Serambo Dyaks, I established a friendship, which lasted during the whole period of our stay; he frequented my house daily, apparently from no other motive than that arising out of a certain degree of attachment, as he did not appear either to desire or covet anything we possessed, whilst his anxiety to procure wild Hogs for our men, as well as Fowls for our mess, always afforded sufficient proof of his disinterestedness. On one occasion having to complain to him of a theft committed by some of his people, he exhibited great firmness on the subject, gave his orders, and those orders were *effectual*. I observed that our having witnessed any crime committed by his people pained him much; it depressed his spirits for the day; he went home earlier that evening, and his return the day following was, on the other hand, as much delayed. It is by these traits that we can properly estimate the character of these people; they reminded me more of the original characters of Tahiti, on Cook's visit, where each man selected his Taio, or friend, and devoted himself to him.

He gave me much interesting information relative to

their communications with the interior, and even volunteered to convey a letter for me to the city of Brunai. I immediately caused one to be written by Tuan Hadji, assisted by our interpreter, and on presenting it to be forwarded, he asked for a piece of white cloth to put round the head of his messenger, informing me that it would reach the Rajah Muda Hassim, to whom it was directed, in ten days. Within was a note to Mr. Brooke, in English. I inquired if he would take *me*; his reply, with a very animated expression of countenance, was, "yes, if you will put a white cloth round your head, I will do the same, and with this symbol of peace we can pass through all the tribes safely; I will answer for your life with mine!" This post, he informed me, "can go from Gunung Taboor also, but the Sultan of Gunung Taboor is not so friendly to the Sagais; too much powder and guns for their habits." The more I saw of these interesting people about Borneo, the more am I inclined to coincide with Mr. Brooke, that they required but gentle treatment, and encouragement, to become our most useful commercial allies. Here they could turn out the Bugis Malay race whenever they felt disposed, but the people of Bulungan are not warlike; their town is not stockaded, nor have they anything resembling a battery. Their guns, which in these countries are merely reckoned as *plate* with us, may be brought out upon state occasions for rejoicing, or perhaps as in our case, for defence, but otherwise they are concealed in their houses. Their external commerce is so very trifling that they are frequently distressed for Rice, and of this we ourselves had proof; it is brought here from Celebes and the Kotaí river, by the Bugis traders who obtain the Sagai gold, said to be the purest in Borneo, in exchange. I observed that they pronounce the name of the *Cotí* river as *Kotai*, and causing the Tuan Hadji, a well educated man, to write it, he articulated it clearly, *Ko-tai*.

All the available lands, which are very extensive below Bulungan, are under cultivation, but as the surrounding Sagais are frequently distressed, it bears out their assertion as to the immense population of this region. Wishing to test their disposition towards us, at the moment that we advanced on the town, I enquired of my Sagai friend "how would you have acted had our boats opened fire," he replied, very naively, "*then*, I would have resisted you, *now*, I know you, and your power, I perceive that it would have been very foolish. And now we *know* what the English are, none of my people will ever fight against them." This was followed by locking my forefinger energetically with his, and holding it up to illustrate the league of friendship. It is not to be imagined that this scene occurred with a ferocious looking, heavy built, savage, "or wild man of the mountains," as the Idaan race are termed; the actor in this ceremony was a light but strongly knit, beautifully modelled individual, about five feet seven in height, rather silent, with a mild speaking eye, exciting our admiration and good feelings more by his quiet winning demeanour and cordial pressure of the hand, than by any declaration of attachment. We could only converse with him, first through a Malay interpreter, and then through Tuan Hadji in the Sagai tongue; still his eye might be detected following every word and gesture, and when the reply through our interpreter came to English, holding his hand up at times to signify that he understood sufficient to perceive that his meaning was misrepresented. His intelligence in explaining, by bits of grass and leaves, the route ,by which my letter would reach Borneo; up the river by canoe, up one side of the mountain, crossing the Idaan pass, through hostile tribes, &c., and down the other on foot, re-taking a tributary stream by canoe, and at last reach the main river of Brunai, was a masterpiece of savage ingenuity; and when he saw it traced upon paper in accordance with his description, he was delighted with the transcript, asking for it, as well as for a supply of paper and pencils to make similar sketches. Nothing would have afforded me greater pleasure than to have undertaken this overland journey, had I been unshackled: but this was impossible.

We had now penetrated further into the interior of Borneo, and under more friendly auspices, than any European who has been in this region, and the question often occurred to me,—what might have been the result of poor Murray's expedition, had he selected either the Pantai or Bulungan instead of the Kotai? The trading advantages here are more important than upon any other part of Borneo, and at Bulungan, particularly, the Sagais, the richest of the Idaan tribes, are brought immediately into contact with the traders, instead of, that bar to every improvement in this country, the intervention of the Malay, or more wily Bugis of Celebes.

The people of these two rivers are extremely anxious to induce Englishmen to settle amongst them, *offering* ground to build houses upon, gratuitously; protection in person, property, and freedom of religion, with the sole trade, and to *secure* cargoes for any vessels which I would send with papers bearing my seal. With respect to trading up this river, I am afraid that until the mouth of the Sabanoon is more closely examined, vessels drawing above ten feet would find difficulty in getting over the bar, but once within any of the mouths, there is sufficient water for a frigate. It would be easy to transfer goods, by prahus, from hence to Gunung Taboor, where the principal trade would flow, and where we have proof that the 'Samarang' could safely enter and depart, and by care, and lightening, could even be taken up to the city of Gunung Taboor.

On the evening of the second day, ten Lascars were sent in, several ill, and very weak. It is almost needless to say that they were delighted at this unexpected release, but it grieved me much to learn that so much duplicity had been practised, and that they were all in the town, and neighbourhood, at the time of our arrival; however, the Sultan appeared to be really pleased when he had it in *his power* to release them, and I believe that the cause of delay arose principally from the reason, that the Malay masters to whom they had been assigned, were, not able to arrange about their missing clothes and effects.

Some difficulties were now interposed on account of the two Lascars still missing, but upon my reply that "come they must," and that any delay beyond the time stipulated, would be fatal to some fat Bullocks grazing near us, as well as to the various fowl preserves; and further, that a tribute of Rice for the Lascars, would be exacted from the Bugis traders, they began to be more anxious for our departure. The people in Tuan Hadji's prahu had also exhibited symptoms of insubordination, declaring that they must return for food; and, eventually, started without further permission. I was perfectly satisfied that this was another attempt of the ill-favoured chief to try to retain these two Lascars, for on the *fourth* day they were sent in, having been near enough in the *first instance* to have been delivered over with the others. I determined, therefore, that no presents should be given to these chiefs.

The Sultan now became anxious for my departure, indeed the flight of Tuan Hadji had rendered him uneasy, fearing, perhaps, the enmity of the Sultan of Gunung Taboor. I offered him tea, sugar, and other articles which I knew he was anxious to obtain, if he would send a canoe with us to the ship; but his anxiety "that I should carry off the Lascars, lest any of them should escape, and involve him in further trouble," overpowered every other feeling.

Having executed a treaty with the Sultan, similar to that completed at Gunung Taboor, in which he invites the friendship and alliance of Great Britain, and engages in future to behave with kindnes to her subjects; and having fully impressed both the chiefs, as well as himself, with the conviction, that Great Britain would severely punish the repetition of any such conduct as that which they had lately exhibited towards the Lascars, and that nothing excused them on the present occasion but their ignorance of our laws, I took my leave of him and my friend the Sagai chief, to each of whom I made various useful presents, and about 3 o'clock, P.M., on the 10th of January, 1845, quitted Bulungan.

The following is a copy of the Treaty with the Sultan of Gunung Taboor, of which that with the Sultan of Bulungan is identical.

"The SULTAN OF GUNUNG TABOOR is anxious to enter into friendly relations with Her Majesty the Queen of Great Britain, and is willing to execute a formal Treaty of Friendship and Commerce whenever Her Majesty the Queen of Great Britain will send any duly authorized person.

"The SULTAN OF GUNUNG TABOOR engages, that the subjects of the Queen of Great Britain shall always meet with friendship and protection within his dominions.

"On the part of the QUEEN OF GREAT BRITAIN, Sir Edward Belcher, commanding Her Majesty's Ship 'Samarang', engages, that similar friendship and protection will be accorded to the subjects of the Sultan of Gunung Taboor, should they visit any of the Ports belonging to Great Britain.

"(*Signed.*) SULTAN MAHARAJAH DINDA,
Gunung Taboor.
IBUNO MARAHOM.
SULTAN HADJI KUNING,
Gunung Taboor.
EDWARD BELCHER.
Captain of Her Majesty's Ship, 'Samarang.'"

About 10 o'clock on the morning of the 11th we reached the Sãbãnoon mouth of the Bulungan, and as it was requisite that its position should be determined, I selected a huge tree which had been driven down by the floods, and became partly embedded in the mud, for this purpose. We had frequently heard the Lascars speak of the oysters which they had been sent in search of at the River's mouth, but never could understand how they were procured, supposing them to be, as we had generally observed them, firmly attached to the rocks. As the tide bared the shoals which surrounded us, I sent to examine what I imagined to be rocky ledges, when, to my surprise, they proved to be literally *banks of large loose oysters*, with the hinge planted, and their mouths upwards, rather unpleasant to the feet of those not provided with shoes. Aided by iron levers we soon made an opening into this living pavement, and getting some of the larger boats alongside the reef, they were, in a very few minutes, laden with as many oysters as they could conveniently carry. About 6 o'clock, we quitted the river, and without being able to discover any deeper channel in our outward route, reached the 'Samarang' about sunset.

On the morning following, the ship was shifted to a convenient and well sheltered position within *Karang Ujong* (or point of the reef), on which the remains of the 'Premier' lay, and leaving a party for surveying and examining the wreck, we proceeded on the morning of the 13th with our boat force (within the reefs) to Gunung Taboor, in order to make our final arrangements with the Sultan, and to receive his letter for Sooloo, protesting against the conduct of Si Dawut. We reached Gunung Taboor on the evening of the 15th, where we found the Sultan very anxious about our return.

The chart designates the river and outer coast-line generally, as *Curan*. *Curan* is the territory, and the part of the river, indicated by that name, is about midway, where a large branch leads northerly. The river above this branch is the Brraou, (pronounced Brow, as one syllable) and the people inhabiting its banks are specially termed *Orang Brraou*, or the Brow people.

The Sultan's name is Maharajah Dinda, and he is also called Si Atap,* but he dislikes being addressed by this latter name. The Rajah Muda, who has established himself, in defiance of the Sultan's authority, at Sambiliong, and assumed the title of *Sultan Muda*, (or young Sultan,) is a cousin of Si Atap, but, as before noticed, having quarrelled about the Europeans, has been closely shut up in his fortress, and will probably be destroyed; I used all my efforts to induce the Sultan to permit me to visit him and effect a reconciliation, but he would not hear of it. He denounced him "as an artful undermining serpent, who had been using every effort to embroil him with the surrounding powers, as well as the Dutch authorities, and that he never could be safe until his removal, and that after such a breach of faith he would not be respected by his people." He asserted that the Rajah Muda enticed the Europeans over to him under false promises of aiding their removal, but that he wrote at the same time to Kotai, asking what his uncle, the Sultan of that place, wished done with them. That for himself, at the first moment after their return from the wreck of the 'Premier' he had suggested their going to Sooloo with Si Dawut, but they declined going by that vessel, as it appeared their pride recoiled against their being associated with the Lascars. That in return for his civility, by affording them fowls and rice for their own use, and treating them as equals, he had not received even thanks; and that finding their conduct disagreeable to his people, they had been put on board of a prahu and taken proper care of; finally, after making him

* Atap signifies a covering, roof, thatch, &c.

sundry presents, including the desk before alluded to, that everything had been demanded back before the departure of the Dutch vessel, therefore he has not in any way been recompensed even for the maintenance of these people, nor has he required it.

His statement charges the master of the vessel with conduct, which is, to say the least of it, very nearly allied to giving up the Lascars as *slaves*, by denying all knowledge of them as his people, and using the terms "Do what you please with them, sell them"; of drunkeness, falsehood, and gross language between him and his crew. Much allowance, too, may be made, for the feeling of Malay *versus* English, but I regret to say, that upon a close examination of the evidence taken at Manila, compared with the story told here, as well as the character given by the twelve Lascars, recovered from Bulungan, of their treatment at the time of their being wrecked, that there is strong presumptive, if not conclusive, evidence, that the charge of the Sultan is correct, and the whole story narrated to me by Tuan Hadji, in my cabin, during the passage from Pantai to Bulungan corroborated every part of the assertion of the Sultan. The Lascars in their account assert "that the Captain ran away with the boats during the night, leaving them to famish on an uninhabited island." The four unfortunate Lascars who trusted their lives on the raft, have not since been heard of. The rapid tides which set to the S.E., added to the powerful streams entering the sea about this region, must have driven them to sea, and if saved by any of the Illañon pirates, which scour this coast, they will probably be sold at Kotai, the nearest and surest mart to prevent discovery. The act of the master of the 'Premier,' of setting fire to his vessel, was highly injudicious and unwarrantable. It was, in the first place, a beacon to attract the pirates of this region; in the second, he was bound to save the property as far as he was able; had he not acted as he did, the masts, sails, &c., would have been saved, and the Sultan of Gunung Taboor would have been satisfied with reasonable salvage; or, if demanded, would even have restored the whole. Upon these subjects he has now written instructions, drawn up as an agreement between us, and distressed foreigners will, I am satisfied, find as friendly reception, and as just dealing with the Sultan of Gunung Taboor, as they have any right to expect from more civilized nations.

The Sultan informed me that by his Treaty with the Dutch Authorities at Benjarmassin, he had already engaged to assist all Europeans, and that under the spirit of that agreement, he was willing to render the master of the 'Premier' every assistance, and would have saved the entire property in the vessel, but that the act of his firing the ship "divided his power", and he could not be answerable for what the people of Bulungan did; when the vessel and her stores became "as fish", every one took what he could catch. He was still willing to deliver up any article belonging to the 'Premier', which could be traced within his town; he, however, placed himself entirely in my hands, consented that my wishes should be law, and that if I would instruct him (give him a writing) how to act in future, he would most willingly adhere to it.

In proof of his anxiety to befriend the English, the

R

Sultan offers to give them a separate place within his town to live in, to protect them, to give them a preference in trade, and as a further exhibition of his sincerity to open trading connexions, he gave me a letter* under his official seal, containing the list of goods which he would engage as certain cargo, to any vessel which I would send in the May following; he further volunteered to cede to Great Britain any of the outer islands which might be adapted for a settlement, and which I promised to examine, particularly Maratua, after quitting the river.

During these proceedings, it became necessary to attach my seal to the Treaties; they are not in the habit of using wax, and were much pleased with the sharp impression produced by it. He inquired very earnestly whether he could obtain a seal exactly similar to mine, adding, "that will be more lasting than writing, no one can alter the meaning; any letter I send with it will be immediately understood, and any which you may send will instantly be attended to by my people, who cannot read, and the persons bringing it will be assured of the kindest reception." Fortunately, I possessed a duplicate, and this, together with some wax and a supply of stationery, were forwarded to him. The Sultan having expressed a wish that I would procure him two seals similar to his own, but with his titles in Roman characters as well as Malay, I promised, on reaching China, to comply with his wishes. Two of these were duly executed, one in Malay, the other in English characters,

* This letter was delivered to Mr. Wyndham, and I have the satisfaction of learning from him that the vessel he sent was very handsomely received, and that great anxiety was expressed for his personal visit.

the inscription being similar to that subscribed to the Treaty, and with a handsome rose-wood desk and other presents, forwarded by Mr. Wyndham.

Having obtained a document from the Sultan of Gunung Taboor, addressed to the Sultan of Sooloo, denying *in toto* having, directly or indirectly, warranted Si-Dawut in demanding ransom for the six Lascars sent in the prahu to Sooloo; but on the contrary, asserting that he had sent them free to that Port, in order to their reaching their own country, which Si Diwut had informed him could be effected through the agency of Mr. Wyndham. I was preparing to take my leave when a new case presented itself in a native of Manila, who had been captured by the Balligñini pirates, sold at Sooloo, and escaped hither. Having contracted a friendship with one of the Lascars, and being anxious to return to his native country, he had been advised to ask for my intercession. The Sultan immediately summoned him, and to convince me that he was sincere in his professions, relative to slavery, told him, in my presence, that if he thought he would be happier in his own country, he had his free consent to return; but having married a Malay woman, a slave of the Prime Minister, that it was requisite that he should leave something to support his wife and child. The Manila man offered to transmit ninety dollars as soon as he could earn it, and would engage himself on the public works in that city until this was completed. I informed the Sultan that I had no power to engage for any question relating to the Spanish Government, and that the arrangement could only rest upon the man's promise. But he immediately replied, "I shall be per-

R 2

fectly satisfied if you will only mention to the Governor of Manila, that you heard him *promise* to remit the sum as soon as he could earn it." The manner of performing this act, added to his confidence in what he thought honour would compel the Governor to do, made a much stronger impression on my mind than could otherwise have been conveyed, of the fine feelings which generally actuated this young man. I think him quite equal, if not superior, to our favourite Budduruddin, at Sarãwak (now at Brunai).

The Prime Minister is also a very superior person. He does not chew betel, but preserves his teeth, of a pure white, and his frequent and last expressions to me, with a gentle pressure of the hand, were, "I wish to be an Englishman, when you come here again, bring me English clothes, and I will be dressed as one." His son, is also a prepossessing young man, about twenty years of age, very sedate and stately, at the same time very good-natured, and the handsomest Malay I have seen. All the Chiefs of Gunung Taboor eclipse those of Bulungan, indeed, I know not of a single friendship formed at the latter place, excepting with the Sultan and Sagai Chief.

At my last private interview with the Sultan, at which he would only admit Tuan Hadji and our interpreter to be present, he conveyed into my hand, suddenly closing it with great mystery, what they term here the "Snake Stone." This is a polished globe of quartz, about the size of a musket ball, which he described as of infinite value, an "heir loom;" and reported to have been extracted from the head of an enchanted snake. At first, I suspected it to be a Bezoar, but, on inspection, found it to be merely quartz, the grinding and polishing of which, to a globular form, must have required some art.

Tuan Hadji had at his last interview earnestly solicited a letter from me, which would enable him to pass on the sea without molestation. He holds the position of Chief Captain, or Admiral, and being anxious to become "a great navigator," purposes visiting Singapore the ensuing season, when he expects to induce the Malays of that place to open a direct trade with the Curan district, or the *Tanah besar* (great country), as they term this archipelago. He appears to be possessed of considerable knowledge of the geography of the eastern part of Borneo, and coasts of Celebes, Sooloo, and Bisayas, as far as Luzon. He informed me, that immediately behind the Bulungan range there is a very extensive lake, which is connected with the sea by many different rivers. It is probable that the Sãbãnoon, and all these rivers, which we found fresh nearly at their embouchures, are fed from this reservoir. He was very assiduous in explaining to me the different inaccuracies which he noticed upon our charts, furnishing me with a mental sketch of all the Islands, Points, Rivers, &c., between Bulungan and Point Kanioongan of the charts. This latter point, he states to be Tanjong Manäaliak, and that *Kanioongan besar* (great) and *kichi* (little), are islands.

On the 15th we parted from our friends at Gunung Taboor, and on the 19th reached the ship off Premier Reef. Upon a review of our proceedings at this place, I feel great satisfaction in having effected the entire object of my visit without recourse to violent measures; it was considered by many that the rescue of the people of colour, and who would probably be carried far into the interior, was almost a hopeless pursuit, and that nothing less than summary punishment on the people and the destruction of their town, hitherto suspected of being little better than a pirate retreat, would follow. I am, however, inclined to think that our countrymen have been better treated than they would have been upon any other part of uncivilized Borneo. After the burning and abandonment of the vessel by the master, I cannot but consider that the property saved from her belonged, by the custom of the country, to the power upon whose territory she became a wreck; at all events, remained in their keeping until formally demanded by competent authority. We found that the powers, into whose hands our people fell, fed them, took care of them, and exacted no harder labour than was requisite to earn their subsistence, and moreover, when demanded, readily giving them up, refusing to make any charges, even for their sustenance. To have made these powers feel, even if they deserved punishment, that Great Britain is not too anxious to revenge an act, which however open it might have been to our animadversion, appeared in accordance with their customs, is one great point gained towards their viewing us with respect, as well as kindly feeling, even to *wish* for, and *court*, our alliance. I firmly believe that they now entertain a greater dread of the force we could bring against them, than if we had destroyed their towns; no such power has been exhibited, but I have reason to know that they have magnified it in imagination to such an extent, that any distressed British subjects will in future meet with a *home*, instead of that *revenge* which harsher measures would have inevitably entailed.

On the 20th we quitted our reef-bound nook, and beat to the eastward, intending to examine the Island of Maratua, which had been painted in very glowing colours by Tuan Hadji. We found the currents pressing so strong to the southward that we were unable to hold our own, and it was not until the 22nd, and then by dint of very close attention, that we effected our object, and ran down its eastern side; but no sufficient opening in the reef warranted my pushing the ship in, although I could clearly perceive by the deep blue tint of the sea that there was sufficient water within. I had also despatched a boat round the western and southern end of the Island, which on rejoining, did not, from the report furnished by her, afford hope of a harbour, and consequently no plea for further detention. Severe illness had also deprived me of power for further exertion, and giving orders for hoisting in all our boats, we shaped a course to seaward, expecting to be well clear of the land before midnight. Before that hour the breeze failed, and at daylight, I was informed not only that it was nearly calm, but also that the ship was drifting rapidly upon an extensive reef. We had little time for reflection, the boats were hoisted out, and all efforts made to tow her clear. Directions were issued to attach four four-inch whale lines to one of the kedges, and to unite the hemp and chain stream cables, and bend them to the stream anchor. Shortly after I reached the deck, we obtained soundings in 146 fathoms, and orders were given to let go the kedge. This fouled, and the stream was then ordered to be let go; it held, leaving us with 114 fathoms under the stern, and within thirty fathoms of the reef! Our only chance now was to await the sea breeze, but this did not visit us until nearly two o'clock, during which interval we were in a state of dreadful suspense, as in the event of blowing from its old direction nothing but certain wreck awaited us, and from the very small quantity of water which remained on board, it is probable that we should have experienced the greatest distress.

Fortunately the kedge, or the hawser attached, had fouled sufficiently amongst the rocks to serve the purpose as a spring for canting us, and having already brought a fair strain on it, we watched most anxiously for the coming sea breeze. About 1. 45, when a light air sprung up, sail was made, the cable and hawser cut in succession, and once more she glided on in safety, but it was not until the 26th, after a most tedious and harassing beat, that we recovered our ground and weathered Maratua; and by getting in with the Borneon shore, cleared this overpowering current, which had so long held us embayed, with reefs under our lee, as far as could be seen to the eastward, from our mast-heads.

It was, indeed, fortunate that we made the mistake we did on first sighting Maratua, on the 25th, as the pilot most certainly intended to have taken us to the eastward of Maratua, which would have entailed certain loss. The safe channel in approaching the Pantai is by the *western* sides of Maratua and Kakuban, and round the eastern end of Sangalaki, hauling up westerly until the mouth of the river bears W.N.W., when that course will carry you in. The 'Samarang' drew sixteen feet, and nothing going in or coming out, brought her up on that line.

The bottom is very oozy (creamy mud). No vessel should attempt to enter the shallows until daylight, and if caught to the southward of Sangalaki, or Samasama, after sunset, should anchor with the kedge, the moment she gets less than twenty fathoms, until daylight, as there are reefs lying off the southern edges of all the islands, as well as the northern coast-line, which would be clearly discernible with a morning sun.

This unexpected distress for water, reduced us to two pints per man, and rendered it imperative that we should seek some spot upon the coast where it could be replenished. Maratua, as well as Derawan, were pointed out as islands on which it could be procured, but we had already seen enough of them; we therefore pushed in for the coast to the southward of Si Amcel. On the morning of the 29th we found ourselves completely surrounded by reefs on the north-west and south, and had proof of being so hemmed in, by *feeling* the coral *beneath* us. Fortunately, we had sufficient breeze to clear us without having recourse to anchors, and noticing a gap to the westward we stood towards it, hoping that it might lead up to the land. We were not mistaken, although compelled to anchor to await the examination by the boats, as well as for winds to carry us forward.

During this delay, we had a magnificent view of the submarine coralline gardens over which we were floating, animated by the graceful gambols of the beautifully painted *Chætodon*, and other varieties of fish, which were most abundant. Many attempts were made to entrap them, but they were cunning enough to elude any baits which we could offer.

As misfortunes not unfrequently turn to our advantage, so it was in the present instance; by this delay we discovered the only access to the main, which offered on this coast; as had we not touched the ground I should most certainly have stood to seaward, and thus missed this opening. As we neared the land, I noticed a prahu moving along shore, and despatched Lieut. Roberton in one of the cutters to obtain information as to anchorage, as well as where water could be obtained. This perhaps was a solitary instance in which I omitted the order "to arm complete," she left her gun behind. About noon, Lieut. Roberton came up with the prahu and requested, through his interpreter, to learn where fresh water could be procured, as well as to pilot the ship to safe anchorage. At first they appeared to be inclined to meet his wishes, but evil counsel prevailed, and supposing our boats too weak to resent insult, they pointed a brass gun they had on board at the cutter, and assumed an attitude of defiance, calling out in Malay, "fire, do not be afraid, fire!" and suiting the action to the order, they kept whirling the lighted match in the air, to render its action more certain. Lieut. Roberton behaved with great coolness, desiring the interpreter to inform them "that they were friends lately from Bulungan, and not to be afraid, that he had no desire to injure them, and merely asked for information." With Malays, as well as with all uncivilized nations, passive measures are always interpreted as weakness. Deeming our cutter too insignificant to resent insult with their supposed superiority of the brass gun, and continuing to point it towards the boat, with the match frequently near the vent, repeating their exclamation, "do not fear them, fire ! fire!" Lieut. Roberton deemed it imperative to put a stop to these insults, and to prevent the death of some of his crew. Pulling therefore sharply across their line of direction, he desired his men to lay in their oars and prepare their muskets. The Malays discharged their gun thrice without effect, but the musketry from the cutter soon taught them their inferiority. Grounding the prahu they fled over the reefs to the jungle, where they concealed themselves, carrying their wounded with them. Lieut. Roberton being unable to get the prahu afloat, in order to bring her out, took from her the brass gun, and other articles denoting her piratical complexion, and set fire to her. Her equipment was evidently Illañon, and from information obtained the same evening, we learned that she probably belonged to a reputed pirate den at Tooncoo, situated about thirty miles to the northward of our position, and had in fact committed an act of *piracy* upon one of our allies, not many hours previous to her destruction, as will be noticed presently.

The channel between the reefs having been declared safe, we ran in with a fine sea-breeze, and obtained very snug anchorage in ten fathoms, within a convenient distance from the shore, where we had the further good fortune to discover a small rill of tolerably pure water; this by judicious management in clearing its source inland, was found sufficient to keep two boats employed watering. The remainder were employed in the examination of the coast, and outer dangers, as well as ascertaining the possibility of getting to sea by a more direct or wider channel. We found, very large, and most delicious oysters in abundance, and they were much enjoyed; but whether owing to previous severe illness, or to some poisonous quality in those which I had eaten, I was attacked with an illness similar to that resulting from poison, which affected me most severely. The evening after we anchored in this position, the prahu which accompanied us from Sooloo rejoined her crew, expressing most unequivocal joy at finding themselves again under our protection; and for this they had certainly great cause to be thankful; for the Nakoda informed me, he had been plundered of all his Rice, as well as water, by the very prahu which had been destroyed by Lieut. Roberton. He was anxious to ascertain what implements had been found on board of her, and upon seeing them, his attention instantly fixed on an instrument, which we had mistaken for "grains," or a "fish-gig," an article used for spearing fish, but which we were now informed was for taking men! This instrument is bifurcate, with a sufficient spread between the points, which are barbed internally, to include the neck of a man; the weapon is thrown with almost unerring aim, so as to secure the victim by the neck, and jerking it back with a sharp motion, fixes him within the barbs, setting all opposition at defiance. Immediately they had examined this weapon, they observed, "then those in the prahu were *Orang Lanoon jahat* (bad Llãnon men), belonging to Tooncoo."

On the 2nd February, having failed in finding any other channel than that by which we had entered, we hoisted the prahu of our ally on board, very much to the delight of her crew, and by stationing one of our boats on the shoalest position, reached the offing in safety, but not without being compelled to run ten miles to the southward, to clear the outer group of Islands. We now began to derive assistance from our Sooloo pilot, who, in addition to much general information afforded, regarding this part of the coast, acquainted us with the names of the islets which we had just surveyed, and which proved to be the inner group belonging to Si-Ameel. The position upon which our observations were made, a small sand island within one mile of the Borneo shore, was determined to be in Lat. 4° 19′ 6″ N., Long. 118° 33′ 16″ E., Var. 0° 45′ 3″ E.

Being too unwell to endure the harassing duty of working up in shore, we stood to the eastward, and on our western tack did not reach more than two miles to windward in three days. I therefore determined to make a longer stretch easterly, and found that the current was not only weaker, but slightly in our favour, enabling us to reach Si-misa, on the eastern side of Sooloo, on the morning of the 8th. I would not advance this, however, as any guide to navigation, for I am well aware that the currents among these islands are irregular, and that the tides, when the sea breezes act in concert with them, would lead a casual observer to anticipate a northerly, instead of southerly, set, which latter would invariably prevail during calms. We had a proof of the uncertainty of these currents previous to reaching Si-misa, having experienced a strong northerly current, attended with heavy overfalls, instead of the southerly set anticipated. On the night of the 8th we were, however, forced by a strong *southerly* set on the shores of Si-misa, and compelled to anchor in ten fathoms, close to the reefs, with a velocity of current of three knots. Near midnight, a different current compelled us to weigh, to avoid being forced on a spit which then became astern of us, the current forcing us towards the Sooloo shore, but *not northerly*; about dawn, on the 9th, however, we again experienced the northerly set, and on passing Bi-ti-nan, the eastern island off Sooloo, although going at the rate of eight and a half knots, found it entirely destroy our steerage, giving a shower bath to the master on the *bowsprit end.* This ceased immediately after rounding this island, and we shaped our course for the anchorage at Sooloo, where we were secured by 3 o'clock, P.M.

Here we found the French squadron, composed of the 'Cleopatra', sixty, Rear-Admiral Cecile, having on board Monsieur Lagréne, the Ambassador to China; corvette, 'Victorieuse', and steamer, 'Archimede.' Officers from each vessel waited upon me, offering the customary civilities, and shortly after, I paid my respects to the Admiral and Ambassador. Their visit here, which I contemplated before quitting, related to the melancholy affair which had taken place at Basilan. The Admiral wished the interference of the Sultan, but although his *mediation* might, in the first instance, without calling upon the Spaniards, have proved important, and saved money, still he had no *power*, and, moreover, declared, "that the people resident there, although nominally tributary to Sooloo, were Illañons, and set him at defiance."

This declaration induced the French to assume the people of Basilan to be Pirates, and upon the plea of ridding that island of these people, and forming a French establishment there, endeavoured to persuade the Sultan to sell the island. This was for some time rejected, but conditions were finally agreed upon, which were communicated to me by the Sultan. The terms were nearly to the following effect: that the French should, upon payment of one hundred thousand dollars, *govern* Basilan for one hundred years, but the Sultan declined attaching his seal until confirmed by the French Government. As the possession of Basilan, by the French, would cause a discussion with Spain, which also lays claim to the island, and would, further, create a jealousy amongst other nations; this treaty has not been recognised by France.

By the information which I obtained from Admiral Cecile, they appear to have suffered greatly in their rencontre with the pirates of Basilan. It appears that the channel of the river was barred and staked, and that they were reduced to the necessity of carrying the boats over these obstructions. The enemy had laid their guns accurately for this point, as well as others to enfilade any such attempt, hence, the attacking party were much cut up before they could advance to the conflict, which the enemy evaded by retreating to the jungle.

Madame Lagréne accompanied her husband in the 'Cleopatra', and during our stay in port I experienced many civilities from the Admiral and party on board that ship, they also did me the honour to become my guests on board the 'Samarang', it was not, therefore, without some feeling of regret that we parted, the French squadron preceding us on the 22nd for Singapore and Batavia.

This visit of the French had delayed my affairs with the Sultan, but we now commenced on a more intimate footing, as his fear of the French had induced him to look more narrowly into his relations with Great Britain, in order to discover some pretext by which he might claim his right to refer the discussion, relative to Basilan, to his Old Ally, as he was pleased to acknowledge us. His observation to me was, "We owe all to Great Britain, the cession of Balambangan, part of Borneo, and Toolyan, on this Island, are not to be taken as precedents by any other nation; the British are our natural allies; they brought our ancestor, the Sultan Alimudin, from Manila, where he was a prisoner, and replaced him on his throne and possessions, and no concession, even to ourselves and all we have, can be too great for such obligations." A special meeting of all the Chiefs was summoned to decide upon the letter sent by the Sultan of Gunung Taboor, which I delivered under the customary ceremonies. The letter was prefaced by certain religious perorations, invoking punishment if he stated anything untrue, and then proceeded to declare, the denial on the part of the Sultan of Gunung Taboor, to any permission, directly or indirectly, given to Si-Dawut, the Nakoda of the prahu, to demand any ransom for the six Lascars. That they were sent by him to the Sultan, in order to find their passage to their proper country, through Mr. Wyndham; that he was still a debtor to Si-Dawut to the amount of one hundred and eighty dollars, for certain goods left behind, which were to be paid for in fish and shell on the return of the Nakoda, the following season. At any other period, vengeance would probably have fallen upon the head of Si-Dawut, and have compromised some of the Datoos, his supporters; the Nakoda, too, evidently felt himself in a very awkward situation, although strongly asserting his innocence, in which no one, however, believed.

Fully aware that I had gained my object, as well as the satisfaction of having afforded them a wholesome warning that all such transactions will, in future, be narrowly inquired into, and punished; and further, being unwilling to disturb the warm feelings which appeared at present to be entertained towards our country, I intimated to the Sultan, that with respect to Si-Dawut, I considered the loss of six hundred dollars ample punishment; and as the British Government would never permit such a subject as *ransom* to be named, I expected the formal release of all demands on account of these Lascars.

The Sultan immediately declared them free, and further engaged to secure the repayment of the six hundred dollars, in goods, by Si-Dawut, or the Sultan of Gunung Taboor, with whom he would hold further communication, until he ascertained the truth, when Si-Dawut, if guilty, will probably pay for his misdeeds.

Having thus fully completed the object of our mission, and the monthly magnetic term day having arrived, we began to look around for some convenient spot where these observations might be satisfactorily made. Under the present excited state of the populace, it was not considered either safe, or politic, to erect tents, and land armed men to protect us from the visits of those who might be inclined to be troublesome, or disposed to approach too near with their iron implements of war; it was therefore proposed by my kind friend Datoo Danielle, (and with the permission of the Sultan) that I should make these observations within his grounds, which were enclosed

s

by a very substantial stockade, and where a convenient shed, detached from his private residence, afforded us much greater convenience than could be obtained within the restricted limits of our magnetic tents.

The house of Datoo Danielle is situated upon a rising ground, about half a mile inland from the northern limit of the town, and but for the occurrence of occasional disturbances, which render it necessary for each chief of a clan to make his establishment a fortress, would be termed a neat farm. He is surrounded by his relatives at very short distances from his house, forming together, the superior class, or aristocracy of the island. Here we experienced not only the utmost kindness and attention from our excellent host and his connections, but were freed from the visits of impertinent curiosity. Some of the inland or mountain chiefs, noted for their total disregard of all restraint, paid me a visit at the house of the Datoo, and expressed themselves much attached to their old allies the English. They exhibited great anxiety to view our instruments, but evinced some little restlessness when they found that a compliance with their wish would be attended by disarming; such an operation being deemed nearly tantamount to disgrace. The character and weight of Datoo Danielle was, however, deemed sufficient guarantee against any loss of *caste*, and they were much delighted by the beauty of the instruments; more particularly by Fox's dipping needle, placed beyond the limits of influencing the more delicate magnetometers. Of the uses of this instrument they appeared to comprehend more than I had given them credit for, although I have remarked, as a general feature amongst the better educated Malays, as well as Chinese, that they understood more of the properties of the magnet than many educated Europeans. I expected to excite their surprise by the reversal of the poles of the Dipping Needle, and I was assisted by my very intelligent friend Mr. Wyndham, as interpreter; but the better informed of Datoo Danielle's family, gave me to believe that they understood it perfectly. Indeed I was told that the younger brother, Udin, was an ingenious mechanic, and could take a watch to pieces, and clean or repair it. He attached himself particularly to the observing position during the whole period, and seemed to take great delight in the interchange of English and Malayan terms, explaining the differences or additions of Bisayan which renders the *Soög** language almost distinct. To Datoo Danielle we were indebted, not only for the flattering hospitality during our temporary occupation of his grounds, but through his exertions were enabled to purchase the best cattle at reasonable prices, in addition to several pet animals, which at this, and our previous visit, he, as well as his mother, had been kind enough to send as presents. His fine figure, mild countenance, as well as manly independent bearing, obtained for him a most marked distinction amongst his own community. He was evidently considered by the Sultan and his wily Prime Minister, (*Datoo Muluk*) as a man neither to be despised nor trifled with. With us, he was an especial favourite, and I am sure that no one could wish greater prosperity to the Sooloo nation than the elevation of this chief to the government, either as Sultan, or Prime Minister. He is warmly opposed to the piratical dispositions of some of his

* Soög is the language of the Sooloo Group.

brother chiefs, as well as to the system of slavery which is its foundation, although he could not help expressing some chagrin at losing one of his lads, which escaped to the 'Samarang' and claimed our protection, as a subject of Spain captured by the pirates.

During our stay here many had sought protection on board the French squadron, as well as the 'Samarang', and were thus rescued from slavery. One, a relative of the deceased wife of Mr. Wyndham, a lady of Ilo-Ilo, on the southern coast of Panay, was still a captive, but beyond the reach of even Mr. Wyndham's interest. I was informed "that he might be fortunate enough to reach the 'Samarang'" but the moment the chiefs were aware (on the application for the release of the first that reached our decks,) that having once set foot on board of a ship of war, they could not be released, the others were more sharply looked after, and marched into the interior until after our departure. From two of these refugees, lately captured by the *Moros,* (Balligñinis and Illañons), taken to Balligñini, and subsequently sold at Sooloo, I learned that the pirate den at Balligñini, might be destroyed very easily, by making the attack during the interval of their cruizes, which would happen between the months May and October. That previous to quitting the stronghold, upon this service, their guns and valuable property are buried, and the entire establishment left to the care of their old men, cripples, and women, the entrance being so staked as to prevent any, but a person in possession of their secret, from gaining entrance during this interval; but that any of the lads at Sooloo, lately captured, would prove sufficiently expert to lead a boat force in without the chance of resistance. These liberated slaves would thus become valuable, as pilots, to the Spanish authorities at Manila, who were, as I understood, on the point of sending a frigate, accompanied by a powerful flotilla of *Faluas*, which would assemble at Samboangan.

During the sojourn of the French squadron at Sooloo, the disaffected people of the suburbs, or interior, or possibly those who had sustained the loss of slaves, by escaping to the ships of war, made several attempts to poison the springs at which the boats were procuring water. It was evidently intended to injure the French, as on the arrival of one of our boats, early in the morning, one of the natives immediately prevented their making use of the water, until he had cleared the spring by digging down with his hands, and throwing out from beneath the stones and sand overlying, about a dozen of the fruit of the Gomuti (*Borassus gomutus*) which, although it might not produce death, would cause great pain and vomiting. The infusion, in its powerful state, as examined by us, produced great itching of the skin, and when taken into the mouth, was excessively acrid, producing instantly a stinging and prickling sensation on the fauces and glands of the throat. The French were disposed to take the matter up warmly, but it was utterly impossible to attach the act to any particular individual, and probably was solely to be attributed to the mountain Chiefs. This same fruit is used generally both at Sooloo, as well as Borneo, to poison fish. After the water is impregnated with the infusion, they become intoxicated, swim in circles near the surface, and are then easily speared or netted. The *Tephrosia toxicaria*, and other plants are used for the same purpose, for account of which see Appendix.

CHAPTER VIII.

ILLANON PIRATES AND SOOLOO TERRITORY.

History of the Illanon pirates—Established in a spacious lagoon with a Chief of their own—Ingenious ways of escape—Their mode of construction—The Illanon vessels—Range of piratical incursions —Mode of eluding the Spanish forces—The Ballignini pirates—Court of Sooloo—Notes from Oriental Repertory of Dalrymple—Sooloo group of Islands—Toolyan—Tawee-Tawee—Bangene—Palawan—Tiroon—River Barow—Sicatack—Siboccoo—Maratua Spanish account of the origin of the friendship between the British and Sultan of Sooloo and occupation of Balambangan by the English—Instructions upon these matters from Madrid—Proceeding of Governor of Samboangan—English attacked and expelled from Balambangan—Summary of the English privileges on northern coast of Borneo—Dalrymples's account of the Sooloo independency.

THE following particulars relative to the history of the pirates infesting these seas, and known under the names of Illañon, or Lanoon, and Ballignini pirates, has been drawn up from information obtained from Officers commanding the Spanish gun boats, and employed for their suppression, and particularly from conversations with my friend Captain Villavicentio, Commandant of the Arsenal of Cavite, and to whom I am indebted for much valuable information, relative to the whole of the coasts within the Mindoro and Sooloo Archipelago, as well as for great personal kindness and attention experienced during our visit to Manila. Captain Villavicentio received his promotion about the year 1838, for his gallantry displayed during his employment in the suppression of piracy amongst the southern Philippine Group.

The Illañons, commonly termed by the Spaniards *Lanoons,* and *los Moros,* are a distinct race, inhabiting the great Bay of Illañon, on the southern part of Mageendanao, or Mindanao, having for its capital the city of Mindanao, where the Sultan resides, and where, even in the pirates' nest, Europeans and other traders meet with hospitable reception and protection! The shores of this immense bay, the eastern arm of which forms a peninsula with a very narrow neck, is closely wooded with Mangroves, running out, in most instances, into six or nine feet water, and affording sudden shelter, or concealment, to vessels drawing about six feet water. These trees, springing from roots which firmly support their main trunks, at a height of seven or eight feet above the flow of high water, cover the swampy ground which intervenes between them and a spacious Lagoon. It is this Lagoon which is the stronghold of the Lanoon pirates, and gives to them the appellation of "*Los Illanos de la Laguna*"; where, it is highly probable, they submit to their own pirate Chief, and who, acknowledging the supremacy of the Sultan of Mindañao, shields the latter from blame by this semblance of independence; it is well known, however, that any matters referred to the Sultan of Mindañao, respecting the acts of the Lanoons, especially upon questions of ransom, are speedily and effectually arranged by the Sultan.

But to return to *La Laguna*; throughout the vast range of the bay connected with this Lagoon, the Illañons have constructed numerous substantial escapes, being ways of timber, which permit of their hauling their vessels into the Lagoon upon any sudden emergency, and so amazingly expert are they in this manœuvre, that when in hot chase, my informants have pressed them close, and considered their escape impossible, they have seen them dash suddenly into one of these escapes, and before their *faluas* (or launches) could reach the spot of entry, they had been hauled out of sight, and upon presenting themselves at the opening, were saluted by a discharge of round and grape, from heavy brass guns placed in battery, and so far within this dangerous jungle, that attack was impossible. It is a well known fact, also, that the whole line of the bay is rigidly watched by *vigias*, or small look-out houses, built in lofty trees, and immediately on the alarm being given, ropes are instantly led to the point of entry, and the home population in readyness to aid in hauling them through the mangroves, as well as to defend them from further attack. The method of constructing these escapes is very simple; strong mangrove trees are driven at opposite angles, obliquely, into the mud, and their upper ends securely lashed to the growing, standing, mangrove trees, forming a V-shaped bed at an angle of one hundred and twenty degrees. These trees being stripped of their bark, are kept very smooth, and when wet, spontaneously exude a kind of mucilage, which renders them very slippery. The outer entrance of this angular bed is carried into deep water, and at so gradual an inclination, that the original impetus given by the oars, forces them at once "high and dry," and by the ropes then attached, they are instantly drawn by their allies into the interior, at a rate, probably, equal to that at which they were impelled by oars.

The vessels of the Illaños are very sharp, of great beam, and exceed ninety feet in length; they are furnished with double tiers of oars, and the largest generally carry about one hundred rowers, who are slaves, and not expected to fight unless hard pressed. The "fighting men", (or chiefs) as they are termed, amounting to thirty or forty, occupy the upper platform, and use the guns as well as small Leilas or swivels. The whole of the main interior, occupy ing about two-thirds of the beam, and three-fifths of the length of the vessel, is fitted as a cabin; it extends from one-fifth from forward, to one-fifth from aft, and at the bow, is solidly built out to the whole beam of the vessel, with hard wood baulks of timber, calculated to withstand a six-pounder shot: a very small embrasure admits the muzzle of the long gun, which varies from the six, to a twenty-four pounder, generally of brass; independent of numerous swivels, of various calibre, mounted in solid uprights, secured about the sides and upperworks of the vessel. Above the cabin is the fighting deck, upon which their heroes are placed, and upon any chance of action, they dress themselves in scarlet, and are equipped very much in the style of the armour furnished for the stage property of our theatres, varying from steel plate to ring chain, or mail shirt. Their personal arms are generally the kris and spear, but they have also a huge sword, well known as the "Lanoon sword", which has a handle sufficiently large to be wielded with two hands. In place of a mast they have sheers, capable of being raised or depressed suddenly, upon which a huge mat sail is hoisted.

The fitting of these sheers is as follows:—on the fore part of the fighting deck is a small pair of bitts, each bitt-head being placed about three feet on each side of the centre line; through the head of these bitts a piece runs, windlass fashion, its outer ends being rounded, which pass through the lower ends of the sheers in holes, this arrangement completes a triangle, having this windlass base of six feet. The heads of the sheers are joined by a solid piece of wood, perforated as a sheave hole for the halliards, by which the sail is hoisted; a third spar is attached, which, taken aft as a prop, instantly turns this mast, upon its windlass motion, to its vertical, and, almost, as by magic, we find the sail expanded or reduced instantaneously.

The slaves who have escaped from these pirates assert, that within the Lagoon they have extensive building establishments, and the means of repelling any attack which may be made upon them. The old prahus are used instead of houses, and in them they have their wives, families, or treasure, in readiness for removal to any part of the Lagoon, upon any sudden emergency. In this respect they assimilate to the Tartar race, in the Tanka boats of China; an isolated and distinct community, subject alone to the rule of their Admirals, under whom they proceed to sea in divisions, and which divi-

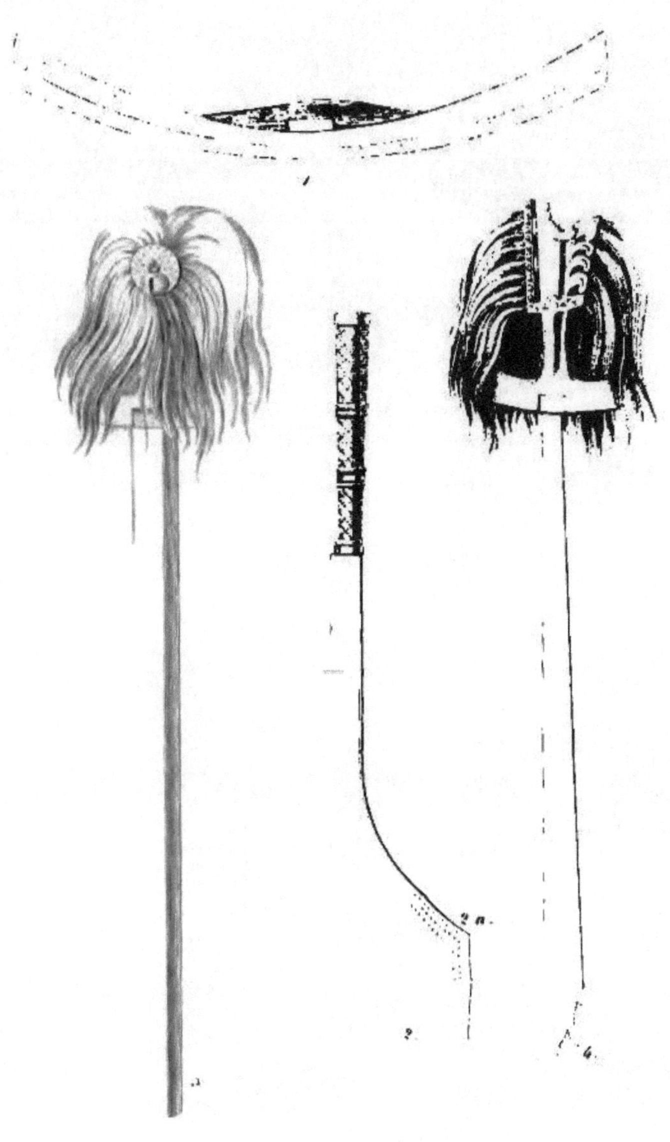

1 Ielele Shield *3 Scabbard of Kampilan*
2 Beheading Sword Illanoon *4 Kampilan Illanoon*
2 a Holes signifying the number of victims

sions occasionally unite for special purposes, amounting at times to as many as four hundred sail.

The limit of their cruizes are not confined to the neighbourhood of the Sooloo or Mindoro Archipelago, they have been traced entirely round the islands of New Guinea, on the east; throughout the straits, and continuous to Java and its southern side; along the coast of Sumatra, and as far up the Bay of Bengal as Rangoon; throughout the Malay Peninsula and islands adjacent, and along the entire range of the Philippines. Their attacks are not confined to small vessels, for we have instances as late as 1843, of their molesting the Dutch cruizers, off Java. They, however, generally act with great caution in their approach to square-rigged vessels, and can readily distinguish the difference between merchantmen and vessels of war, by the colour of their canvas. Along the entire coasts of the Philippines, they attack villages, and carry off boys and girls for slaves, and in some instances do not hesitate in kidnapping a *Padré*, for whom they demand heavy ransom, (as upon a late affair they obtained upwards of one thousand dollars.) Upon one occasion, they ventured as far into the Bay of Manila as Cavite, and captured two boys who were in a fishing boat. They had also, in this bay, within the Corregidor, where there is a Gun-boat establishment, a very severe action with this force, commanded, I believe, by a Lieutenant Elliot, an Englishman in the service of Spain. The result of this encounter was the crippling of the Spanish force, so severely, that only the Commander himself, although wounded, remained to serve his gun, and was not displeased to notice the enemy draw off; had they attempted to close with him, he had no further means of resistance. They also made a very determined attack upon one of the villages in a bay on the eastern side of Luban, and took many captives. They are particularly careful, in their habits of plunder, not to incommode themselves with any but articles of value, seeking gold, silver, arms, or ammunition, and cautiously avoiding any objects which may be recognized so as to bring them under the fang of the law; and it is to this extraordinary cunning, that, although frequently captured by the Spaniards, it is difficult to attach to them any tangible fact of piratical complexion.

At Samboanga, the Spaniards have a large force of *faluas*, commanded generally by one of their most expert officers, and promotion usually follows success. It is seldom, however, that they are fortunate either in coming up with, or in capturing, these Illañons, who, by the measures before alluded to, not only elude pursuit, but also compel them to haul off in discomforture upon reaching their ambuscade. Upon finding themselves too closely watched at the mouth of the Bay of Illaña, they have been known to drag their vessels over the isthmus, and get to sea by the north eastern coast of Mindanao, and maintaining the *ruse* by keeping up sufficient excitement to amuse the Spanish force, collected in the Bay of Illaña, commit, without restraint, the most bare-faced acts of piracy upon the shores of the Philippines, thus left exposed by the assemblage of the Spanish force to the southward.

These are the famed Illañons; but we have another notorious station in sight of Sooloo, upon the Island of

Ballignini, or Baugene of the charts, which may be considered a branch of the Illaňons. Their island affords them, at present, as much security as La Laguna does at Mindanao. It is not approachable within distance of attack, by reason of the reefs which environ it, and there is not anchorage near the edge of the reef. It is a Lagoon Island, and the entrance is so narrow that it is staked precisely similar to the *ways* alluded to at Illaňon, only admitting one vessel at a time, and that by preserving her keel exactly in the centre; consequently, the Spanish faluas cannot enter, and if they did, they would be met by batteries within, mounting above one hundred guns, all laid with great precision to this very point of entrance. There are seasons (probably May or June) when they quit the Lagoon to join their allies on their extended cruizes, when only the females, old men and cripples, are left to defend their property; and I was informed that two *faluas* entered the Lagoon on one of these occasions, by surprise, but hesitated to follow up the advantage, by retiring, without any act of hostility on either side.

These Balligñinis are considered to be under the jurisdiction of Mindanao; they have numerous haunts throughout the islets of the Sooloo Archipelago, and particularly at Malozo, and other harbours, upon the Island of Basilan, from which they attack the Spanish possessions near Samboangan. We noticed several prowling off that island when on our passage to Sooloo, The connexion is carried on complete to the eastern side of Borneo, and may reckon upon Tambisan, Maludu Bay, Tampassook, Borneo Proper, and the off lying islands of Banguêy and

Balabac, on the north, and the whole eastern coasts southerly, as far as Benjarmassim. These, although I have heard strong assertion to the contrary, I know, from sound information, as well as personal experience, to be connected by *family ties*, and although petty wars have occurred amongst them, still, upon any great question, they will unite, and act, under any great Illañon Chief. They have been traced along the whole coast of Borneo, into the Archipelago off the Malay peninsula, and I am credibly informed (indeed I had it from a Chief, whom I believe to be a *Pirate leader*) that they trade to Singapore, leaving their war boats at the Natunas, or Anambas.

The Spaniards, and, I believe, the British Government, also, still labour under the impression, that the Sultan of Sooloo has power over, and acts in concert with, all these pirates. I have taken very great pains to arrive at the proof of any such fact, and my conviction is, that he has not the *power*. He is too weak to oppose the interest of some of his Datoos, or leading Chiefs, who exhibit much greater interest in the success of the pirates; they *participate* in the *profits*, are *receivers* of, and *traffic* in the *plunder*, and will afford them every assistance in their power. But this applies only to a particular set, at the head of which is, probably, the present Prime Minister, Datoo Muluk, as arrant a rogue as any in Sooloo; he and the opium smokers are the supporters of piracy. The other party, headed by Datoo Dacola, Datoo Danielle, and their connexion, are as anxious for its suppression. I have reason to know, from my communications with the Spanish Authorities, with the Sultan of Sooloo, and Datoo Danielle, assisted by Mr. Wyndham, the resident at

Sooloo, and confidant of the parties, that the Sultan has no real power, and in the case of the appeal of the French Admiral, for his active interference at Basilan, he declared, distinctly, "that he was not responsible for any acts of aggression committed within his territory by persons who were, not only, not subject to him, but whom it was quite out of his power to control, being natives of Mindanao."

The Sultan of Sooloo was deemed the virtual Sovereign, and exercised entire control over all the northern and eastern coasts of Borneo, comprised between Pulo Tiga, near Brunai, and Cape Kanioongan, near the river Kotai; as well as throughout the Sooloo Seas, including *Banguey*, *Balambangan*, *Balabac* and *Palawan*, in so far as relates to the Malay population. Of this sovereignty, Balambangan, and that part of the coast of Borneo, comprised between Pulo Gaya and the eastern head of Muludu Bay, was ceded to Great Britain about the year 1763, at the period when the English forces took Manila, and finding the Sultan Alimudin a prisoner there, restored him to his throne and possessions. Gratitude, for this benefit conferred, induced him to adopt England as his firm Ally, and in proof of his sincerity, and by the consent of his Chiefs, perfected the Treaty of Alliance by the above cession.

The following notes, relating more particularly to this connexion with Borneo, are collected from the 'Oriental Repertory', by Dalrymple, and are extracted as far as they are borne out by our own observations.

"The limits of the Sooloo Sovereignty," as given by Dalrymple,; "are to the eastward and northward, the Philipines; westward, Borneo-Proper; and southward, Idanea, or the *inland* of Borneo.

"It is composed of an Archipelago, of which the three most considerable islands are Sooloo, Baseelan, and Tawee-tawee; of many districts on the east, north, and north-west coasts of Borneo, and of the better half of Palawan, or *Paragoa,* and of Dumaran.

"*Sooloo.*

"Sooloo comprehends the Sooloo *Islands, Tapool Isles, Palecangan Isles,* and *Pangootaran Islands.*

"Under the denomination of the Sooloo *Islands,* I consider *Sooloo, Nosa Salé, Tulëan, Bankoongan, Panganak, Koohangan, Toolyan, Boolé Kootin, Kapooal, Beeteenan, Saang, Dong-Dong, Tamboolean, Pata, Dammokan, Loombeean, Patëan* and *Teoombal.*

"There are, perhaps, few places in the world more agreeable than Sooloo, particularly in the arrangement and figure of the hills, some whereof are covered with stately woods, others with clear grass land, delightfully verdant, except in spots, where it had been burnt for cultivation, and which, from the variety it affords, conveys more the idea of pleasure than of barrenness. Many of the hills are cultivated almost to their summits, and these fields, surrounded with clumps of woodland, afford a delightful prospect to the eye, which only wants country seats, churches, and such decorations of a civilized people, to form a complete landscape, as the huts, which appear scattered over the country, are but a poor substitute for the want of better habitations. The coast is generally woody, so that it is no small pleasure to the eye, as it were, to steal through this barrier into the cultivated scenes.

Town of Sooloo.

The climate of Sooloo, although so near the Equator, enjoys a much more even and cooler temperature than that of Mindanao. The nights, in particular, are sensibly cool, and although the island abounds in water, mosquitoes are not troublesome. The range of the thermometer during our different visits was between eighty and eighty-four; highest, eighty-seven; Samboanga, eighty to eighty-eight.

Upon the authority of Dalrymple, as well as that of the present resident, Mr. Wyndham, and the living Datoos, it appears that these islands are seldom, if ever, visited by gales, although strong winds and heavy falls of rain are not uncommon, something of the nature of hurricane, or possibly an earthquake, seems to be on tradition, and is mentioned by Dalrymple.

Elephants formerly existed, but in consequence of the destruction they caused amongst plantations, they have been exterminated. This has also been the case with Unsang, in Eastern Borneo, where they were once supposed to be numerous. As they are not now known in a wild state in Borneo, it is highly probable that they were originally imported in their tame state, as presents* to the rulers, otherwise their entire destruction by the very small portion of Malays inhabiting merely the coast-line of the island is highly improbable. Deer abound in the mountains, but as their flesh is not much valued by the natives, they are seldom disturbed, and as they could not be induced to bring them to market, it is possible that they are averse to their destruction.

Of the off-lying islands, Toolyan, said to have been

* This conjecture is confirmed by Dalrymple.

T

presented to Dalrymple, by the Sultan Alimudin, is situated in the North-eastern Bay, and is described by the former as follows:—

"Toolyan is high land. The hills form an amphitheatre with a large valley in the middle, to which two or three brooks between the hills form a passage, particularly on the south part, where there is a large plain between the *Peak Hill* and the Green Ridge covered with woods; the island is not, at present, inhabited, but formerly it was, and had then many cattle, cocoa-nut, and other fruit-trees, which were destroyed by the Spaniards in their last expedition against Sooloo.

"The woods are not in general large towards the shore; they are of various kinds, and many of them good timber. The *Alexandrian Laurel* is common enough, and by much the largest I have seen, one of them, growing on the shore, being above two fathoms in circumference. There are several *Poot trees* on the island; the leaves are dark green, pretty large, and high ribbed. The Dammer is in general as white as milk, and has the consistency, and somewhat of the smell, of turpentine, it seems to ooze entirely from the bark.

"The shore is, in some places, so steep, that a large ship may careen by it, but the island is but ill supplied with water. The bay is very commodious, and secure for a few ships."

None of the other islands immediately connected with Sooloo, appear to be deserving of particular notice. *Tawee-Tawee* is termed a small, low, woody island, belonging to the Sooloo Group, but the Tawee-Tawee Group, situated on the east of Unsang, is described as a group containing fifty-six islands, and rocks; they are described only upon report.

He observes:—"In the interior of *Tawee-Tawee*, there is a lake, named *Lanän Toong-ang*, with an island in the middle, which in one place approaches so near the main that the roots of a large tree there (probably the *Ficus Indicus*) hangs over the island, and affords a passage to fugitive slaves, who have fixed themselves on the island. The lake is full of crocodiles.

"There is another lake on the island of more consequence, it is named *Doongon*, and was for some time the residence of Sultan *Badarodin*, (from thence commonly called Sultan *Doongon*) two rivers fall into the lake, and the coast between them is steep, rocky cliffs, the lake is fresh at low water, and has eight fathoms. The river leading from it to the sea, has five, six, and seven fathoms. But on the bar, which is of black sand, only one and three-quarters at low water, and about four at the height of the springs. *Towsan Doolangdoolang* adjacent to *Doongon*, has very many pearl oysters.

"The chain of islands on the south east of *Tawee-Tawee* are all low, with an infinite number of shoals between them and *Tawee-Tawee*, through which the channels have six, seven, and eight fathoms, but are extremely intricate, and so narrow that the Chinese junks used, in some places, to be pushed on with poles. These gutts are the most valuable Pearl fishery, as accessible at all times, and fish of various kinds are amazingly plentiful, and of great size. The Island of *Tawee-Tawee* has but few people, but abounds with excellent timber."

The natives of Sooloo, which composed the crew of the

prahu which accompanied us to Curan, describe these people as being of the worst description of pirates, seldom affording quarter, and feared by all the surrounding islands. They allow that they possess excellent harbours, but the musquitoes are a perfect *plague*.

"The *Sunken Island*, *Apo Lamboo*, (Sooloo Group,) within the memory of man, was above water, but is now, where shoalest, four fathom under the surface. It had a Lake three fathoms deep in the middle, without any entrance through the bank of sand which surrounded it, and was covered with trees. A hard storm overwhelmed the island, the trees, which are all dead, being still visible under water."

Bangene.—The residence of the present Balligñini Pirates has not been described, as, in the period at which Dalrymple wrote, it is probable that what are now termed piratical actions, were merely considered as the lawful pursuits of that race, and confined to vessels and people of their own colour and neighbourhood, with occasional skirmishes with the Spaniards, with whom we find them at war. No such concealment, as that now required, was then necessary; they found a welcome reception at Sooloo, and were doubtless deemed the naval heroes of that Archipelago.

The name of our friend *Budduruddin*, of Sarãwak, but latterly of Borneo, has been spelt in various ways, sometimes, *Bedruddin*, *Badruddin*, and *Buddur-uddin*, the latter being, I believe, the most aristocratic. But as he was the issue of one of the *Sooloo* Princesses, and we find the Sultan residing (temporarily, perhaps,) in *Tawee-Tawee*, called *Badarodin*, this latter, if correctly given by

Dalrymple, (which is not the case, as many of the Malay terms are now written,) is probably the true source from whence it is derived.

With respect to the Island of Palawan, which Dalrymple claims as part of the Sooloo territory, he observes :—

"Although the greatest part of Palawan be under the Sooloo dominion, yet I cannot enter into a minute description. The country, in general, is described to be plain and flat to the bottom of the hills, and no country in this quarter, abounds more in valuable productions. The Canes are esteemed the finest in the world, Cowries are very plentiful, Wax, Tortoise Shell, Baat, or Sea-slug, (*Beche de Mer*,) &c., are in abundance. Most of the *Idaan* live on the east side, for which reason it is best frequented, but as there are few *Bajows* (Sea Gipsies) the utmost benefit is not derived from the innumerable banks there. There has lately been found the *Tenjoo*, which is the gum or resin of a very large tree, it much resembles amber (Tenjoo is little different from gum copal) and forty or fifty picul may be had of it yearly. There is much Ebony and Laka, and it is said there are hot springs, and mines of gold. The best side is chiefly inhabited by a savage people, who seldom frequent the coast.

"The Sooloo dominions, *on Borneo*, are distinguished into four districts; *Tiroon*, *Mangeedara*, *Maloodoo*, and *Keeney Balloo*, or *Pappal*. The first extends from *Kanneoongan* to *Sibocoo*, which is the last river of *Tiroon*. *Mang-eedara*, extends from *Sibocoo* northward to *Towsan Duyon*. *Malloodoo* comprehends the north end of the island and *Pappal*, the districts adjacent to Borneo

Proper. However, the limits of each are not very definite. Besides these districts on the main, there are many islands adjacent to almost every part of it, which I propose to mention in succession to the district they are nearest."

Those parts of the Sooloo dominions, which are situated easterly of Sampanmangio, the island situated off the western horn of the Great Bay of Maludu, I shall extract as belonging to that part of Borneo lately visited by us; but those westerly of that island will be reserved until called for by our subsequent examination of Northern Borneo.

" *Tiroon.*—The coast is all low mangrovy land, the mountains very distant in shore, are inhabited by *Idaan;* all the country is covered with the *Sago trees*, which, being the chief sustenance of the natives, they plant in great numbers every year, to prevent any deficiency, as they are long in growing. The rivers are many, very large, and navigable. The produce of the country is chiefly Sago, and Birds' nests, both of which are in great perfection and abundance; it also yields Wax, Canes, Rattans, Mats, Honey, and some parts of it Gold, Goolega, and Baat, or Sea Slug; and it is affirmed there is great plenty of Saltpetre, and many Capis.

" The first river of *Tiroon* is *Tapeandurian* or *Tapedurian*, chiefly remarkable for the bad disposition of its inhabitants. The next, is a small river named *Samontay*, and to the northward of it *Dumaring*, which is a considerable place. A little further is *Talisyan*, to the northward whereof is a point with a hill towards the shore. There are several banks along the coast, where they collect *Baat*.

"The next river is a very large one, sometimes called *Barow*, and sometimes *Curan*, from different places near it; the first is an independent state, in alliance with Sooloo, the other is subject to Sooloo. The river has three fathoms at the mouth, but there are several shoals which require a pilot."

This river has been already noticed. It is the Pantai, one of the branches, or properly the main stream, which takes the name of *Brraou*, and gives its name to people of the district, the city being Gunung Taboor, before described. It is only in the state of Curan, and the state, at present, as in Dalrymple's time, in alliance with Sooloo. The river has eight and ten fathoms at its mouth, but for ten miles seaward, not more than three fathoms at high water. Probably the last eighty years have rendered it a fathom less, not having *now* more than two fathoms at low water.

"There is a considerable trade in Cocoa-nuts carried on from *Tuallee*, or *Celebes*, to *Barow*, which they call *Barong;* according to their accounts, the river is very deep within, and the country yields much Bird's nests, and other valuable commodities. But, although the Sooloos agree in the magnitude of the river, they deny that their country is of much consequence with respect to its produce. This river is in the bottom of a deep bay, the land running from thence to the eastward, terminating in a point of red land, called on account of its peculiar colour, *Tanna Mera*, (Red land,) off which are many islands. The northern part of this point is called *Sabannoong*, from whence the land runs as much to the westward to a large river named *Baroongan* or *Booloongan*, which is a considerable place, formerly under *Passir*, and besides the common produce of *Tiroon*, yields much gold; a very rich mine having been lately discovered. It also yields earth oil."

Dalrymple was misinformed here, the first *river*, the Sabañon, is one of the mouths of the Bulungan, and the information as to the value of its produce is nearly contradicted by the "much gold" to be obtained there. The rivers of the Curan and Bulungan districts are probably the richest in Borneo, and in the latter, *sixty thousand* Sagais are said to be located on its main branch, near the city of Bulungan. But to proceed with Dalrymple, he observes, without recording any of the other mouths of the Bulungan, which are fed by a great inland lake.

"Adjacent to this is *Sicatack*, or *Lalawang*, it is represented to be a fine bay, into which the small river of *Tolangang* falls on the south side, and that of *Mantabuling* on the north. The productions of this place are one hundred picul Black Birds' Nests, besides a little White, and the other *Tiroon* commodities.

"There are many islands close to this part of the coast, where the river of *Leeleedong* disembogues itself into the sea; one of these, named *Tarakkan*, yields twenty or thirty jars of earth oil per annum. This river is capable of receiving the largest ships, and is very populous,* it is sometimes named *Leo* and *Leedong*, from different places situated on it; inland it produces much rice, which they sell, living on Sago, as on other parts of Tiroon.

* (Bantilan) 10,000 people, twenty-five picul Birds's Nests, Wax, Sago, and Boory Mats.

"There is adjacent to this place, another red Land, called also *Tanna Mera.*

Sambacoong, which, according to the Sultan's account, yields above twenty piculs of bird's nests. It is also a large river though less than *Leo,* but it has some shoals at the entrance, and several islands divided by creeks, and covered by Nipa trees. The outermost of the islands, which terminates in a sharp point, is named *Pedadda,* it forms, on the south *Sibocoo Bay,* in which the river disembogues.

"*Sibocoo River* is larger than *Sambacoong,* but is said to have some shoals at the entrance. The current is very rapid, so that the tide never runs up, the flood only slackening the stream. All these rivers are very deep within. Off this river's mouth are situated two pretty large islands, named *Samangkarroo* or *Samakadoo,* and *Leebattick,* the last is high, and yields much Dammer.

"*Sibocoo* has more than thirty towns inland; produces forty piculs of birds' nests,* according to *Alimudin,* fifty piculs by *Bantilan's* account, 100 piculs Wax, Canes, Rattans, very fine Sago, Honey, Boory Mats, and 1,000 people."

The folowing islands belong to Curan district, and are situated immediately off the point of *Tanna Mera.* The only one deserving of notice is *Maratua,* which the natives declare to abound in valuable woods, and to be one of their most valuable fisheries. Dalrymple describes it as follows:—

"The *Maratua Islands* are six in number, *Maratua,*

* Each picul of birds' nests is reckoned in the present day at between 500*l.* and 550*l.* sterling.

Kakabban, *Sangalakee*, *Seemamak*, *Dalawan* or *Darawan*, *Pulo Panjang* and *Raboo-Raboo*.

"*Maratua* is reckoned moderately high, without hills, and has some wells of fresh water, made by the Sooloos, who go thither to collect Sea Slugs, which are in great plenty on the banks near it; it produces also great plenty of the *Coolit Sawang* or Clove Bark, there being scarce any other trees on it; there are also very curious Corallines found there, plenty of *Keema* and some *Teepy*."

No notice appears to be taken of the Ligitan group, but he passes on immediately to the district of Mangeedara, as follows:—

"The district of *Mang-eedara* is the most eastern of Borneo, extending itself towards the Sooloo *Archipelago* in a long narrow Point, called *Unsang*. This district produces Birds' nests, Wax, Lacka-wood, Dammer, and plenty of fine Gold, which is soft like wax; the most remarkable place for this is *Talassam* within *Geeong*, but the river disembogues into the North Sea, between *Tambeesan* and *Sandakan*.

"The first river in *Mangeedara* is *Tawao*, opposite to the island *Seebattick*, to the eastward of this is a Point with a high land, named *Pallass*, at which place are many cattle. The land from thence to *Geeong Bay* is divided by creeks into several islands, the southernmost and largest is called *Cooly Babang*, the northernmost, *Tanna Baloo*, the southern point of it is named *Tanjong Timban Matta*.

"The south coast of Unsang, from hence to the eastern extremity of Borneo, has many bays and rivers. These comprise the Bay of *Salooroong*; *Babatoo* a small river, where there are cattle; *Malaboong*, a river adjacent to it; *Tooncoo*, the next, and *Leebait* the last. Unsang terminates eastward by the Bluff Points, and on the northern rounding lies Tambeesan, which forms a harbour between it and the main, having about four fathoms. The country in the neighbourhood produces the Alexandrian Laurel, or *Palo Maria* of the Spaniards, much esteemed for masts. The north coast of Unsang has many bays, but none which afford shelter in northerly winds. There are on this coast many large rivers, thirty in number, from *Tambeesan* to *Sandakan*, all (except *Maroak*) branches of the *Kinabatangan* river, which comes from the Lake of Keeney Balloo."

These are the principal points and rivers mentioned by Dalrymple, and these copious extracts are given of the coast not visited by us, as a guide for those who may chance to visit those regions without being able to obtain access to the works of this persevering and intelligent navigator, the want of which I much felt. Where we have come into actual contact with the places which he has described from the reports of others, and when we consider that some errors may be attributable to the intervention of the Malay language, they have been found to be tolerably accurate. But it would be well to caution those intending to navigate the eastern limit of Borneo, that numerous dangers are reported to exist southward of Maratua, which have no place upon the charts. They were all distinctly pointed out and named by Tuan Hadji, the pilot of those regions.

Having now adverted to the authority of Dalrymple, as to the state of the Sooloo Sovereignty in 1763, I will add a few observations taken from a recent Spanish work on the Philippines, '*History of Manila,*' 1842.

As the following extracts are translated from a language in which some of the idiomatic phrases are very peculiarly expressed, and can only be properly understood in the original, I have merely to offer to my readers the general meaning of the matter made use of as relates to the islands of Sooloo and Balambangan, placed in comparison with the extract from Dalrymple, both bearing on the relations of Great Britain with Sooloo.

Speaking of the attack of the English forces, under Admiral Drake and General Draper, in 1753, the writer goes on to observe:—"The King of Sooloo, who was defending a position with the people of his tribe, delivered himself up a prisoner. The English fortified it and maintained it until the peace.

"We have already seen that Alimudin shewed himself inclined towards the Spaniards in this affair of the war with the English, probably because he perceived some booty or prize fall into the hands of Great Britain which he coveted himself.

"The Commander of the British Expedition on withdrawing his forces from Manila, offered him his protection, which he accepted, embarking with the English Admiral, who sailed from Manila, with part of his squadron and troops, which had been disembarked.

"The Admiral arrived at Sooloo, and having been detained some time there, succeeded in obtaining from Bantilan, the Sultan, the cession of the Island of Balambangan to the English East India Company, believing that having once gained a footing there, he could easily extend his command over the whole Sooloo Archipelago. At that time the English did not possess Singapore, Penang, or Malacca, and spared no means to establish themselves near China. On the arrival of Alimudin at Sooloo, he confirmed to them the cession of Balambangan. Shortly afterwards they endeavoured to transfer their forces to Tandun Dalaga, in the Island, and near the capital of Sooloo, but this they were unable to effect.

"The Governor of Zamboanga, Don Raimundo Español, endeavoured to fathom the intentions of the English. Accordingly, in conformity with instructions already received from Madrid, relative to this subject, he directed Anda to leave Manila with an Expedition consisting of a galley and two Schooners, well armed and manned, and commanded by Lieut. Col. Don Juan Canceli. His instructions were to direct his course between the Mosquito Islands, apparently with the object of pursuing the Illañon pirates, especially those of the Island of Cagayan (Cagayan Sooloo), in the neighbourhood of Balambangan, and then, under pretext of watering, or bad weather, to enter the same harbour, manifest surprise at finding the English in the dominions of His Christain Majesty, and send an official letter to the Governor, requesting him to retire immediately, and likewise acquaint him, that he would instantly inform the Governor of Manila of this affair.

"He was then to visit Sooloo, and deliver his dispatches to the Sultan; he further received instructions respecting the stipulations he was to make with him, in the event of his finding him disposed to expel the English from the establishment, and whether he required our assistance to effect this object.

He had especial orders not to make use of arms, even should he find himself possessed of superior force. This order, which deprived him of the power of acquiring laurels, added to the old enmity which existed between him and the Governor of Zamboanga, and were, without doubt, the cause which induced this vile man (in whom Anda had great confidence) to lay open his natural turbulent, envious, and domineering character. As everything was to be executed in conformity with the plan conceived and contrived by the Governor, Don Raimondo Español, Canceli did everything in his power to mar the project.

On quitting Zamboanga, by a plot contrived between himself and Aviles, an Officer equally perfidious, the supply of fresh water on board was found to be exhausted; under this pretence, instead of proceeding first to Balambangan, they presented themselves at Sooloo, before Español had informed the Sultan of that island, as previously agreed, of the sailing of the Expedition, its objects, and his intended arrival there. He so manœuvred as to alarm the whole population, and caused them to to put themselves on the defensive.

Finally, he despatched a boat to seek for water, as if he had arrived at a desert island, and wrote by this opportunity to a Chinese resident there with whom he was acquainted, to send him him twelve Princesses of that country, for himself and his Officers, and that he in return, would remit him, as payment, a good fat hog.

He knew, of course, that this letter would reach the hands of the Sultan and Datoos.

He then attempted to land, but as they would not permit him he threatened to fire on them, and would have done so had he not been restrained by the Officers of the Expedition.

He returned to Zamboanga without having been at Balambangan, or without having delivered his dispatches to the Sultan of Sooloo; which caused great disgust to tho Governor Español; he likewise meddled much with his conduct, received official complaints against and censured him: in a word, insinuated at this critical moment, into this fortress, so near to the English at Balambangan, disorder, anarchy and sedition.

Various letters passed between them, in one of which Español requested assistance to restrain his garrison, and insubordinate convicts; Canceli replied, that the only assistance which he could send him, was one mistress out of three which he possessed, of different colours.

This soldier (who was an Italian), on his arrival afterterwards at Manila, without permission, solicited orders to attack Sooloo in order to revenge the insults he had received, and instead of meeting the punishment which he richly merited, merely received slight censure from the Governor, D. Simon de Anda, and took command as Colonel of the King's Regiment, which appointment had become vacant during his absence. This is the same person whom Basco soon afterwards sent to New Spain under arrest. Español recovered the despatches and sent them by two of his Officers in a *panco* or boat to Sooloo, writing particularly to the Sultan and Datoos, and using every argument in his power to redeem the evil impression resulting from the conduct of Canceli.

At that period there were two factions amongst the chiefs of Sooloo; one party for the Spaniards, the other for the English. The latter were bought by their presents; the others were composed of those who possessed more independence and *amor patriæ*; they knew that the vicinity of the English would in the end prove their inevitable ruin; and, on the other hand, that they had nothing to fear from the Spaniards. In this party were Israel and his father. Alimudin, on account of age, had abdicated his throne in favour of his son, who, when a child, had been at Manila with his father, had been educated in the college of San José with the Jesuits, and spoke Spanish. The Sultan was much pleased on reading the letters of his friend, the Governor of Zamboanga, notwithstanding that the Datoos in the English interest answered them in rather an angry manner. This is literally their letter.

"This is the answer which we the Datoos, illustrious councillors of the kingdom of Sooloo, give to Don Raimundo Español. As regards the letter, which the two Ambassadors delivered, we must say, that we ourselves act with honour, and do not require any foreigners to direct our concerns, because we are not quite children at the breast ('*Ninos de têta*'). Above all things, we pray, that the Being who occupies heaven and earth, and governs the wills of the living, may preserve you many years."

The English invited and admitted the people of Sooloo to Balambangan, but punished them when they committed their customary cheating tricks, in a severe manner, placing the heads of the greatest princes in the stocks.

In the letter which the chief Tenteng wrote to Español, after his banishment, he complained of the Sultan having been termed in his presence a lying, prating person, "a sweet potatoe root",* and added, "what would you have done had you witnessed such treatment of the king of Spain?" This Datoo, Tenteng, was one of those who exerted himself most to show the necessity of expelling the English from that position, but could effect nothing, as the Council was divided among themselves. Finally, in consequence of having himself been placed in the stocks, he joined another chief, who was his cousin, named Dacula, in the island of Banguey, contiguous to Balambangan, together with some Illanos and slaves of his own, in all about 300. These, with merely the hope of booty, decided on attacking the English. The difficulty which Tenteng and his companions experienced was the mode of transporting their party across to Balambangan, in order to surprise the English. The latter, when they first established themselves, possessed a force amounting to 400 men, composed of Europeans and Sepoys, but the bad climate had reduced them by degrees to seventy-five infantry, and twenty-eight artillery, who now accustomed to the country feared nothing, and cared little for the *Moros*.

"At that period, Balambangan was garrisoned by that number of troops, without including the Governor, Commander of the troops, and Officers, a Commissary, and Commander of the Fort. They had a lofty and respect-

* *Y raiz de camote.*

U

able battery, whose guns all pointed seaward, having the rear cleared to the forests. On the lower part was a battery with guns, &c., *en barbet,* having a covered way, which formed the street to the Governor's house, the storehouse, and other quarters, the extremes of which were closed with a gate and portcullis.

"Tenteng and his people knew that it would be easy to attack the battery from the forest in rear, where his people could unite and hide themselves, and thus they took advantage of this want of care of the English, who had neglected to defend that side, not dreaming of attack from a point from whence they did not expect an enemy. In the meantime, those at Banguey exerted themselves, transporting the people across the sea to the woods of Balambangan, and without being discovered by the English; the natives had only three small boats, each of which would scarcely convey seven persons, but these boats, after many trips, succeeded in transporting all the people to Balambangan, disembarking them on the opposite side of the island, where the English were established, and in this manner they approached silently, concealing themselves in the wood immediately behind the Fort.

"The English little dreamed of what was about to happen, and the officers slept profoundly, having enjoyed themselves at a fete given the day and night preceding, in celebration of the Governor's birth-day.

"At dawn on the 5th of March, 1775, they formed in three divisions, attacked and burned simultaneously the Governor's house, fort, and barracks; shouts and shrieks on both sides were dreadful, those who died from wounds, as well as those who conquered, seemed to unite in fearful din to celebrate this easy conquest. At that period there were in the port two brigs, two pontoons, unladen, and a large bark belonging to the English; the Governor always had a small boat in readiness at the gate of his house; he, with six men, escaped to one of these brigs; those that were armed with guns opened a brisk cannonade towards the land. The Chief, Dacula, who had made himself master of the fort, returned this fire, and, by a chance shot, cut away the only cable of one of the brigs, which was anchored nearest the land, the sea breeze driving her on shore. The crew jumped overboard, some were drowned, and a few gained the other brig, where they met the Governor. A flag of truce was hoisted, but he did not succeed in saving any of those remaining on shore, therefore, making sail, he quitted the smoking ruins of this position, over which he now ceased to have command.

"Tenteng captured forty-five cannon, two hundred and eight cwt. of powder, two hundred and fifty muskets, twenty-two thousand shot, a great deal of iron, lead, tin, and gold in bars, more than fourteen-thousand dollars (Spanish) in coined silver, a large quantity of muslins, and other kinds of merchandize, the whole valued at one million Spanish dollars.

"The Datoos, after this act, fearing the vengeance of the English, declared Tenteng unworthy of the privileges of a Sooloo Chief, and banished him the kingdom, with all his followers.

"The Sultan wrote to the Governor of Zamboanga, informing him that neither he nor any of the Datoos took part in this *unlawful* affair, and begged him to send him

U 2

some books on the right of nations, to enable him to answer the charges that might be brought against him by the English.* In another letter he *re-claimed* protection and assistance, in virtue of the Treaty celebrated in 1737, and begged a remittance of arms, ammunition, and his little squadron. Don Raimundo Español answered, that he could in no way assist him, either with arms or troops, but as to the books he would do so willingly, though, at that moment, he did not know if any such were in his possession.

"On the 23rd of March, Tenteng arrived at Sooloo with his brig and rich trophies. These were such convincing proofs in his favour, that he was immediately admitted. He delivered up all the munitions of war to the Sultan, with two thousand dollars as homage, and desired to divide the booty with all the Datoos, as if they had taken part in the enterprize. Enthusiasm reached its height; they not only annulled the proscription, but, if they had known the title, would have declared him 'Most High and Eminent Servitor of his Country.'

"With this supply of guns and ammunition, they now believed themselves independent of the assistance ar alliance of the Spanish, and thought they could face any English force which might appear.

"On the 6th of July, an English ship-of-war arrived to reclaim Balambangan, and the effects robbed from that establishment. She remained five days. The Sultan communicated this to the Governor of Zamboanga, Bayot, telling him, 'that the Captain, on hearing the firm answer of the Council, seemed greatly vexed and

* Be it remembered that he had studied with the Jesuits.

astonished.' The same Chief, Tenteng, attempted to do at Zamboanga as he had done at Balambangan, but a slave, named Reyes, disclosed the project to Bayot, and by this means frustrated his design, and he was unable to surprize the garrison. His designs being thwarted, he crossed to the Island of Zebu, where he committed a number of piracies."

As all this narrative relates particularly to our former privileges on the northern coast of Borneo, and our independent right to maintain our territories in that region, either increased by new Treaties, or continuing those which were executed of old, I think that my readers will excuse the digression from the main points of our own immediate voyage, particularly as the Sultan of Sooloo, has been pleased to admit England as "her old and staunch Ally." Indeed, it is probable that by the very act of forgiveness, mentioned by this Spanish writer (not evidently a friend of England), they became by gratitude more distinctly connected. The object of the work in question has evidently been directed to the assertion of the Spanish claim on the entire Sooloo Territory, including our undoubted position on Balambangan. I am, therefore, tempted to add a few further extracts from Dalrymple, who, in concluding his 'Essay on Sooloo,' observes:—

"The chief object of this Essay is to evince the Sooloo Independency, to which these historical anecdotes are only an introduction; and for this reason it has been thought expedient to make a separation of the ancient and modern history; refering to the former all incidents which occurred before 1734; when the present Sultan succeeded to the throne: and to the last, all the circumstances which I have been able to collect of the late transactions, whether regarding the Spaniards or others."

"As the proof, deduced from original papers, will plainly evince the modern independence, it will excuse a discussion of the ancient Spanish pretensions in that quarter." *

"The present Sultan has promised the author a detail of all the circumstances since his first accession; particularly regarding the Spaniards, whose protection he claimed, and by whom he was afterwards put in irons! The *Marquis* of *Ensenada's* letter plainly confutes the *Spanish allegation* in defence of their conduct, 'that the *Sultan* was detected in illicit correspondence and double dealing.' Were the proofs much clearer than they are, the most they could make of it would be, 'the biter bit.' As it is evident, from that letter, the *Spanish plan* was formed before the *Sultan* had given any ground for their perfidy; although they were fairly outwitted, if not outbullied, by the *Sooloos*; for it is obvious that the *Spaniards* suffered more by the *expences* of the *expedition* and the *disgrace* it did them, than the *Sooloos*, by any mischief from the *Spaniards*; and from a full knowledge of both, the author is convinced that the *reduction* and *maintaining* Sooloo, under the *Spanish yoak*, is beyond the power of the *Philippine Government*.

"The *reduction* of the *Moorish States* has been a favourite object with the *Manila politics*, ever since the

* *Vide* 'Full and clear proof, the Spaniards can have no claim to Balambangan.' 8vo. 1774.

Spanish establishment there; but it has always been much easier effected in *speculation* than *practice*; for many years past the *Spaniards* have been losing ground; and perhaps arming the *Indians* is the only method of freeing the *Spanish Islands* from the *invasion* of the *Moors*. However, this is not a step consistent with *Spanish caution*, and, perhaps, too dangerous ever to be attempted. This subject will particularly occur hereafter, and the author means to be very particular on this head, as it may be extremely useful, in case we pursue an interest in this quarter.

"To Sooloo, (which as well as the Philipinas was anciently under the *dominion of Borneo*) then an obscure place, a *Bajow* from *Jehore* retired with a *beautiful daughter*, whom the *Jehore Sultan* wanted to place among his *mistresses*. The *fame* of *this beauty* drew many of the *Eastern Princes* to Sooloo, and amongst the rest, one from *Java*, who won the Prize; executing the penalties enjoined by the father; which were, to introduce *Elephants, spotted Deer*, &c., the *Javan* making a *voyage* to *Siam* for that purpose. He continued at Sooloo until his death, which happened soon after, leaving his *beautiful widow*: sometime after, a *Serif*, driven hither by stress of weather, was compelled by the *Natives* to an agreeable penance, in the enjoyment of *Beauty* and a *Crown*; and from this *descendant* of *Mahomet* the present *Sultan* is sprung."—*Dalrymple*, 1792.

*** The Italics are Dalrymple's.

CHAPTER IX.

BATAN, HOA-PIN-SAN AND LOO-CHOO.

Take leave of Sooloo — Cagayanes Group—The Natives—Camden Shoal—Loss of Jib-boom in a Squall off Point Calivite—Arrive at Manila—Return to Hong-Kong—Examine Defences of Canton —Leave for Batan—Excursion to Ibayat, accompanied by the Dominican Padres—Difficulty of landing—Explore Interior—Embarcation hazardous—Island of Samasana—Slight shock of Earthquake—Sail for Y-nah-koo—Beneficial results of the transportation of Plants—Visit Hoa-pin-san—Attack of Mosquitoes—Tia-usu—Geological features—Proceed to Loo-Choo—Anchor in the roads of Napa Kiang—Loo-Chooans visit to the Ship—Droll curiosity of one individual in taking its dimensions—Find French Priest and his Servant.

On the 24th of February I paid my final visit of ceremony to the Sultan and chiefs of Sooloo, and at this visit I endeavoured to impress upon them the great pleasure I anticipated in being able to communicate to the British Government the very decided proofs of friendship which they exhibited in the case of the Lascars; the disavowal of anything approaching to ransom, and of other releases of British subjects at the request of Mr. Wyndham, previous to my visits to his territories. To that gentleman himself, I feel the Government are particularly indebted for his great personal sacrifices; indeed, I wish most sincerely that he may recover the sum of six hundred dollars for which he made himself liable, on account of the Lascars. Independent of this, his entire time was engrossed during our detention, and his mercantile pursuits much damaged by the prosecution against Si-Dawut, to whom he had made extensive advances. To myself, personally, I feel that his services were most kind and disinterested, and at my night conferences with the Sultan and Chiefs, divested of ceremony (and also of jackets), without his powerful assistance and interpretation, my objects, which, as it was impossible to have conversed about them in public meetings, could not have been explained, and therefore would not have been achieved.

Numerous friendly questions relating to their general conduct; the altered state of affairs in Borneo; the determination of European Powers to suppress piracy, as well as slavery; and the punishment which had already ensued, and would certainly fall upon those who continued such practices, aided or abetted the actors, or even admitted them into their ports, were all gravely discussed; and I feel persuaded that more moral good was effected amongst the leading powers by this mode of argument, than would have been by more violent measures, whatever force might attend them.

On the 25th of February, we bid farewell to our Sooloo friends, and experiencing very light airs had not progressed further than the island of Salleolookit, on the morning of the 27th: and as the result of our Magnetic observations at Samboangan gave the dip of the Magnetic Needle northerly, and those at Sooloo nearly an equal quantity southerly, it was highly important that we should take advantage of every available spot of *terra firma* included within those positions, to determine, approximately at least, the Zero curve. Independent of this, our friends in the French squadron had informed us, that they doubted the correctness of the Longitude of the Duo Bolod Islets, which they considered to be about fifteen miles in error. This position on Salleolookit offered the means of approximating this point very satisfactorily, as the bearings were very little to the eastward of south. Our observations place this rock in Lat. 6° 40′ 52″ N. Long. 121° 24′ 30″ E. Dip. 0° 17′ 30″ Var. 0° 17′ 20″ E., and by the bearings and assumed Longitude of Sooloo, we found no reasons to suspect it to be out in *relative* position.

On the 28th we succeeded in crossing the stream which sets strongly through the Straits of Basilan, and fetched in with the land about twenty miles to the northward of Calderas, when by making short tacks along the western coast of Mindanao we succeeded in making better progress.

On the 28th March, we stood off to seek the *Cagayanes* Group, about which we had received very conflicting accounts, and about nine, A.M., of the following day effected a landing on a small rocky islet, situated in the channel between the two largest islands. A rapid survey was made during our short detention of six hours, by which we discovered that neither the Charts nor the sailing directions, by Horsburgh, afford any correct information regarding this group. Three more islets and very extensive reefs, extending as far as the eye could reach from our most elevated station, which was about 100 feet above the level of the sea, will have to be added to those before known. The islets are situated upon the outlines of the northern reef, the most distant about ten miles, but as they would become a subject for further enquiry, no further delay was incurred. During my detention at our observing position, we were visited by a boat from the Pueblo, where we noticed a white-washed fort and church, as well as a pretty large village; we had not time to examine it, but one of the authorities deputed to make enquiries about us, and who endeavoured to make himself understood in a jargon composed of bad Spanish, Malay and Bisayan, assured me, that everything which I enquired for (consisting principally of Bullocks, Vegetables and Fowls,) could be procured at the Pueblo, and from the general tenor of the enquiries made by him, I was led to infer that Whale ships frequently touch here for water and refreshments. The object of our visit, particularly as none of our people visited the Pueblo, was a matter of deep mystery to them, as they could hardly be brought to imagine that so many human beings could be induced to broil themselves for six hours under a tropical sun for pastime.

The bays or creeks, situated in the interior of the extensive sound, formed by the two greater islands, are very picturesque and retired, and have, at their entrance or chord of the bay, a depth of not less than three and a half or four fathoms.

If the entrance to this sound from the northward should be found clear from danger, or even accessible by dint of pilotage, this group would form a most important naval position, commanding the entire range of these seas, and be a most convenient spot for relief or recruit to cruizing, or disabled, vessels. The cottages which lie scattered in the little nooks or bays, did not present, as viewed from the boats, either a neat or cleanly appearance but the race composing the crew of the boat which visited us, probably Bisayans, were clean-limbed, light coloured, and vigorous; very respectful and courteous in manners, inheriting the politeness of the Spaniard and superior Malay: a combination resulting, probably, from Malayan fathers, and Spanish mestizo mothers. The rock upon which our observations were made, is situated in Lat. 9° 35′ 30″ N., and Long. 121° 15′ 30″ E., Var. 0° 45′ 3″ E. Dip. 7° 37′ 0″.

Horsburgh in his notice of this group, p. 573, makes some remarks upon the depth *within* this Sound, although he passes at six leagues! The interior soundings obtained by us, varied from four to fifteen fathoms (some few casts much deeper) in the great Sound, and at its northern outlet, where I hoped to find a channel of sufficient depth to admit the 'Samarang', I could not find more than twelve feet. On quitting this group I had intended working along the western shores of Panay, or as generally termed by those navigating these seas, "the *Antique Coast*", and passing to the eastward of Semirara and Mindoro, take that channel for Manila This is considered the most certain course, and is adopted by all the small traders employed about the Philippines, in consequence, as they assert, of strong north-easterly winds prevailing on the east of Mindoro, when calms and light airs are experienced on its western side. But the breeze leading me off shore in a line for one of the reported shoals, I could not forego the opportunity of searching for it, and if possible securing its position. We did not succeed, and as I subsequently found that it was termed "Camden shoal"; I suspect, therefore, that it was only an erroneous position for the Panagatan shoal, on which we *know* that the 'Camden' was wrecked.

On reaching the northern extremity of Panay, we found by our sea reckoning that the three islets of Moralisan, Balbatan and Napula, were situated much more to the eastward than where they are placed upon the recent Spanish Charts, and on sighting Quiniluban, the southernmost of the Cuyos Islands, I observed that the second island in sight, then bearing S.W., when Quiniluban bore W.S.W., was not placed on the Chart furnished by the Admiralty; but on the private set of Spanish Charts furnished by my friend Capt. Salomon, I noticed that they were nearer the truth, although not correct. Having also on my passage up these seas, in December last, noticed the appearance of rocks and islets to the westward of the Cuyos, which are not placed upon the Charts, I am disposed to think that the entire Cuyos Group, indeed, all southerly of Capt. Ross's Survey, terminating I believe about the southern limit of the Apo Bank, and Eastern Calamianes, are very much in error, and render the passage eastward of Palawan unsafe, until further surveys have been effected in that region.

A favourable leading wind, enabling us to make

northing at the rate of ten knots an hour, decided me on giving up the passage eastward of Mindoro; before midnight we had reached the southern limit of the Apo Bank; and passing between it and Mindoro found ourselves a little before dawn on the morning of the 10th, off Point Calivite, the north-western extreme of Mindoro. Here we experienced a very sudden squall, from one of the ravines under this very high land, which taking us under all possible canvas snapped off our jib boom short at the cap, without affecting the royal masts, or giving the ship any great careen. This happening nearly at the moment that it became requisite to haul sharp up to beat through the passage between it and Luban, I was afraid that the loss of such an important spar would cripple our progress, until we could replace it by another; this, however, was very speedily effected. About ten o'clock we lost the second under nearly a similar squall, but this was apparently a defective stick, and as we were now reduced to the spare mizen topmast, it took some time to adapt this for a jib boom. Very much to our astonishment we found the ship cared little for its loss, *staying freely*, and going nearly ten knots, close hauled, notwithstanding the absence of this most important spar and its canvas. About three, P.M., we cleared the islands, and with a leading wind reached the entrance of Manila Bay, at ten, P.M., and at noon on the 20th, reached our anchorage off the city.

Referring to my extracts from the Spanish work upon the Philippines and Sooloo, it will be remembered that the author advanced pretensions to great part of the islands composing the Sooloo Archipelago, but as they consider that their influence extends more particularly to the island of Basilan, immediately in connexion with Mindañao, the intelligence brought by us caused a very considerable sensation. As it frequently occurs in arguments of this nature, that partizans, in their eagerness, forget their principal object, one of the strongest advocates in favour of the Spanish claims, forgetting his object in proving the Spanish authority, observed: "but we can even prove the fact of tribute having been received from Basilan by the Sultan of Sooloo, within the last five years, that is, of birds' nests and Pearl shell"!

During our detention, refitting, the French frigate, 'Sabine', arrived from Basilan, when we were informed that the French force had been engaged two days against the town at Malozo, which they had destroyed, suffering on the part of the French, a loss of three men killed and several wounded.

On the 20th of March we took our departure for Hong-Kong, and on the 22nd, about five miles to the southward of Port Calaan, on the Island of Luzon, grounded upon a coral ledge, which we found *outside* of us, on the off shore tack; showing the Charts off this river to be defective, but as it was almost calm, and without swell, no damage was sustained, although we were somewhat puzzled to find our way out of the dilemma. On the 28th, we reached the Batanes Group, and remained a day at San Domingo for observations and stock, and with a fine breeze from thence reached Hong-Kong on the 1st of April, where we found H.M. Ships 'Castor' and 'Iris'. Gapt. Graham of the former, being left senior Officer during the absence of Sir Thomas Cochrane at Singapore, Trincomalee, &c., &c.

Nothing important transpired during our refit. On the 28th I made an excursion up the river to Canton in a chopboat, attended by my gig, in order to examine narrowly the state of the defences and difficulties to be encountered, should it be found necessary to carry vessels of war up to Canton. The result of this examination showed me, that although the Chinese had used great efforts to raise obstructions to the navigation, that nature, assisted by a little naval energy, which can generally be found when required, would not render our advance impossible; and as to the fortifications, I could plainly perceive that we had not taught the Chinese any of that art, as positions could generally be taken up where their batteries would be powerless, and this nowhere more conspicuous than upon our old friends the Wangtong Islands. Returning by "Blenheim Channel," I found that they had been more successful in blocking the river on that line, and that our native vessel was for some time delayed by the rocks which had been placed there. Nevertheless I am confident that these could easily be removed, and leave even a deeper channel than we had before, if *required.* But should our forces again be called into requisition on any of these waters, I trust the boats of the squadron will be found fully equal to any service of this nature which may required. Indeed, I cannot see of what use anything beyond our smallest steamers were in this river, beyond housing the crews of the acting force.

On the 9th of May, we quitted Hong-Kong, in company with H.M.S. 'Castor', parting company off the Lema

Islands, she for a cruize in that neighbourhood, for exercise, and ourselves for Batan, Meia-co-shimas, Loo-Choo, Korean Islands, &c. On the 14th, we passed close to the Pratas Bank, the weather fine, with light winds, but rather hazy. At noon, just as we were about to send the crew to dinner, we found ourselves embayed by the shoals which had not been distinguished by the man on the look-out at the mast-head. We fortunately tacked, and cleared these difficulties, which, at night, would have proved of dangerous importance, although a course very wide of these dangers might have been adopted, had it not been our object to make this close examination by day. One thing, of which we were not before aware, was discovered; viz., that the line bounding the Pratas dangers is not circular, but, as far as we could observe, runs in bays formed by projecting points of the reef. After clearing these dangers, our course was directed for Batan, with the view of completing some unfinished parts of that group, which the present condition of the weather seemed to favour, or even, failing in this, to complete our stock, and obtain a more eligible departure for verifying the Longitude of the Meia-co-shimas.

We reached our anchorage at St. Domingo on the 7th of May, and on mentioning my intention of attempting a landing on the Island of Ibayat (considered almost inaccessible) the Dominican Padres of the convents volunteered not only to accompany us, and afford their valuable aid, as interpreters, but also their almost absolute power in procuring the services of the native population of that island, who, although termed *Indios Christianos*, are very little removed from *Los Bravos* (wild Indians), or those

X

who have not yet been admitted as members of the church. As landing is at all times hazardous, and can only be achieved by the aid of a body of men prepared for this service, the Padres had sent forward notice of their intended visit by one of their boats; the ship quitted San Domingo on the afternoon of the 22th, and favoured by light airs, and a smooth sea we effected our landing at the western side of the island, about five, P.M. Even under these very favourable circumstances, it was far from agreeable, charged as we were with the care of valuable instruments; free and unshackled by such cares, and in pursuit of pleasure or adventure, it is probable that I should have thought little beyond the cold bath which momentarily appeared to threaten. Immediately our baggage, &c., was landed, it was shouldered by the natives in attendance, and we now commenced the ascent of the cliff, (a perpendicular height of ninety feet) by the aid of zig-zag paths and very indifferent ladders; fifty feet more, of rather steep work brought us to the summit of the outline, putting our lungs to the proof.

The exterior of the Island, as viewed from the sea, is dismally uninteresting, presenting a blank barren outline, defying disembarkation to any but those acquainted with the locality, and defensible against any attacking force; and moreover, without anchorage. Great was our surprise, then, on entering, what may be termed the crust of the island, at beholding a highly cultivated and gently undulating surface at a slightly lower level than its coast-line, and in many spots exhibiting patches of good timber trees. After a pleasant walk of about two miles, we reached the Pueblo of San Rafael, where we took up our quarters at the house devoted to the Padres, which had been already cleansed for our reception, and where our good friends Padres Remigio and Tomas, used every exertion to render us comfortable. As the uncertainty of embarking became an important consideration, and I have often experienced that the delay of one unhandy individual has risked the lives of all, I determined on reducing our number to the *minimum* requisite for conducting the service on which we were engaged. It consisted of Mr. M' Dougall, my amanuensis, coxswain, two seamen, and the optician. The ship had orders to remain 'off and on' under canvas, and in addition to sounding, had instructions to light beacons at points, already fixed upon. We were hardly housed when bad weather came on, and during our stay we had reason to think, as we had no "chimney pots or tiles" over our heads, and knew that the good ship 'Samarang' had plenty of sea-room, that we were quite as happy on shore; although at times, when rain confined us within doors, reduced to the necessity of going to school to the Padres, who strove hard to instruct us in the language of Ibayat.

This visit of the Padres was connected with their pastoral duties, and had not at this period, I believe, been performed for several years. Those who visited Batan in their boats were in communication with the Padres, and were consequently accustomed to pursue their religious exercises; but the women were seldom included in these excursions, consequently those inclined to marry could not put off the ceremony, to the almost *sine die* visit of the pastor, for whom, not having seen, they probably cared but little. The routine duties of worship had been per-

x 2

formed by persons brought up in the convents of Batan and duly deputed by the superior authority to act here; but their province did not exceed the repetition of prayers, consequently the duties of our friends, registering, baptizing, catechizing, and marrying, throughout five Pueblos, formed no light occupation.

The marriage arrangements seemed even to puzzle the Padres; there were numerous candidates awaiting their arrival, some to be married according to the rites of the church; some who had not thought this ceremony of sufficient importance to delay their union, but now wished to come under the wing of the church; others, whom the acting ministers, or Captains of the Pueblos, suggested as likely to follow their own inclinations after the departure of the Padres, were persuaded to be united, in anticipation, in order to secure them under church discipline. The assemblage of these parties and the pairing off, sometimes a husband missing, at others the wife, boys of sixteen to women of twenty-six, and *vice versâ*, with many other irregularities, or inequalities, apparent to civilized life, rendered the scene ludicrous in the extreme, and I am fully satisfied that three-fourths of the parties concerned, understood as little of the ceremony as the natives of the South Seas before the visits of the missionaries.

During our detention on this island, we visited the Pueblos San Rafael, Santa Rosa, and Santa Lusia. The two highest elevations on the islands are Santa Rosa, on the north, and Mount Riposet, on the south, the latter of which became my principal position, in sight of Batan and Dequey. The houses are constructed similar to those on Batan, with very strong timber frame work, put together with great skill, much in the style of ship-building, and thatched with fine grass, resembling rush, but very strong. The population of each Pueblo is estimated at 400 souls, which will give about 1,600 for the whole island. The people appear to be of a peculiarly mild disposition, lighter coloured, better formed, although less civilized, than those of Batan, and from the difficulty of following any maritime vocation, are completely devoted to agricultural pursuits. Notwithstanding the unpromising exterior of this island, it is infinitely more fertile, as regards its produce, than Batan; the latter has, however, a richer volcanic soil, better adapted for garden than agricultural produce, although many fruits are abundant here which fail in Batan, particularly Limes and Pine Apples. This may result from the perfect shelter of this basin-formed island. The rocks and cliffs even to their summit, on the western side of Ibayat, are coralline limestone, apparently upheaved: on the eastern side generally of black basalt. The only two elevations are of a red steatitic clay, with occcasional streaks of a whitish substance, like baked pipe-clay, or porcelain. Their exports to Batan consist principally of maize, fowls, and timber, the latter generally of hard woods and ebony, for anchors. As money is not current with them, our payments were in calico (provided for such purposes, before leaving England), a yard of this substance proving far more attractive than a dollar at Batan. Their services were very freely and cheerfully rendered, and many expressed the hope of meeting us again, during our visits to Batan, where they promised to bring objects of natural history, for which we had made inquiry, and which our short visit precluded obtaining at present. We now found that quitting the island was not such an easy matter, and our patience was severely tested, it being necessary to transfer instruments backwards and forwards as often as opportunities for embarking seemed to offer. Even when attempted it was hazardous; but trusting to the skill of my own well-tried crew, added to the superiority of our pet cutter, it was achieved without damage to instruments; although with rather more of the cold bath than suited the constitution of some of our party, having to pull some distance in their wet clothes, exposed to a glaring sun before we regained the ship. After being forced by the currents past the north end of Ibayat, we bore up for Batan, and reached our anchorage on the 28th, completed observations, stock, &c., and again quitted on the 29th, coasting the eastern sides of Ibayat, Siayan, &c.

The following morning we found ourselves close off Yámi or the northernmost of the Batanes Group, and were fortunate enough to effect a landing on a detached islet, and obtain its position. This enabled us to efface from the chart the islets termed North Bashees, which have no existence in the position assigned to them, nor in the visual radius from the mast-head position of the 'Samarang', 108 feet above the level of the sea. The channel between the two northernmost islands is safe, and carries soundings, but too deep for anchorage, as well as the bottom being rocky. The position of the islet lying off the south extremity of Yami, is in Lat. 21° 5′ N. Long. 121° 54′ E.

Our next object was to search for Ladd's rock laid

down to the southward of Botel Tobago, but although our reckoning placed us near enough to observe any breaker, the placidity of the sea rendered this impossible as twelve feet water on it is assigned by Capt. Ross, the latest authority. Passing to the eastward of Botel Tobago, we found ourselves on the morning of the 3rd of June near the Island of Samasana. This being a doubtful position, a landing was effected, and a cursory survey of its southern features completed. We found a very snug little village concealed within the bamboo hedge skirting the sea, and a population probably amounting (after the Chinese habit of reckoning, ten souls to one house) to 150. Two small junks were on the beach, which they informed us belonged, as well as themselves, to *Tai-wan*, the general term for Formosa in these regions. The island appeared to be under cultivation, chiefly Rice, and the village valley laid out in gardens, producing Maize, Cucumbers, Cabbage, and customary Chinese produce. As the sun at this season was rather beyond the limits of observation by sextant, we were reduced to remain on shore to obtain the Latitude by the stars. About six, P.M., just as we were all comfortably seated upon the apex of a small hillock, discussing the dinner sent on shore to us, our nerves were somewhat disturbed by the sudden shock of an earthquake; the sensation to myself, seated upon a keg, was as if the hillock was about to burst at its apex, and disperse our comestibles in *radii* from the centre. The state of our appetites, after fasting since 8 o'clock, A.M., soon, however, enabled us to resume operations, the shock having failed either to disarrange our table, or disturb the crust of the wine. At the same instant the 'Samarang' having got into troubled water (heavy overfalls) to the westward, records, "6. 45, ship touched the ground", but no bottom with fifty fathoms; and it is, I believe, at this moment firmly adhered to by the unbelieving, that she did touch, but did not *stop* or receive any *damage*.

Having completed our operations here, making the position of the N.W. end of the island in Lat. 22° 38′ 20″ N. Long. 121° 26′ E., we embarked at 8. 30, the following morning, and shaping our course for the Meiaco-shimas, on the 6th of June, reached the Island of Kumi of the charts, Y-nah-koo of the natives. Provisioning one of the cutters for seven days, the master was despatched in her to land, erect stations, and make the necessary preparations for the survey of this island; but the immediate object in view was to prepare the inhabitants for my visit, and to find out the best position for landing, in order that the delay arising from explanation, &c, might not frustrate the measurement of the meridian distance within the shortest interval. Passing on in the ship we reached Port Haddington on the 8th, about two, A.M. Our friends were not, however, so soon at the beach as we had anticipated, and after the chief had made his appearance, and resumed his customary familiarity, I thought that I could discern something not exactly like a want of cordiality, but rather a fear of some influence which prevented the exhibition of that *natural feeling* of friendship so freely exhibited at our last visit. Having completed water, we quitted on the 9th and on the following evening landed at Y-nah-koo, where we found that the authorities had behaved very civilly to the master and his party, and appeared to be fully prepared to further our wishes in the examination of the island:

of which intention they had already received notice from Pa-tchung-san.

The day following was chiefly devoted to preparatory arrangements, Astronomical observations, measuring Bases, &c.; and as no convenient anchorage was found, the 'Samarang' was compelled to continue under canvas, depriving some of those wishing to stretch their legs of the opportunity of mounting the hills. At an early hour the following morning, reinforced by some of the civilians from the ship, and amply provided with horses by the authorities, we commenced our examination of the island; the master having also received instructions to endeavour to complete the circuit in the opposite direction, by the west and south-east. Although this was strictly a surveying expedition, yet being all fairly mounted, and the delays at the stations affording time to look about us, we enjoyed ourselves amazingly, ascending gradually until our advanced position, where we interlaced with the signals of the master below, afforded us a complete view of the island, at an elevation of 700 feet above the sea.

Y-nah-koo has four villages, one on the west, one on the south, and two on the north, one of which is inland, in a basin-shaped valley. The principal town and Port is Pseu-bang-yah in the north, in which we noticed several junks of about fifty tons riding; but the entrance from the sea is so very narrow and shallow, that ingress and egress can only be effected at Spring tides, and very smooth water. We noticed the operation of getting one to sea. The inhabitants are a still poorer description of people to those on Pa-tchung-san, and as the island is not so fertile, we did not notice the same luxuriance of growth in the vegetables which they presented to us. Cattle, Horses, and Goats appear to be pretty abundant, which the greater extent of grazing would tend to favour.

From the condition of these people, their natural timidity of strangers, difficulty of landing, &c., it is not an island calculated to afford refreshments or supplies to any visitors. On the contrary, I was so much impressed with this fact that I took care to accept nothing from them but vegetables, and left them various seeds, potatoes, and tops of Pine Apples, in the hope of improving their gardens. During our intercourse with all of the islands in these seas, from Singapore, northerly, it has been an object with me to introduce from one place to another all the most useful trees and vegetables, making the Island of Batan our chief depository; and we have the satisfaction of knowing, that in the latter island all the objects introduced have flourished beyond our most sanguine expectations. It is to be hoped that at some future day this may be found to be successful also at Samasana. One case occurs to me where this habit has not been productive of the intended benefit. It is perhaps travelling a little out of my present limits, but as a fact bearing on the introduction of trees, &c., is not unworthy of record: Capt. Bligh originally introduced the Orange and Guava trees at Point Venus, Tahiti, both have produced finer fruit than in the places from whence they were transported, the latter is now deemed a pest; it overpowers everything, destroys vegetation near it, injures the cattle, and is there considered the promoter of dysentery. A law had been passed

PA POO-HOO

Native of Fee kien san.

previous to 1839, requiring the destruction of this tree. It must have increased prodigiously between 1825 and 1839, as I recollect but one tree at the former date bearing fruit, not exceeding a billiard ball. In 1840 they exceeded the size of a cricket ball, and were in great profusion, the entire underwood of Point Venus being composed of this tree.

The composition of Y-nah-koo differs from its nearest neighbours, Koo-kien-san and Pa-tchung-san, being chiefly of coralline limestone, its highest peak attaining the elevation of 770 feet. All the ranges are capped with trees and brush-wood, but excepting the Pine Fir, which contains a great portion of resin, rendering it specifically heavier than water, none attain any size. The position of the northern beach to the west of the town of Pseu-bang-yah, is in Lat. 24° 25′ 58″ N. Long. 122° 55′ 53″ E.

During the interval employed in the examination of the island the ship discovered a bank of soundings to the north-eastward of the town; it is apparently a coral ledge, but affords tolerable anchorage in fine weather.

Quitting Y-nah-koo, which is conspicuous from the sea by the peculiar sharpness of its single peak, we returned to Port Haddington, to rate, and sailing the same evening, shaped our course in search of the group Hoa-pin-san of the charts; although not known by this name by our Pa-tchung-san pilots. Indeed, we found that the names assigned in this region have been too hastily admitted, as may be remarked in Meia-co-shimah and Y-nah-koo, for Madjicosima and Kumi.

On the morning following we were sufficiently near to

Hoa-pin-san to secure a landing for the meridian distance, but here as in other positions near the Northern Tropic, the sun at this period being nearly vertical at noon compelled us to have recourse to star observations for Latitude. Towards sunset the ship found anchorage on a bank to the eastward of Pinnacle Island, and thus prevented her being drifted beyond our sight before the morning. Had such an event occurred, it would have placed us in rather an awkward dilemma, as the strong eastern currents, attended with very light airs, would have prevented her recovering her ground, and our eatables were already reduced to a low ebb, although most delicious water abounded. Every luxury they say has its evil, and not long after sunset we had reason to repent of the proximity of this same luxury. Scarcely had we commenced with the stars than the mosquitoes attracted by our lamps, attacked us in the most merciless manner. A determined action, with these pests, was vigorously maintained for nearly half an hour, at the expiration of which period, the exclamation of my assistant and boat's crew, added to some very *piquante* hints, that we had enough to satisfy any opponent as to the actual Latitude of the position (differing merely two seconds north and south), induced me to withdraw my forces to the salt water, leaving the instruments until the more powerful sun dispersed our enemies. Hauling off to an anchorage about 100 yards from our position, we obtained a release from further punishment, and enjoyed tolerable repose. Having embarked our instruments in the morning, and obtained another station on the Pinnacle Island, we rejoined the ship.

On the 16th, we endeavoured to obtain observations on Tia-usu; a landing was effected, but the absence of sun prevented our obtaining satisfactory observations, and bad weather coming on hastened our departure. This group, comprehending Hoa-pin-san, Pinnacle Rocks, and Tia-usu, form a triangle, of which the hypothenuse, or distance between Hoa-pin-san and Tia-usu, extends about fourteen miles, and that between Hoa-pin-san and the Southern Pinnacle, about two miles. Within this space lie several reefs; and although a safe channel exists between Hoa-pin-san and Pinnacle Islands, it ought not, (by reason of the strength of the tides destroying steerage) to be attempted if it can be avoided. This is also very deceitful, as the slight deviation of course which would change the current from the weather to the lee bow, would also most materially change the rate of sailing particularly under the variables which prevail here, and from the reliance on what would be deemed a commanding breeze, the vessel would be suddenly found unmanageable. To those employed on these critical examinations, and who are daily if not hourly, subject to these nervous predicaments, these facts are keenly felt, as the lives of all are constantly in their keeping, and it is on quitting the ship at such moments that the Commander feels the responsibility he incurs, and which for the due execution of his peculiar duties it is requisite for him to transfer into the hands of his Lieutenant. Fortunately I felt that to no one could I entrust this charge with more satisfaction than to my zealous supporter Lieut. Anderson. But with the command I could not give him the breeze which had accompanied us, and I had the mortification to see him baffled all day, without being able to examine any of the space alluded to, and barely to save his distance on a casual bank discovered, as before-mentioned, at sunset; once driven easterly in this region, it would be impolitic in us to lose time by the attempt to recover it. The extreme height of Hoa-pin-san was found to be 1181 feet, the island apparently cut away vertically at this elevation, on the southern side, in a W.N.W. direction, the remaining portion sloping to the eastward, where the inclination furnished copious rills of excellent water. There were no traces of inhabitants or visitors; indeed, the soil was insufficient for the maintenance of half a dozen individuals.

The composition of this island is trap, including masses of Basaltic Hornblende, Amygdaloid, &c., but the inclination of the upper strata, as viewed from the ship, exhibited lines of stratification deeply inclined to the N.E., facilitating the flow of water to the beach on that side. That this supply is not casual, is proved by the existence of fresh-water fish, found in most of the natural cisterns, which are connected almost to the sea, and abounding in weeds, which shelter them. Traces of the wreck of Chinese or Japanese junks were noticed. The position of the south-east angle of this island was found to be in Latitude 25° 47′ 7″ N., and Longitude 123 26′ E.

Pinnacle Group is connected by a reef and bank of soundings with Hoa-pin-san, allowing a channel of about twelve fathoms between it and Channel Rock; it presents the appearance of an upheaved, and subsequently ruptured, mass of compact grey columnar Basalt, rising suddenly into needle-shaped pinnacles, which are apparently ready for disintegration by the first disturbing cause, either gales of wind or earthquake. On the summits of some of the flat rocks, long grass, similar to that usually noticed on rocks frequented by sea birds, was found, but no shrubs or trees. The rocks were everywhere whitened by the dung of marine birds, comprising the Booby, (*Pelicanus Sula,*) Frigate Bird, (*Pelicanus Aquilus,*) and various Tern, (*Sterna*), the noise from which, intended to frighten us from their eggs, was almost deafening. Tia-usu appears to be composed of huge boulders of a greenish porphyritic stone, probably a Basalt, cemented by coralline and amygdaloidal matter, the upper surface being loose plates of greyish Basalt, occasionally cemented by the same amygdaloidal mortar. Some distressed beings had evidently visited this island, not Europeans, as their temporary beds were constructed of materials which belonged to canoes, palmetto thatch, &c. They had probably selected this cave as furnishing water by percolation from above, and were probably sustained by the bodies and eggs of the sea-birds which abound in the brush wood. In addition to the sea-birds noticed on Pinnacle Island, we found here the gigantic Petrel in all its stages. At the first discovery of the young in its unfledged state, I had some idea that I had been fortunate enough to hit upon a specimen of the long-extinct *Dodo*, but on proceeding further, I found the parent to differ materially from both that and the *Solitaire*. The capping of this island, from about sixty feet to its summit, which is about six hundred feet above the level, is covered with a loose brushwood, but no trees of any size.

We now sought Raleigh Rock, situated to the eastward, but were equally unfortunate in the want of sun, and the weather continuing still to threaten, did not warrant further detention, particularly as it was my intention to revisit them on my southern route. I found landing practicable, and remained on the reef, upon which it rises, as long as any hope remained, either of seeing the sun, or obtaining the bearing of Tia-usu from it, but a heavy squall put an end to any further exercise of patience. Raleigh Rock rises abruptly from the reef to a height computed at ninety feet perpendicular on all sides, and covering an area of probably sixty feet, in diameter, appearing in the distance, as a junk under sail. As we found it upon the computed bearing as given in the charts, from Tia-usu, its position cannot be much, if at all, in error.

Giving up for the present any further delay in this uninhabited and not very interesting region, we pushed on for Loo-Choo, with no small degree of anxiety on my part, from having reckoned upon gaining some insight into northern politics, and upon making them acquainted with the probability of our coming into contact with those whom I knew they now considered their lords and masters.

On the 19th we anchored in the roads of Napa Kiang, and were immediately visited by the Officers of State, &c., requesting, in their set form, to be made acquainted with the object of our visit, and what supplies we stood in need of. The reply, "water and the sun", seemed in no way to disconcert them; they were evidently aware of the object of our visit, and did not appear to be quite so well satisfied when apprized of our intention of sailing either the next, or at latest, the following day.

Presents of one bullock, two hogs, three goats, and

vegetables, followed this visit, and the next morning I landed nearly opposite to the town, in order to obtain our Observations. Here we were visited by some of the minor Mandarins or Secretaries, evidently deputed emissaries, and much interesting matter was communicated through my Chinese interpreter, who informed me that our visit had been for some time expected, that they had received full reports of our proceedings at the Meia-co-shimas, and that they knew us to be people who did not offend their prejudices, or wantonly enter their towns. Upon mentioning the chances of my communicating with the Japanese, they were silent, but some scraps were written, and hastily destroyed the instant my interpreter read them, which implied that we might succeed, but beware of being entrapped. To use the expression of my Chinese interpreter, it would stand nearly thus:—"He say Japan man very cunning; suppose he see you strong, he very civil; suppose he catch you too civil, he take you head. He give plenty to eat, but no let you walkee on shore." To my enquiry, if they had any idea of our visit, "they thought—*yes.*"

Our communications were interrupted by the visit of a French priest, who came to pay his respects and ascertain if we either brought him letters, or could afford him any intelligence of the movements of the French squadron in this direction. He acquainted me that he had been left behind by one of the French frigates, about sixteen months since, under the pretence of learning their language, and teaching them French; and that they were not then aware that he was a priest from Macao. Since this discovery had been made they had restricted him in his liberty of rambling, confined him within the walls of his garden *(where Basil Hall was similarly confined)*, and that upon several occasions they had *forcibly* carried him home when he straggled. I found that I had now a difficult game to play; the Frenchman desired me to impress them with the probable vengeance such treatment might evoke upon the return of the frigate, which he hourly expected; and the poor Loo-Chooans besought me in the most touching manner to carry him off; supposing that as we had punished the Chinese we were masters of the world.

A middle course was adopted, in which they were warned, as the Frenchman wished, of the impolicy of affording any ground for French interference which might eventually risk the *transfer* of this island. On the other hand they were told, that if the priest wished to proceed to Macao, on my return from the north, (at which period, tired of his confinement, he might give up all hope of the visit of any of the French squadron for the season), that I would willingly afford him a passage in the 'Samarang', but I thought for the interests of all parties, that they should continue to treat him with the most marked civility.

The ship was visited by numbers of the inhabitants, but not to the extent that I remember in the 'Blossom', in 1827. The customary form of measuring the ship was also gone through here, but I understood with rather less precision than formerly. "Among the visitors," relates our second master, Mr. Richards, "was a singular individual, who brought on board with him a rope, composed of twisted hay, for taking the dimensions of the ship, he measured every part, and the gravity with which he adjusted his spectacles, and conducted his operations, amused us exceedingly. He seemed rather puzzled where to begin, but this important point determined, he proceeded to call out the measurements most lustily to his amanuensis who was in readiness with ink and paper."

Having completed the object of our visit and obtained a distinct permission to make surveys of this group, on our return, influenced doubtless by anxiety to secure such a chance of taking away their visitor, we quitted Loo-Choo on the 21st of June.

CHAPTER X.

QUELPART, AND THE KOREAN ISLANDS.

Island of Quelpart—Landing at first opposed by the Fishermen—Observations effected on shore, by appointing Sentinels to intercept the curiosity of the Natives—Symptoms of hostility—Surprised at midnight by a body of the inhabitants with torches—Disperse quietly to their homes—Watch-fires on the Great Island—Visit of the Chief to the Ship, accompanied by most discordant music—Dress and Manners—Visit to a superior Chief on the Great Island—His curiosity to understand the object of our Expedition—Punishment of an Offender—Make the Tour of the Island—Proffers of hospitality from a young Chief—Arrangements for making a formal visit to the Examiner—March to the City—Misunderstanding and return to the beach—Proceed to the Southern Islands, and are visited by an intelligent Civilian Chief—General remarks on Quelpart and the Quelpartians—Departure for the Archipelago of Korea—Survey estuaries—Features of the Country—Habits of the People—Return to Quelpart—Sail for Japan.

As the summer Solstice had now arrived, when very heavy gales are expected in these seas, I was exceedingly anxious to get into some of the northern ports of the Korea before its effect might disturb the efficiency of our Chronometers. On the evening of the 23rd of June, we sighted the Island of Gotto, situated at the south-western extremity of the Japanese Group. Here we met the anticipated gale, but by dint of carrying canvas, crawled under the lee of Gotto, which we rounded about seven on the following morning, experiencing a very heavy squall as we opened the land westerly. That night as the gale moderated, we increased our canvas and fetched over to the Island of Quelpart, under the protection of which we continued beating, until we got its northern island under our lee. At daylight we bore up, and about 6 o'clock anchored off the southern bay of this island, which here forms a channel with the great island, about two miles in width. The current set strongly through to the southward.

As soon as our sails were furled and boats equipped, preparations were made for landing the tents and instruments; upon which a body of fishermen, natives of a small village on the near slope of a hill, assembled to receive us, and motioned to land at what they considered a more eligible spot. Being inattentive to their wishes, one of them deliberately placed his shoulder to the stem of my gig and pushed her off, the others at the same time waving either to depart or land more to the left, which was clear of rocks. Our Chinese interpreter was unable to make them comprehend, and probably mistaking his attempt to parley for indecision, I thought it better to put the matter beyond further doubt; directing the men, therefore, to pull in, I leaped on shore, with a musket, followed by my crew, with their arms, and took possession of the mound. They instantly perceived that we were not to be trifled with, and a better understanding was soon established between us. One of the elders, who appeared to understand Chinese characters, was informed in writing of the object of our visit, which as explained by our interpreter, "to catch a small piece of sun, and measure the land," was probably equally unintelligible. It is very probable, however, that our mysterious dealings with the sun had a much stronger effect in preventing any further opposition, for we soon found them disposed to be friendly and assist our people in bringing water, erecting the tents, &c. On the arrival of the barges for orders, they were very anxious to inspect them, and on noticing the brass six-pounders in them observed, that they had much larger guns in the great island. We several times endeavoured to ascertain the name of the island on which they were, but could gain nothing beyond O-tcheou-san, which I well knew was merely their term for the land. As visitors increased they began to be more inquisitive, and so troublesome, that I was at length compelled to post sentries to keep off those who had not permission to approach; the parties, moreover, with which we were now in contact, were so filthy in their manners and persons, that it became a matter of necessity to keep them aloof. With some their curiosity, or impertinence, carried them so far beyond the bounds of decorum, that they were very soon taught that the white-faced foreigner was able to punish their presumption, even without the assistance of weapons. As some doubts were entertained of the amicable disposition of these people, who quitted us rather sulkily and as if by signal, due care was observed shortly before sunset, in doubling our guard at the tents, by the crew of one of the cutters, whilst the further force of the barges moored in the bay, made it sufficient to have repelled any attack.

Shortly after midnight, however, whilst taking a nap, during a cloudy interval, which prevented my observing the stars, I was awakened by cries and yellings in our rear, followed very shortly by the natives rushing towards us, each brandishing a torch. These sudden alarms afford excitement and excellent practice to Officers and men, and in no point more so than as a trial of their coolness and forbearance. Both barges were ready for action on the instant; eighteen loaded muskets, with bayonets fixed, awaited the approach of the enemy, and close as they were, not a mistake occurred. Many were "eager for the fray", but it was not our province to commence hostilities, nor do I think at this moment that the natives came down upon us with any warlike intention, for I afterwards found that an inferior Officer and his party from the great island landed about that time, and probably conceived it to be his duty to inspect us, and show his people that he entertained no fear. It was rather a hazardous experiment, as the mistake or want of nerve of one man might have sacrificed a dozen; it is also possible that these villagers might have deemed us weak enough to be frightened by their display of torches; their surprise to find so many muskets pointed towards them caused the greater body, however, to retire with more precipitation than they advanced. A few of the band advanced in a friendly manner, and among them the chief alluded to, but the nature of his errand did not transpire, as we could only communicate by the Chinese written characters, and darkness did not at all favour his trusting himself in our hands. They very shortly dispersed to their homes, leaving us to take care of the stars; and it is highly probable that to this early lesson, teaching them that we were ever on the alert to any interruptions inimical to our duties, rendered our subsequent transactions with them more easy. We found that a vigilant look-out was also maintained on their part on the summits of all their high hills, where guards in little square forts were always to be observed moving about, and at stated hours, near sunset, and during the night, signal fires were passed along the posts, in succession, commencing from that nearest to the ship or boats. By day, this was effected by smoke, which was very cleverly, as well as prettily performed, by throwing wet chopped straw, and sometimes paddy husks into the fire, producing instantaneously a dense white column, afterwards used, in imitation, by ourselves for surveying signals. Some of the Officers thought that they could distinguish symbols in the *form* of the lights, but these I did not perceive, and when we consider that their telescopes are of the most miserable description, and that with ours, of the very best quality, that it was but a conjecture, and the distance also between the objects in question being, at least, three miles, I think there is no ground for that inference.

Preparations were now made for carrying on the survey of the island by the ship and boats, in the event of any difficulty arising on the part of the authorities; my instructions strictly prohibiting any measure of this nature being effected by force or against their consent. On the 30th of June it was intimated that one of the Quelpart Generals would visit the ship. Every preparation being made for his proper reception, shortly before noon three large boats were noticed coming from the main island, but as both wind and tide pressed them southerly, they made but slow progress. The largest boat, which bore the Chief and his party, consisting of his suite and band, the latter producing the most discordant sounds that were ever emitted under the name of music, from brass tubes, at length reached the ship, and the General stepped upon our quarter deck, where he was duly received by the Officers and guard, and saluted with three guns, the customary compliment to a Chinese of similar rank. He was a light built, but compact man, about 5ft. 6in., of rather handsome features, inclined to Grecian, with rather sharp forehead, small eyes, but intelligent, and with feet very small in proportion to his size. His hair appeared to be dressed much in the fashion of the people of Loo-Choo, but in place of the Cameesashee and Oosisashee pins, it was confined by a delicate net-work bag, composed of brown silk. The hat, which is a light fabric, and most beautiful piece of workmanship, is composed of the fine outer fibres of the bamboo, dyed black, and woven into a gauze, like our finest wire-work.* The rim is about two feet in diameter; the cone rises to nine inches, having a diameter at the truncated vertex of three inches, where it is slightly convex, and has one or more peacock's feathers attached in a kind of swivel,

* The hat is also furnished with a fine covering composed of very fibrous paper, so well glazed, at the same time so flexible, that it was generally mistaken for oil silk. This is prepared both by the people of Loo-Choo, as well as the Chinese, by a solution of the gelatinous sea-weed, Agal Agal (one of the Algæ), which will be noticed hereafter.

forming a graceful head-dress, and one not unbecoming a military character. Beneath this hat our chief was decorated by two necklaces or collars, one composed of large ultramarine-blue balls, apparently of porcelain, the centre being about nine-tenths of an inch in diameter, diminishing in size towards the extremities. The other fastened behind the left ear and crossing the breast, but this was composed of long tubular pieces, about a quarter of an inch in diameter, by two inches in length, tapering at the extremes, and apparently amber, having a dark coloured red bead between each. In his hand he carried a wand of office, of a dark black wood, with a black silk braid, plaited about six inches inwards, from the greater, and terminating in fringes. These constituted his official marks, or *bâton*, of rank and office.

His personal dress consisted of a fine loose shirt of grass cloth, trowsers and stockings in one, of a species of nankeen, and leathern boots of very neat workmanship, in the loose Wellington style, the upper part being of a black velvet; a loose tunic, of open texture, approaching to coarse grass cloth or muslin, having the cuffs lined and turned up with scarlet silk, confined by a broad sash of blue at the waist, completed the house dress. But in the costume of state now before us, there was superadded a military cloak or scarf, descending from each shoulder in folds behind and before, turned up at the cuffs with red silk, representing two very useful sleeves. The attendants were dressed similar to the people of Loo-Choo, some with boots, others with sandals, constructed very neatly of straw; and those of military habits performing the duties of Sergeants, Provost-Martials, or personal guard, wore a kind of gaiter, protecting the leg from the knee to the ankle.

Our guest appeared to be quite at his ease, and on going round the ship, paid the most minute attention to every object likely to interest a warlike people. The size of the guns, weight of the shot, chain-cables and cooking apparatus in the galley chiefly attracted his attention. If I should venture to select any particular object which appeared to make an impression of *power*, it certainly was the chain-cable; he recurred to it several times, and observed, to use the interpreter's words, "he say must have strong man do that work." His merriment was very much excited at our sheep, goats, fowls, &c.; "he say all got proper house"; but in descending to the lower deck, its comfort, arrangement of the seamens' messes, &c., a sight of admiration at any time, even to our own countrymen, perfectly astonished him. He trembled, I even suspect, to find another world, and more men lower down, and wished to return to the cabin, where he was greatly delighted with the performance of a musical box.

After partaking of sweetmeats and wines, &c., he acquainted me that a greater General than himself, the Commander of the forces, expected me to visit him at the great island; we therefore proceeded thither with our boat force in state, taking every Officer who could be spared. Having landed in a very convenient spot, sheltered by two reefs, we were conducted to the presence of the Chief, under a very miserable military tent, which would not even shelter us from the sun, where we found him seated within a space, enclosed on three sides by a folding screen, so contrived as to form (by additional pieces) small chambers behind him. He received me sitting, when to put an end to any forms of *etiquette* which might be in contemplation, and in order to arrive at that point of equality upon which all our measures were to be conducted, I planted myself *sans cérémonie* on the mat near him, and shook him by the hand, in true English style, a compliment which I observed somewhat to discompose him, although his assumed gravity quickly vanished.

The customary formal questions were then put. From whence do you come? What do you want? When do you go, and where? To these interrogatories I made a general reply:—"that my Queen had sent me to visit foreign countries, in order to correct the charts by which our vessels might navigate in safety, and that it was important we should obtain a knowledge of the hidden dangers surrounding their island, in order that none should be wrecked upon its shores; that to effect this in a proper manner, it was necessary to observe the sun and stars, and make other measurements from the various hills about the island; but that we had no wish to enter their towns or interfere with their people, and I therefore hoped that he would give them strict injunctions not to interfere with any marks which we might erect, and that our operations would not disturb the harmony which ought to exist between all nations; that our object was for the benefit of mankind in general, and that he must not consider me as the servant solely of my Sovereign, but as that of all nations; that immediately our operations were completed, we should proceed to Korea, and endeavour to see the ruling power there, and then call at Japan for refreshments on our return to China."

He appeared to comprehend these matters clearly, issued his orders in compliance with my wishes; and expressed himself very anxious to see the map of the world, to understand the very great distance which the Queen of Great Britain had sent one of her great war-ships to work for their benefit, which he remarked, showed a very kind disposition. This map I promised to give him when we met again at the great city, where he had arranged that I was to be introduced to the Examiner, the *de facto* Governor of the island. As to Korea, he considered that we should not be able to meet any great men, but very many soldiers, and very brave ("large hearts"), cautioning me at the same time, not to allow myself to be entrapped by them.

Everything having been satisfactorily arranged between us, sweetmeats and saké (or Sam-schoo) were introduced, and the customary curiosity about the texture of our clothing, uniforms, &c., was indulged in. Anxious to procure Bullocks and vegetables for my ship's company, I had taken the precaution of bringing with me samples of the different supplies of cloth, flannel, cotton, &c., as a means of exchange, and enquired if such could be obtained. This point being also satisfactorily arranged, we were preparing to take our leave, when I found that an inquisitive member of the rabble which pressed upon us, almost beyond the controul of their police, had been carrying his curiosity to an impertinent excess upon one of the Officers, who in his indignation had repelled him more roughly than he anticipated. This circumstance, however, soon proved that they possessed the power to punish an offender when necessary. Without any forms of enquiry, or drum-head court martial, the delinquent was pointed out by the Provost, suddenly seized and brought before the police magistrate, by four sturdy fellows, and he was then made to kneel uncapped, with his hair untied, or, as a seaman would term it, 'adrift'; this condition of the hair serving with the Chinese and other tailed nations, as an important hold on refractory characters. His crime, as I supposed, having been recited to him by the head policeman, or Provost, the magistrate bowed towards him, which being construed into passing sentence, he was, with very great rapidity, bared from the waist to the knees and forcibly thrown on his face; being confined in this position by the four policemen, a fifth now appeared, a distinct official, prepared to carry out the sentence. The instrument used for this purpose may be compared to a huge bat, or Harlequin's wand in shape, but longer, wider, and heavier, with a long handle; it appeared to be of ash, and bent freely like the wand alluded to. The operator placing himself in a convenient position, and measuring his distance from the culprit so as to inflict his blow with the knees almost bent to the ground, swung this instrument over his head, and brought it down flat over the back part of the hams, a little above the knee joint, with a force apparently sufficient to break the limb, but for the flexibility of the instrument. I interceded to prevent the repetition of such torture, but at least a dozen of these terrific blows were inflicted before my wishes could be explained and acted upon. It appeared to me to be a most severe punishment, yet the instant the culprit was released he nimbly tucked up his garments and fled, possibly accustomed to this mode of castigation.

Taking leave of the Chiefs, we returned to the 'Samarang', and on the day following commenced our tour of the island, the ship accompanying us within short signal distances, and anchoring at night. During our progress we were very strictly escorted by the military guards, which maintained a respectable distance inland, probably to preserve order, and prevent our free communication with the natives; wherever we reached their batteries or military stations, there was a great display of banners, spears, &c., but no communication.

The several districts of the island appeared to be under the control of independent chiefs, or magistrates, and according to their disposition did we find our operations facilitated or retarded. About the third day of our progress, it was found convenient to sleep in the boats, in a very well sheltered and retired little bay, about one quarter of a mile from one of their towns. The chief personage, a young man about five-and-twenty, and of very prepossessing manners, came down to visit me at the station, examined the instruments, and issued very decided orders in our favour. When he understood that it was my intention to sleep in the boat, he endeavoured to persuade me to accept the use of his house, and to render me the more independent, offered to vacate it, and allow my own people to guard it. Aware of the general craftiness of these people, and suspecting that they would be glad to make one of us a prisoner, I still felt so much confidence in the genuine feeling of this chief, that, had it been consistent with my duty, I should have gladly taken advantage of this opportunity of seeing more into their habits, &c.; but considering that on these occasions, the leader of such expeditions should "in his own person and place", set the example of endurance, and not accept a luxury which his officers could not enjoy, I declined the invitation. Another important consideration which occurred to me, was, that if I had been either willingly or unwillingly detained, either by design or mistaken hospitality, the zeal of the Officer left in command of the boats, might have led to some untoward misunderstanding. As the fishermen had disturbed our marks, and were not friendly, there were many of our party who were not inclined to give our new acquaintance credit for the integrity of his intentions; they were, of course, on the alert, and suspicion, heightened by the exhibition of some flashes of fireworks during the night, put us on the *qui vive*, or under arms, and somewhat troubled our rest.

On the morning following, we found the people well-disposed; and moving onwards to the next station, I was again favoured with a visit from our friend, the young chief, inviting me to breakfast, but finding that I still declined the honor, he caused a small basket, or canteen to be put into the boat, containing what evidently had been prepared in case of my declining his invitation, and motioned me to take them with me. The contents were fish, vegetables, pickles, rice, and Saké, in white metal and porcelain vessels, the latter certainly of some value to them. Even this did not satisfy the suspicions of some of our gentry. However, about noon, at a station, a little inland, and about five miles in advance, and apparently beyond the limits of his district, we found that he had followed us in one of their unwieldly boats, and mounting to our station, set all the people at ease about our penetrating so far into the interior. My friend now acquainted me that the Examiner had sent me a present of Bullocks, which were on their passage from the city, and intimated a wish that I would go there with all convenient despatch to visit that personage, and that he would be there to receive me. Returning him his canteen and vessels, and exacting a promise that he would visit the ship on her anchoring, we parted, and, about 4 o'clock that evening, met the boats containing the Bullocks, which had been sent off to the ship to be embarked. The ship anchored about a mile from the landing-place, and early the ensuing morning, a special invitation was forwarded to a ceremonial breakfast, and introduction to the Examiner in the city, which was accepted; and as the chiefs thought the ship too far off to visit, she was moved as close to the shore as *safety* admitted, her fore-foot having at one time touched a rock, which *ought not* to have been *under* us. Selecting a party, including marines and blue jackets, of thirty men, under arms, as a guard, and accompanied by about six officers, we landed at the beach, in front of the city, where several thousand people, including troops, with their banners, were drawn up to receive us. My friend was not amongst the officials, and considerable shuffling and evasion appeared to mark the conduct of the military chiefs. At length mats were brought, and the chiefs and myself being seated, some little communication took place about horses, the number of attendants, &c., all of

z

which appeared to have been satisfactorily arranged, and the horses led out in readiness to mount. Still some unseen difficulty seemed to cause a restlessness amongst the chiefs, whilst messengers were repeatedly passing between them and the city. I shall therefore take advantage of this pause, and describe the outer parts of the capital of Quelpart.

The space on which the city stands, is in a broad valley, situated about the centre of the northern coast-line, having a conspicuous flat eminence on its eastern side, and a small river, or copious stream, on the west. The country immediately surrounding it on all sides, being peculiarly barren. The city wall, on the face exposed to the sea, occupies a line of about 500 yards, containing seven bastions, apparently with embrasures throughout; but no guns were noticed, excepting in these bastions, and from their report, when saluting, of no importance. The depth of the walls, which form a parallellogram, is about 200 yards. The main gates, which are inland, and seaward, are in recesses formed by two of the bastions, with apparently one additional gate on the eastern angle. The height of the walls is about twenty-five feet, and from their structure here, as well as in other parts of the island, I am induced to believe are of European design. They are unlike the works of China or Loo-Choo, and manifestly convey the impression of a knowledge of the art of defence. Their present condition and appearance, added to the slovenly manner of repairs, where attempted, tend to confirm the opinion, that they were designed by a more warlike people, and that the present race have neither the tact for keeping them in a condition for action, nor are possessed of the ordnance for rendering them respectable. Their force, therefore, could only be reckoned as to numbers in hand to hand conflict.

Matters being now arranged, I was informed, after a delay of, at least, an hour, that they were prepared for our reception. The officers mounting their horses, which, fortunately, I had insisted upon their providing, and the force shouldering arms, we proceeded to the eastern gate, which we found closed, whilst the batteries above were crowded with people. Under any other circumstances this alteration of arrangement in avoiding the great sea gate, and refusal of admission here, would have touched my pride, and induced me to return to the ship, but I had an object in view of more importance: I wished to enter their town, and make the friendship of their chief, an object, possibly, as related to future communication with Korea, of national importance; moreover I conceived that these disagreeable arrangements might result from the vacillating conduct of some timorous official.

It was now intimated to me that the Examiner desired to pay me the greatest compliment which he could offer, and that he wished me to enter in state by the great city gate, on the land side, the officials having been deputed to arrange this ceremony. I directed them to lead, and conducting us by a circuit of about a mile and a half, we at length reached the avenue which led to the land gate. If this scheme was concocted in order to entrap us, it was well managed, had they possessed the courage to carry it out. To speak the truth, I had already made up my mind to stand the brunt of my act, and had taken into consideration the position of the

z 2

town, as under the point blank range of the guns of the 'Samarang'. The boats also armed with four field-pieces, and congreve-rockets, were at the beach, within sixty yards of the walls, with thousands to fall under a few discharges; and last, not least, the handful of picked men under my immediate command; I could not imagine, therefore, that these people could be such idiots as to provoke hostilities. The avenue in front which led to the main gate, was scarcely more than ten feet wide, not affording room for more than four men abreast, and two for active operations. Their troops lined this road, with spears on our left, and forty-eight matchlocks, with lighted matches, on our right. The projecting bastions, which formed a very deep recess to the gate, were frowning over our heads, at a height of above thirty-five feet, thronged with people, and requiring merely a handful of pebbles to exterminate us. In the face of this we advanced to the gate. A parley was held and a messenger arrived, refusing to admit so large an armed force into the city, "it was against their laws." They were then informed that these matters had been already arranged, and that I declined further parley. The period had now arrived when it became necessary to exhibit to them the contempt which we entertained for their Forces. Assuming the command by the order of "Silence", I reversed my little band, having half of the marines in front, at the charge, the Officers in the centre, and the remainder in rear; and giving the order to "Advance", we steadily cleared our way past the matchlocks and "stone range" of the walls, and then forming square on the nearest commanding ground, gently captured a *stray General*, and gave him to understand that the safety of his head depended very much upon his piloting us safe; these arrangements completed, we advanced very leisurely along the western walls, until we reached the beach.

To show how completely some of our party entered into the spirit of this little affair, I overheard a discussion which took place among the marines, whilst resting in square. One, calculating the odds, observed, "Well, there were enough of them to have smothered us"; the other coolly replying, "Nonsense, they were not more than two hundred to one jolly"! We had yet about 200 yards to traverse, and here we found the ground kept by a regiment of *flailmen*, stationed six feet asunder, so as to admit of the free use of their weapon. The handle of this dangerous weapon was about three feet in length, with an arm of eighteen inches, jointed in iron, and studded three inches from the extremity by nine studs, or nails, similar to those used in portcullis gates, &c. A single blow from this weapon would probably indent a musket, and render it useless; against cutlasses it might become superior; and to unarmed men, terrific. Between these lines we continued our march, and reached the position, covered by our boats, in safety. Here I summoned one of their chiefs, and informed him, by a written communication, that I was ashamed of their conduct, and that I could no longer consider them entitled to respect. This produced a fresh invitation. "The breakfast was prepared, the chiefs awaited me, and the sea gate was open, to enter upon my own terms." To have accepted their hospitality under these circumstances would, I considered, have lowered the character of the Flag; I therefore caused the interpreter to commit the following to paper, and forwarded it to the Examiner:

"I regretted that either bad advice, or pusillanimity, on the part of the Chiefs of Quelpart should have marred the pleasure which I had anticipated, of paying my respects to the Examiner, to whom, personally and individually, I felt under great obligation. That notwithstanding all that had occurred, and as a proof that no such indecision would be found upon our part, I should be happy to receive the Examiner, his Chiefs and attendants, to any number, on board the 'Samarang', where they might be assured of a reception befitting their rank, and I should wait until 3 o'clock for their reply." In a short time they acknowledged "that they had lost face" (were disgraced), and further communication being out of the question, I retired to the ship, and quitted the anchorage. I felt great disappointment at the non-appearance of my friend of the two previous days, who had not exhibited himself in any capacity; and as all the chiefs of the neighbouring districts were, probably, present, it frequently occurred to me that he was either a near connexion of the Examiner's, or had been ordered to remain aloof. That he was a first-class Mandarin, or Chief, we knew, from his hat and feathers, as well as from his own people, who showed him greater marks of respect, although unattended by Officers, than any authority I had hitherto met.

It was evident that there existed a party hostile to us on the island, and I am inclined to suspect that it was military. The day previous to our visit to the city, on passing a fortified town at the sea shore, a gun was fired, in the direction of my gig, the shot dropping short.

As this might have been intended for a *compliment*,

and the shot (as I have seen even in a British battery) accidental, I did not notice it further than by signalling one of the barges to close, and pulled directly in for the spot from whence the gun had been fired. A second discharge, which passed the ball quite close enough to our heads to put the *intention* beyond doubt, induced me to return them the compliment, from the six pounder in the barge, *tiro por tiro* (shot for shot), as the Spanish have it; and this put an end to their amusement.

We found, after quitting the city, that a similar feeling prevailed at one of our stations about ten miles to the westward; the report of this transaction, by Mr. Richards, the second master, in command of one of the cutters, was to the following effect. He had been despatched in advance to exhibit a signal upon the extreme point in view, and as the period of his arrival was about the time that his people should breakfast, he landed one of the men to stand by the signal, whilst he anchored off and allowed the crew to get their meal. Shortly after, the natives came down in great numbers, and endeavoured to force the man in charge of the signal, over the cliff into the sea; not being able to effect a landing in time to prevent this act, Mr. Richards fired a musket over their heads, to intimidate them; this they derided, and using brands, which they probably brought from their watch-fires, endeavoured to *burn him out*, by setting fire to his clothes. Further delay was impossible, and the discharge of the brass gun and some muskets, served to disperse them, wounding, as he suspected, one of the most forward in this outrage. On my arrival at the station they had retired, and this proved the last attempt to annoy us, or our marks. As to the act of firing on them, Mr. Richards was aware that upon a former occasion of the people destroying our marks, the chiefs *desired* "that we would fire the guns on them, as they had already sufficient warning." Nothing further transpired until we reached the southern side of the island, where, being short of fuel, I intended to complete from one of the small uninhabited islands; within which a convenient, if not secure, anchorage seemed to offer. A small, flat island within, also presenting a most convenient opportunity for completing our water, I determined upon making it one of our principal stations, particularly as I noticed an extensive walled town immediately within us, where numerous banners were displayed.

We had not occupied our position long, before we received a visit from the chiefs, who professed themselves anxious to be on friendly terms, and brought with them presents of sweetmeats, cakes, saké, fans, writing paper, as well as drawing, envelopes, and the protrait of the Emperor of Tcheousan (or Korea). Amongst this party was another young chief, also a civilian, who very soon contracted a friendship, and promised to use his exertions to obtain for me one of their state hats. After a great deal of communication, carried on by the intervention of our Chinese interpreter, in writing, he consented to visit the ship, in the company of one of my officers, the observations at that moment not permitting me to quit my post. On his return, I found that he had been very sea-sick, probably from having taken wine, but had previously been shown every object of interest, and appeared to be highly delighted. He very soon recovered his composure, and from the various questions which he put, and his enquiry after a map of the world, a telescope, &c., proved that he was a well-educated, and very intelligent person. Having intimated that he was aware that the map had before been requested for the Examiner, and that he should be happy to be the medium of conveying it to him, I lost no time in obtaining it from the ship, promising him the telescope upon our final meeting at the eastern island, where he had arranged to meet, and bring the hat and other objects of interest. I left with him a few seeds of various Melons, Cucumbers, Orange, Shaddock, Chinese Plum, Pumpkin, Mustard, Cress, and Lettuce. This produced a further solicitation from him, which seemed to imply that he undersood something of Pharmacy. He produced specimens of the *Strychnos* or St. Ignatius bean, which he informed me he had obtained from China, through Korea, and that he knew that it was brought to China by an European vessel. I endeavoured to ascertain how he had obtained this fact, and taxed him with having visited China himself. This he denied, but admitted having been at one of the chief cities of Korea, visited by the junks from China as well as Japan. He was unwilling, or fearful, to afford me any information respecting this latter place, but he most distinctly combatted any idea of their being either dependent or subject to any control but that of Korea. I despatched a messenger to the ship for some of the beans of the *Strychnos*, which had been presented to me by the Padres of Batan, and begged him to accept them, in the hope of obtaining further information, but the approach of evening, and the presence of others, who seemed to act as spies, put an end to our conference. They seemed to be very much surprised at the facility with which our Chinese interpreter expressed himself in the court dialect of China, and particularly at his assisting *us*, probably termed here, as in China, *barbarians*. They were so far, or pretended to be, ignorant of our transactions with the Celestial Empire, that they doubted the assertion of the interpreter, that England did not pay tribute to China; and when informed of their submission and payment of six millions of dollars, as ransom at Canton, and further discomfiture, and payment of twenty-four millions, at Nankin, they termed him a very bad man, to tell such untruths of his country.

Another gross insult, similar to that noticed at our first visit, occurred here, but on this occasion, I not only allowed justice to take its course, but insisted on the instant removal of the offender from the island. On the 14th of July we completed our tour, resuming our old position off the eastern island, which, as we were unable to obtain any native name either for it, or any of the other islets, or promontories, I have thought fit to designate as Beaufort Island, after our worthy chief, at the head of the Hydrographic department.

I am not aware that any European has before landed on, or surveyed, this island, although from its representation on the charts of former navigators, it is roughly, but incorrectly, exhibited. Throughout its extent it has but one safe anchorage, and that happens to be on the spot where, with our customary good fortune, we first dropped anchor. The second temporary roadstead, from whence a vessel would be compelled to seek an offing, at the first symptoms of a north-westerly breeze, is off the city first visited. The third affords shelter from the north, by the east, to N.W., and offers an escape to leeward, if requisite; this is on the western extreme, and within its outer islet, which was named Eden Island. A fourth temporary, but dangerous, anchorage is off Hooper's Island, near the southern city, but this is open from west to south-east, and is too confined to admit of beating out, should wind and sea come in suddenly.

Water appears to abound on the southern side of the island, but only in the case of Hooper's Island could it be procured easily. On Barlow Island, the south-westernmost of the group, it is easily obtained, but there is not safe and convenient anchorage near it. At the north city it may also be found. We endeavoured to procure wood by purchase, from the authorities, but it was doled out in such small portions, that it did not repay the trouble of sending for it. Nevertheless it is abundant in the mountains, and on two of the off-lying islets, to be procured by slight labour.

The general appearance of the islands, as viewed from the sea, is inviting. There is a pleasing variety of hill and dale, and on the northern and eastern surfaces much cleared land, cultivation rising probably to the level of 2,000 feet. Above this, all appears to be buried in thick forests of Pines, and other northern trees, even to the highest peak of the island, which, from our computations, from various stations, reaches the height of 6,544 feet. This was named Mount Auckland. Towards the northern and eastern parts, some of the cones, which reach elevations of from 500 to 800 feet, are so very smooth and circular, that, with their little batteries, or watch-towers, on the summit, exhibiting some tiny banners, appear almost be the work of art. This, probably, results from their method of cultivating the sides, as all the furrows appear to be made horizontally, which, in process of time, by the constant falling down of the ridges, would effect such a regular outline.

The productions of the island do not appear to be at all equal to the wants of the population, and are in very small variety; Rice, Wheat, Barley, sweet Potatoe, large Russian Radish, Maize, and small garden produce, comprise all that we noticed, either in the grounds under cultivation, or amongst the people. This does not appear the result of any deficiency in land fit for cultivation, but rather in the very poor nature of the soil. Of their agricultural implements we can afford but little information, as our knowledge of these matters is completely confined to the fields bordering the coast. Hoes and spades, after the Chinese fashion, were the only hand implements; a species of plough of very rude construction, was also noticed, but its perfect inefficiency for the purpose intended, renders it unworthy of description. I endeavoured on one or two occasions, to excite their attention by the offer of useful seeds, which I always carried in my canteen for this purpose, but, with the exception of my second friend at Hooper's Island, no one appeared to attach any value to them. With respect to the materials for clothing, they appear to depend chiefly on home manufacture, whilst all articles of superior quality are imported from Korea.

In the construction of their houses their mode is similar

to that of the people of Loo-Choo; those within cities being covered with red tiles, and otherwise ornamented, but they affirm that these tiles are brought from the continent. The houses of the lower orders are thatched, and very nearly resemble those of the Meia-co-shima; the sides are occasionally built of stone, they are in a similar manner surrounded by stone walls about six feet in height, completely concealing all within; but in this poor region, where soil is possibly in some measure dependent on climate, very few trees or even shrubs are to be noticed. The people themselves appear to be composed of several races; the superior class is entirely distinct, of the small Tartar mould, and very beautifully formed. Although active, and from their general dress, liable to constant exposure, they still exhibit great effeminacy when at ease, being invariably attended by a species of page, carrying boots, slippers, fan, &c.; but these again are far more effeminate than their masters; pale, slovenly, and disgusting, with loose wavy hair, creating almost a doubt as to their sex. These are invariably the military chiefs and their attendants. The second class Officers are robust powerful men, ranging between the height of five feet seven and nine. Their dress is coarse, and their manners in character with their subordinate situations. The soldiers are of the Tartar feature and build, sturdy compact men, of broader features, and probably averaging five feet six to eight. Their dress consists of the simple blueish coarse grass-cloth tunic, confined at the waist with very loose unbleached trowsers, reaching to the knee, and straw sandals, the hat is generally of a dirty brown felt. The civilians are of a superior conformation to the military chiefs, of whom they take precedence, and are of the same class as those of similar rank in Loo-Choo. Probably from less exposure, their complexions are clearer, but their features are more elongated; they are of a larger mould and approach nearer to the European, attaining the height of five feet eight to ten. All the lower classes are nearly similar, being fishermen; they are a very sturdy well-knit race, but do not attain any great height. They are powerful, lifting much heavier weights than our people, who on their part, beat them in activity. Of their women none were noticed but those belonging to the labouring class, excepting an occasional inquisitive portion of face, which merely enabled one to assert that they appear fair. Those of the labouring class were only noticed when taken by surprise, and they certainly had no cause for their extraordinary alarm and rapid flight. They are small, very short legged, particularly from the knee to the heel, with an apparent tendency to heaviness about the feet and ankles, and withal disgusting. Their manners, excluding the superior class, differ from any nation with whom I have held communication: they are filthy in person and habit.

Their fishing vessels are very few, and of the most miserable construction; many rafts were noticed, and from these facts I suspect that fishing is barely permitted to those licensed to pursue this vocation. It is highly probable that Quelpart, occupies the position of one of the penal settlements of Korea, and the information from my friend at the south city, would tend to confirm this opinion; viewing it in this light, we must not feel surprised at the gross manners complained of, and it will readily account for the variety in the races of beings, which were found assembled. This will further account for the low state of cultivation, as no individual would take that interest in improving a soil, upon which his descendants would possess no interest, and from which he would possibly be removed at the expiration of his term of banishment.

The position in the Sandy Bay of Beaufort Island was determined to be in Lat. 33° 29′ 40″ N., Long. 126° 53′ 5″ E., Var. 2° 30′ 33″ W. The geological features of the islands are decidedly volcanic, the entire southern side being either close grained grey, or greenish basalt, or a scoriaceous tufa. The appearance of the highest peak, when free from clouds, appeared to be the lip of a small crater, but from the abundance of trees, nearly to the crater edge, long since dormant.

On the 15th we took a temporary leave of our friends at Quelpart, and steered a northerly course on our now *boná fide* voyage of discovery, into the Korean Archipelago. We had, indeed, charts of this region, but they were of as much use as one of the Antarctic Regions, would be to show where icebergs might be looked for. One comfort we retained, and no doubt many of my readers will smile when I state that we continued to feel the bottom with the lead-line. This is, however, an important relief to one navigating a sea so studded with reefs, islets, and islands, as that of Korea. Our object at present was like that of the dove from the ark, to seek the first dry, or secure spot, on which to fix our first position, and this at 8 o'clock the following morning, was obtained on an isolated reef, affording us, in addition to innumerable distant islets, the command of a very interesting group, distant about three miles; some of its islets, crowned with sharp peaks, rising to the height of two thousand feet. Having completed our work upon this reef, from which we and our instruments were nearly swept away by a sudden wave, we quitted, about 3 o'clock and proceeded to the examination of this new group. It was found to be composed of three islands, two large and one small, deeply indented and forming a most complete harbour within, as well as a very snug bay without. The ship was anchored in the outer bay, and the day following devoted to the survey of the island. The natives, which occupied four distinct and exclusive villages were civil, and conducted one of my assistants to the summit of the highest peak. The necessity for expedition did not afford us time to observe more of these people than that their occupation seemed to be solely fishing, and that they had a tolerable fleet of well-found substantial boats. There did not appear to be any military persons amongst them, the elder of the village, generally well marked by age and silver hair, appearing as the sole authority; they were all clad in home-spun grass cloth, but of very poor material. In compliment to the Secretary of the Admiralty, the harbour formed by this group received the name of Port Hamilton. Quitting this position we made another stretch northerly, and with our customary good fortune discovered another small group, amongst hundreds of islands in sight, offering very complete shelter to the ship, and our term-day being at hand it proved a most desirable spot for making our Magnetic Observations. Here the ship was secured, and leaving the Officer in command to make the necessary clearance of its summit, erect a large cone for a signal, and prepare our tents, we started with the boat-force to explore the *terrá incognitá*, within ten miles to the northward of us, which we

Korean Chief

conjectured to be the main land of Korea, and where I little doubted of meeting with some Magistrate, or other Authority, with whom I might communicate. After four days exploration we found ourselves almost as much bewildered as when we commenced our labours, and notwithstanding that we had ascended what we considered its Rivers, for many miles, and, with the utmost anxiety, had repeatedly drank enough salt water, to satisfy ourselves that no fresh stream entered into their composition, we returned to the ship to complete our term-day, and make one more effort where a final chance yet remained. That also proved unsatisfactory, and from the explorations made, I have every reason to conclude, as well as from the various information picked up from the elders of the villages with whom we communicated, that we were still merely upon the outer islands of the Archipelago; as in reply to the direct question put by the interpreter, they informed me,—that I could not reach the residence of any principle Mandarin in less than twelve days, and they were conversant with the general rapidity of our movements. They, moreover, intimated, that I should not until then, meet with troops, or guns of brass, similar to those they observed, and examined, in our boats. The mountainous district throughout presented a most barren and bleak appearance. Rugged precipitous peaks composed occasionally of Granite, and at times of light-grey Basalt, embellished but rarely with trees, or even vegetation beyond the grey lichens, afforded from their very desolation, when brought into contrast with the few green islets beneath, an interesting scenery. One of my principal stations, elevated about one thousand feet above the sea,

A 2

and from its architectural features termed "Abbey Peak" formed an exception. From the summit of a steep mount covered with a luxuriant vegetation on the north and south, but abruptly cut off from the vertex on the west, the entire cliff was composed of slender Basaltic columns, and by some freak or convulsion of nature, so displaced as to assume the most fantastic, as well as picturesque forms, occasionally enlivened by what I at first mistook for moss, or ivy, but which upon closer examination, proved to be that most beautiful production, allied to the *Lycopodium lepidophyllum*, or stone plant, so common in the vicinity of San Blas, on the western coast of Mexico. Nor were flowers wanting to adorn this interesting little spot. The Tiger-lily abounded and bloomed in great perfection, as well as Heath-bells, Orchis, Fox-glove, &c. As nature seemed to offer but very scanty means of subsistence on land, beyond the artificial collections of earth, forming the gardens to their little stone-built cabins, their resources if not obtained from places inland, were from the sea; but from the specimens of nets and boats which we noticed, they were very far behind other nations in this pursuit. English hooks of various sizes, knives, scissors, and needles, were offered to them, but either from fear of their superiors, or ignorance of their true value, they were declined. On one or two occasions they produced their *Saké* *, in compliment, and I returned it by sweet wine, which they appeared to esteem, but most carefully brought back the bottle, supposing it to be of value. They were surprised to observe it thrown into the sea, and on recovery it was soon conveyed as a treasure to the Chief, or his nearest friend. In all their transactions with us, I noticed an

* Sometimes spelt '*zakki*' by the Dutch.

irresolution, a fluctuation between violent opposition to our landing in the first instance, and after this act had been consummated, an equal disposition to friendship, clouded by the fear of displeasure from some unseen source.

In all our enquiries, here, as well as at Quelpart, the terms applied to the land were, invariably, T-cho-san or O-tcheou-san, and this was confirmed by enquiry, made through the interpreter. As the harbour of Tcho-san, so named by Broughton, should be somewhere in the neighbourhood examined by us, it is highly probable that he was misled, in a similar manner, by their reply to his enquiry for the name of the *land*.* In the same manner it is very probable that Tanna, in the New Hebrides, obtained its name, as the natives did not recognize that name at the period of our visit in the 'Sulphur', in 1840. *Tanah* is the Malay name for *land*, and it is probable that the Malays, which traversed all the coasts of New Guinea, as well as the off-lying islands, extended their excursions even to the Feejees, many of their words evincing a great affinity to that language.

Our boats had penetrated within estuaries which would easily have accommodated the 'Samarang', as high as 34° 40′ N., and at their extreme points the channels appeared still open as far as the eye could reach, without the slightest traces of civilization, beyond the few fishermen at the beach; our provisions had now, however, become so far reduced as to render departure necessary, and we, therefore, shaped our course for Quelpart, where we had yet to obtain final observations.

* Tsyo-syon and Tyo-oo-seyn are the Japanese names for Korea, which favours this observation.

2 A 2

An island not before noticed, invited the delay of a few hours, and measures were taken for making the survey. As it was distant from Quelpart, as well as from the Korean mass, I had not dreamed of opposition, but the master, on landing, in a deep bay on its northern side, was opposed by the fishermen, who made attempts to snatch the muskets from his crew. As they were met with firmness, they fell back, and the Chiefs coming over to my gig, which had then landed on the other side of the bay, everything was soon satisfactorily arranged through our interpreter. These little skirmishes are rather hazardous; a little more violence on either side might have caused the loss of life, and upon no feasible ground, both parties fancying themselves in the execution of what they deemed to be their duty. So far had the feeling changed, that the master ascended the mountain above them (about 1,200 feet), and after taking up other stations returned to his boat; the crowd remaining about me amusing themselves very happily. Before leaving, they brought their *Saké* bottle, which, after tasting, we returned the compliment with sweet wine, and took our leave.

I was not a little gratified to find on my return to Quelpart, that every minute mark which we had left, was still standing, and one which had been beaten down by the rain or cattle, replaced, and the white-washed stones adjusted, as nearly as possible, to their former positions. I mention these little facts in order to show that there were parties who were not unfriendly to us.

A petty Mandarin from the great island waited on me, and informed me, that the Chief was in expectation of a visit on the other side of the channel, but our duties

Group of Koreans.

requiring my presence here, I despatched one of the Lieutenants to go through the leave-taking ceremony, offering to take charge of any letters for Nangasaki. He was further instructed, to enquire most particularly after my two civilian friends, and the state hat, which had been promised. A telescope was sent, to be presented if the hat should be produced: otherwise, not. The return message was quaint, but decisive; no hat; no letters; many compliments; wishing a good voyage, but expressing chagrin that I did not eat the breakfast provided for me. The Chief interpreter who came across explained that the hat and feather were honourable distinctions, like my epaulettes, and could only be conferred by the higher powers. He intimated, that now I was known, the Examiner might apply to the Emperor to have these things presented on my return.

I cannot take leave of the Korean Islands without recording some notice of the change, which appears to have taken place, in the laws and habits of the people, since the visit of the 'Alceste' in 1816; unless the author of that voyage misconceived their feelings and motives, in resisting any desire to land or communicate. The intercourse that subsisted between the Koreans and ourselves, aided by a competent Chinese interpreter, was of the most courteous description; accompanied by an avowal on my part, that I did not wish to enter their towns, and coupled with an assurance that my duties would confine me to the coast-line, or to such eminences only as they consented to my having access.

That they feared the loss of their cattle I firmly believe, for on every occasion of our boats approaching the shore, the herds were driven into the interior. They must certainly have a law relative to the admission of strangers into their towns; and it seems highly probable that some power exists at Quelpart, as at Loo-Choo, by which they are enabled, under due caution, to entertain and facilitate the operations of visitors, according to circumstances. On one occasion, I obtained permission to cut down some Pine trees for spars, but after the third was felled and embarked, the authorities withdrew their consent; not from any *fear* of the consequences, but because one old man chose to embrace the tree, condemned to the axe, terming it his "*child*": doubtless his private property.

One other point, noticed by us, does not coincide with the observations in the 'Voyage of the 'Alceste'. We found the Chinese written characters understood everywhere by the heads of villages, military Chiefs, and civilians, and frequently when a boat landed, the Officer has been shown a paper in that character, which, when brought to the interpreter, appeared simply to enquire, "what is your business?" Two large sheets containing letters, each an inch square, in Chinese characters, came off with the Bullocks from the northern city; they appeared to be public documents, covered with a waterproof varnish, and are now in my possession. The characters under the picture of the Emperor presented to me, were also Chinese.

END OF VOL. I.

Zeitfracht Medien GmbH
Ferdinand-Jühlke-Straße 7
99095 Erfurt, Deutschland
produktsicherheit@kolibri360.de